Risk Arbitrage

Wiley Frontiers in Finance

Series Editor: Edward I. Altman, New York University

CORPORATE FINANCIAL DISTRESS AND BANKRUPTCY
Edward I. Altman

PENSION FUND EXCELLENCE
Keith P. Ambachtsheer and D. Don Ezra

INTERNATIONAL M&A, JOINT VENTURES & BEYOND
David J. BenDaniel and Arthur Rosenbloom

INVESTMENT MANAGEMENT
Peter L. Bernstein and Aswath Damodaran

STYLE INVESTING
Richard Bernstein

OPTIONS, FUTURES & EXOTIC DERIVATIVES
Eric Briys

MANAGING CREDIT RISK
John B. Caouette, Edward I. Altman, and Paul Narayanan

THE EQUITY RISK PREMIUM
Bradford Cornell

VALUATION
Tom Copeland, Tim Kroller, and Jack Murrin

MANAGING DERIVATIVE RISKS
Lilian Chew

DAMODARAN ON VALUATION
Aswath Damodaran

INVESTMENT VALUATION
Aswath Damodaran

PROJECT FINANCING
John D. Finnerty

FINANCIAL STATEMENT ANALYSIS
Martin S. Fridson

M&A
Jeffrey C. Hooke

SECURITY ANALYSIS ON WALL STREET
Jeffrey C. Hooke

RISK ARBITRAGE
Keith M. Moore

CHAOS AND ORDER IN THE CAPITAL MARKETS
Edgar E. Peters

CREDIT RISK MEASUREMENT
Anthony Saunders

RELATIVE DIVIDEND YIELD
Anthony E. Spare

USING ECONOMIC INDICATORS TO IMPROVE INVESTMENT ANALYSIS
Evelina M. Tainer

FIXED INCOME SECURITIES
Bruce Tuckman

EXPORT-IMPORT FINANCING
Harry M. Venedikian and Gerald Warfield

INVESTMENT TIMING AND THE BUSINESS CYCLE
Jon G. Taylor

NEW DIMENSIONS IN INVESTOR RELATIONS
Bruce Marcus and Sherwood Wallace

NEW FINANCIAL INSTRUMENTS
Julian Walmsley

Risk Arbitrage

An Investor's Guide

Keith M. Moore

John Wiley & Sons, Inc.
New York • Chichester • Weinheim • Brisbane • Singapore • Toronto

Published by John Wiley & Sons, Inc.

Published simultaneously in Canada.

This publication is designed to provide accurate and authoritative
information in regard to the subject matter covered. It is sold with the
understanding that the publisher is not engaged in rendering professional
services. If professional advice or other expert assistance is required, the
services of a competent professional person should be sought.

Library of Congress Cataloging-in-Publication Data:

Moore, Keith M., 1952–
    Risk arbitrage : an investor's guide / Keith M. Moore.
      p.   cm. — (Wiley frontiers in finance)
    Includes index.
    ISBN 0-471-24884-3 (cloth : alk. paper)
    1. Arbitrage. I. Title. II. Series.
  HG6041.M655   1999
  332.64'5—dc21   99-18864

10 9 8 7 6 5 4 3

In the memory of James M. Gallagher.
Everyone needs a start. Jim gave me my start in the business
and continued to help me every step of the way.
God Bless you Jim.

Acknowledgments

I owe thanks to so many people that it is difficult to come up with a complete list. A special thanks to my wife, Ginny, and my children, Kimberly and Michael who have always been there with their support, understanding, and love. I would also like to thank my parents Julia and Horace Moore and my in-laws Frances and Norman Garrett for all their love and support over the years.

I have also been fortunate to have had the opportunity to meet with, and work with a tremendous group of people over the years. Albert Cohen and Marty Sklar introduced me to and taught me the risk arbitrage business and have helped and supported me over the years.

Other arbitrageurs have been great friends, including Bob Dryer, Jeff Cohen, George Kellner, Steve Cohen, and John Wagner who all helped me countless times over the years (including with this book).

A number of professionals shared with me their time and wisdom: Frank Lally, Ann Adrian, Bridget Gagen, Jason Dahl, and Peter Ruggiero—thank you for all your help and friendship.

There are many others who have been kind enough to help me over the years, and who have helped me on this book—thank you all.

K. M. M.

Contents

Risk Arbitrage

Chapter 1

Introduction

The sun was barely up and I was on my way to LaGuardia Airport to catch a plane. It was May 19, 1997, and I was flying to attend the first day of hearings on the proposed merger between Office Depot and Staples. The two companies had announced their merger plan on September 4, 1996. Office Depot shareholders were to receive 1.14 shares of Staples stock for each share of Office Depot they held. Since October 9, the two companies had been involved in discussions with the Federal Trade Commission (FTC). These discussions were designed to convince the Federal Trade Commission that the combination of the two firms would not violate the antitrust laws of the United States. The Federal Trade Commission was concerned that if the two companies combined, they would have a near monopoly in the office supplies superstore market. The Federal Trade Commission was seeking a preliminary injunction, in the United States District Court for the District of Columbia, to prevent the two companies from merging.

The Federal Trade Commission was making the argument that the relevant product market to be applied in the merger would be "the sale of consumable office supplies through office superstores." Office Depot and Staples did not agree. Both companies felt that the FTC and the District Court should be considering the sale of *all* office products to be the relevant market. Using this market definition, the companies held only a combined 5.5 percent share of the market, as opposed to a much higher market share under the market defined by the Federal Trade Commission. The companies felt that the market alleged by the government agency was contrived to produce market share levels that would encourage the court to enjoin the transaction. The relevant product market was the most important issue on which the outcome of the proposed merger would rest.

As the two opposing parties headed toward the hearing at the U.S. District Court, my job as an arbitrageur was about to begin. First, I met

1

with my firm's attorney, at his office. The hearing was so important to the arbitrage and investment community that an overflow crowd was expected. United States District Court Judge Thomas F. Hogan, who was assigned to the case, had refused to move the hearing to the ceremonial courtroom, which could accommodate almost all potential spectators. The hearing was to be held in Judge Hogan's courtroom, which could seat only 60 spectators. To arbitrageurs like me, who were trying to predict the outcome of the Federal Trade Commission's suit to block the merger, it was of utmost importance to be admitted to the courtroom. For the first time in my career, I hired a person called a "line-sitter." The "line-sitters" had gotten to the courthouse at 4 P.M. on Sunday to preserve a place on line for admission to the courtroom. For the fee of $150 an hour, they sat in line overnight outside the courthouse, reserving places on line for those who would be admitted to the courtroom on Monday. It was a case of classic American capitalism.

The next morning, starting one hour before the hearing was scheduled to begin, court officers began admitting observers, two or three at a time, to the courtroom. The line of observers dwindled down, and the line-sitters went to the end of the line to start the process all over again. A few potential spectators were out of luck; all the seats in the courtroom were filled. I would not have wanted to be one of those who were not admitted and who then had to inform their firm that they did not get in. "Flying blind" in a case like this could cause a firm to suffer large losses.

As the hearing began, I was seated in the fourth row—on the end, by the aisle. Normally, this would have been a prime seat. I would have been able to leave the courtroom, call my office, and enter orders based on my predictions of what was happening in the court. However, Judge Hogan's instructions warned that if observers left the courtroom, they were not guaranteed readmission. The next person in line would be admitted instead. If I left the room, I might not be allowed back in!

I decided that I would stay in the courtroom for the duration of the hearing. I would call my office only at the end of the day or if something dramatic, revealed at the hearing, caused a need to adjust my firm's position in the securities of Office Depot and Staples.

The first day of hearings lasted over six hours, with only a few breaks. The sessions continued for five days. I, along with many other arbitrageurs and their attorneys, continued to follow their progress. Many experts on mergers and on the office supplies business testified. We heard testimony from economists from Massachusetts Institute of Technology and from Harvard University, along with industry experts and buyers of office supplies. My job—and the job of all the other arbitrageurs and their attorneys—was to predict what Judge Hogan would rule, *before* he actually issued his opinion. At the completion of the hearings, Judge Hogan announced that he would hear closing arguments by the parties on June 5, 1998.

Depending on Judge Hogan's decision, the prices of both Office Depot and Staples stocks would react dramatically, bringing either a loss or a gain to the holders of the stocks. By accurately predicting the ultimate decision by Judge Hogan, an arbitrageur could set up a position that would profit from the movement in stock prices. Conversely, if an arbitrageur predicted the outcome (in this case, the decision), incorrectly, he or she could suffer large losses.

Most of the arbitrage community returned to Judge Hogan's courtroom on June 5 to hear the attorneys' closing arguments. I could feel the tension of the arbitrage community as arguments progressed. At the conclusion of the arguments, Judge Hogan announced that he was taking the case under advisement and that he would try to render his decision by the end of June. "Under advisement" is legal terminology for taking time to decide how to rule.

After a number of nerve-wracking weeks, Judge Hogan finally issued his decision and opinion on June 30. He was careful to issue his decision after 4:00 P.M. so that trading in the two companies' stocks would not occur until the following day.

Most arbitrageurs had predicted that Judge Hogan would dismiss the limited relevant market that was being alleged; the FTC claimed that the relevant market was the sale of disposable office supplies by office superstores. If Judge Hogan did not agree with the market definition offered by the FTC, he would most likely apply a much broader market definition for the sale of office products. The respective market shares of Office Depot and Staples in the larger market would not exceed allowable limits, and the merger of the two firms would proceed. If this occurred, arbitrageurs would realize large profits because the price of Office Depot shares would rise to their merger value. Prior to the decision, Office Depot was trading at $19.4375 and Staples was trading at $15.50. Each Office Depot share was to be converted into 1.14 Staples shares, but because Staples common stock had split three-for-two on February 2, 1997, the conversion ratio had been increased to 1.71 (1.14 times 1.5) to compensate for the split. Each Office Depot share would then be worth approximately $26.50 if the merger closed as planned. This $7.06 or 36.3 percent spread represented a huge potential gain for the holders of Office Depot shares. Its realization depended on the court's allowing the transaction and merger to proceed.

The potential gain from the deal, however, was not without risk. In fact, the unusually large spread was attributable to the risk that the transaction could be enjoined. A court injunction would most likely cause the merger to be called off. (Companies are usually unwilling to wait six to nine months as the case is presented and decided by an administrative law judge appointed by the Federal Trade Commission.) If the deal were to be called off, the prices of the shares of Office Depot and Staples stocks could be expected to return to their predeal levels. Office Depot was trading at $16 per share prior to the deal's announcement and Staples was trading at $12.50. Because arbitrageurs owned shares of Office Depot and sold short shares of Staples, they could suffer losses on both their long and short positions.

The arbitrageurs' and my own worst fears were confirmed when Judge Hogan rendered his decision. He announced that the Federal Trade Commission showed a "reasonable probability that the merger would substantially impair competition and likewise has raised questions going to the merits so serious and substantial to make them fair ground for investigation, study, deliberation and determination by the

Figure 1.1 Office Depot (ODP) Trading Activity,
August 26, 1996, to July 30, 1997

Source: © 1999 Bloomberg L.P. All rights reserved.

Figure 1.2   Staples (SPLS) Trading Activity,
August 26, 1996, to July 30, 1997

FTC in the first instances and ultimately by the Court of Appeals." The merger was enjoined.

The next day, the shares of Office Depot and Staples opened for trading. Office Depot traded at $15.625 and Staples traded at $16.25. Arbitrageurs lost $3.81 per share on their Office Depot holdings and $1.28 on their short positions in Staples ($0.75 times 1.71 shares short). This is an example of why this investment process is called *risk* arbitrage. From Figures 1.1 and 1.2, the reader can see the movement of both companies over time.

Arbitrage situations like the proposed Office Depot/Staples deal create complex and potentially lucrative investment opportunities. This book will describe the process of risk arbitrage investment, help in understanding the business implications, and aid in the decision making in a risk arbitrage situation. We have designed the book so that the reader will initially learn what risk arbitrage really entails and will then explore how it is done. There has not been an authoritative text dedicated to the subject of risk arbitrage in many years.

Chapters 1–3 deal with a detailed description of the risk arbitrage business. In Chapters 4–6, we will explore in depth the key elements of the risk arbitrage process. Finally, we will meld the elements together to demonstrate how to make decisions on risk arbitrage opportunities. We will examine real-life cases in depth. We will also introduce, in the final chapters, information on and insight into the areas of trade execution and portfolio management, which are critically important for arbitrageurs' success.

Chapter **2**

What Is Risk Arbitrage?

Webster's New World Dictionary offers this definition of arbitrage: "A simultaneous purchase and sale in two separate markets in order to profit from a price difference existing between them." This definition accurately describes what is known as "classic" arbitrage, where the investor is purchasing and selling the same security in different markets. An example would be: buying 100 shares of American Telephone & Telegraph at $60 a share on the New York Stock Exchange and selling the same 100 shares at $60.25 on the Pacific Stock Exchange. If these transactions were executed simultaneously, the investor would have a guaranteed profit.

In risk arbitrage, profits are anything but guaranteed.

Webster's goes on to describe risk arbitrage as follows: "A buying of a large number of shares in a corporation in anticipation of and with the expectation of making a profit from a merger or takeover." Do you really have to buy a large number of shares to achieve risk arbitrage? Does risk arbitrage require the arbitrageur to anticipate the announcement of a merger or takeover? The *Webster's* definitions are helpful, but we need to add more depth if we are to understand the investment process of risk arbitrage.

It is always interesting, when reading financial publications, to see the misunderstandings that surround the process of risk arbitrage. An article in *The Wall Street Journal* or *The New York Times* might describe a transaction involving a merger of two companies and then include a misleading reference to risk arbitrage. For example, "Arbitrageurs realized large gains on the announcement of the merger between Company A and Company T. The price of Company T's stock rose $8 to $32 on the announcement that Company A will be purchasing the company for $35 per share." This quite typical comment leaves the reader with the impression that the arbitrageurs held shares of Company T prior to the announcement of the transaction, and realized a large gain as a result.

The newspaper has given a very good description of sheer speculation, but it has certainly missed the mark in describing the process of risk arbitrage. Institutional and individual investors generally benefit from the initial merger announcement. The announcement, however, generally marks the beginning of the process know as risk arbitrage.

Here is perhaps the best definition: The risk arbitrage investment process is the investment in securities involved in and affected by mergers, tender offers, liquidations, spin-offs, and corporate reorganizations. The securities involved in the risk arbitrage process can be common stocks, preferred stocks, bonds, or options. Once a transaction is announced, arbitrageurs try to assemble as much information as possible to help estimate each transaction's risk, reward, and probability of occurrence. Annual reports, 10-K reports, quarterly reports, and reports generated by Wall Street analysts are gathered and evaluated by the arbitrageur as quickly as possible. As can be expected, much of this is done with the aid of computers and various on-line services.

The arbitrageur sets out to analyze all aspects of the transaction. He or she seeks to make various estimates that will help evaluate when a monetary commitment should be made to a particular transaction. Generally, the arbitrageur focuses on three keys to each prospective transaction: return, risk, and the probability of the transaction's being completed. Armed with these estimates, the arbitrageur will determine which, if any, securities will be purchased or sold, and what strategies must be used to hedge a particular transaction.

Risk arbitrage is an exciting and challenging process. Stocks involved in these transactions may become volatile. If the deal works out, the arbitrageur may realize a large gain, depending on the arbitrageur's market position. On the other hand, if the transaction is called off, the securities may drop precipitously and the arbitrageur may suffer large losses. The intensity may be further heightened because these developments may occur very quickly. The arbitrageur comes to work each day not knowing what type of industry he or she will have to be working with, or what companies will be at the center of an analysis. An arbitrageur may spend a morning analyzing a domestic oil deal, and, by the end of the day, will need to present a complete analysis of a transaction involving computer hardware manufacturers.

In addition to the need to be a generalist (as opposed to a specialized industry analyst), the arbitrageur must be able to use various analytical tools. The most frequently used tool is financial analysis, but the arbitrageur must also be able to use various computer and legal skills. Many deals need specific legal analysis centering on antitrust or securities law. Frequently, the arbitrageur will consult with outside advisers on specific important issues related to a particular transaction. These advisers may be attorneys, accountants, or financial analysts. All analyses have one main emphasis: to predict whether an announced transaction will occur and, if so, to decide what securities position to take in order to profit from the transaction. Risk arbitrage is an event-driven investment process.

The arbitrage investment may involve various types of securities. Typically, the arbitrageur is investing in the common stocks of the companies involved in the merger or takeover transaction. If shareholders of the company being taken over are receiving shares of the acquiring company, the arbitrageur will also sell short an equivalent amount of the issuer's shares to hedge the market risk of the transaction. For example, in the Office Depot/Staples deal discussed in Chapter 1, many arbitrageurs expected the court to reject the issuance of a preliminary injunction and therefore allow the merger to close. These arbitrageurs owned shares of Office Depot. To lock-in a spread, they had sold short the equivalent number of shares of Staples that they expected to receive upon the closing of the transaction. (The hedging process will be explained in depth in a later chapter.)

Common stock is not the only type of security involved in the arbitrageur's analysis and investment process. Convertible securities, bonds, and options will also be evaluated to determine whether they offer the arbitrageur an optimal choice of investment. Put and call options will frequently be evaluated once the arbitrageur has determined how to set up a position. The options may be used as a stand-alone strategy or combined with the purchase or sale of common stock to alter the risk/reward framework of the transaction.

In setting up the arbitrage position in the overall portfolio, the arbitrageur is generally trying to profit from the spread between the deal value or takeover price and the price of the securities that are subject to the transaction. The spread or discount from the deal value generally exists for two reasons: (1) the time value of money and (2) a risk premium. Many transactions may be announced, but not all are completed. A termination of a proposed deal is generally accompanied by a drop in the target's security's price, which may cause the arbitrageur to suffer a loss in portfolio value. Therefore, the arbitrageur's overall portfolio management strategy must include various risk parameters and disciplines to ensure an ability to weather individual deal losses or overall general equity market moves over various investment cycles.

There have been a few exceptions, but returns earned in the risk arbitrage business tend to be unrelated to overall equity market returns. This could be an advantage for investors in periods when the stock market declines or has negligible returns. However, arbitrageurs are hard pressed to compete with equity returns in periods of dramatic bull markets such as we have experienced over the past decade. The reason lies in the fact that the arbitrageur is generally trying to earn small increments of return (spread) with a high degree of certainty. The arbitrageur invests in a particular transaction, typically holds it to the deal's completion, and then seeks to redeploy the capital involved in the transaction. By turning over the investment and earning the incremental returns over a forecasted period of time, the arbitrageur hopes to generate meaningful returns that are unrelated to overall equity returns. This low overall correlation to the equity market exists because the individual transaction's occurrence is generally not related to the direction of the equity market. The deal's return is more a function of the merging companies' plans and the passage of time.

In the past fifteen years, however, there have been several periods in which arbitrage returns were related to the equity market. For instance, during the Crash of 1987 and the Mini-Crash of 1989, many announced merger transactions were reevaluated by the acquiring companies' boards of directors. Whenever the transactions were then terminated, the arbitrage community suffered huge losses. The reevaluations were generally done because of the large decline in stock prices. The transactions had been structured in an earlier period, and the higher equity prices at that time had been used as a guideline to determine the price to be paid for a particular company. When stock prices declined dramatically, many board members felt they were overpaying for the assets they were trying to acquire. Furthermore, in this earlier period, a tremendous number of transactions were being driven by entrepreneurs who were trying to buy companies as part of a plan to sell off their assets in a short period of time. Many of these buyers were highly leveraged, and their strategies were dependent on the stock market's remaining healthy. When the market declined, their strategies were flawed and the sources of their financing began to pull their financing commitments.

Barring these few market dislocation periods, risk arbitrage can provide investors with a profitable strategy to generate returns that will not be dependent on equity market moves.

TYPES OF TRANSACTIONS

Mergers

Mergers are the most common type of transaction that arbitrageurs analyze. Mergers may not always start out to be consensual transactions, but the structure of a merger transaction requires the involved parties to enter into an agreed-on transaction to combine their respective businesses.

Mergers are generally announced through a joint press release. Two forms of the initial announcement are possible. The two companies may announce what is known as an *agreement in principle* or they may enter into a *definitive agreement* to merge. Years ago, it was common for companies to enter into an agreement in principle and then proceed to do due diligence on each other's business. When the due diligence was completed to their satisfaction, the respective firms would have their attorneys draft a contract known as a definitive agreement. The boards of directors of the companies would then approve and execute the definitive agreement.

Today, companies rarely announce a merger with an agreement in principle. Most deals are announced when a definitive agreement is already in place. The merging firms try to perform their due diligence procedures in secrecy, and they make their public announcement after they have a definitive agreement. In fact, a deal announced today with only an agreement in principle should be a warning signal for arbitrageurs.

*Notes from the File** ══════════════════════════

An agreement in principle may indicate that the companies felt pressure to release prematurely the news of a pending merger. A leak in the private negotiations may have occurred, and changes in the underlying stock prices of the two merging firms may have been the market's reaction. Rising prices in the target company's stock may serve as a warning to the companies that their negotiations were filtering into public domain. Recently, a number of target companies have experienced a sharp run-up in their stock prices just prior to the public announcement of a transaction. For instance, prior to the announcement on August 3, 1998, that Ascend Communications was going to merge with Stratus Computer by issuing .75 share for each share of Stratus, Stratus's common stock jumped by over 30 percent. This jump was a clear indication that information regarding the transaction had filtered into the marketplace. The likelihood of the transaction's taking place may not be affected, but if the companies have not completed their due diligence, there may be a significant additional risk that the companies may not come to an ultimate agreement. Therefore, compared to deals announced with definitive agreements, deals with only agreements in principle should be viewed as higher-risk transactions.

---

* "Notes from the File" are particular lessons the author has learned during his years in the risk arbitrage business.

After a definitive agreement is negotiated, a registration statement has to be filed with the Securities and Exchange Commission (SEC). In a cash deal, the registration process is simple. If, however, the consideration to be received by the company being acquired is securities, the securities have to be registered with the SEC. This process has several steps. (1) The registration statement, which includes all the details of the securities being offered and the proposed transaction, must be filed. (2) The SEC generally reviews the documents and makes confidential comments to the issuing corporation. (3) After analyzing the comments and consulting with attorneys, the issuer responds to the comments by amending the registration statement as necessary. (4) After the issuer has answered all of the SEC's initial and subsequent comments and has made the required changes in the registration statement, the registration statement may be declared "effective." This does *not* mean that the SEC approves the securities. It merely means that the SEC believes that disclosure of the required information has been met.

When the registration statement has been declared effective, the document must be mailed to shareholders for their approval. If the merger is for cash or involves a small amount of the acquiring company's stock (less than 17.5%), only the shareholders of the company being acquired need to approve the transaction. If, however, more than 17.5 percent of the acquiring company's stock is being issued in the transaction, the New York Stock Exchange requires approval by both sets of shareholders before the transaction can become effective. The New York Stock Exchange does not allow companies to issue large amounts of stock without prior shareholder approval and still maintain their listings on the Exchange.

The shareholder vote required to approve any merger transaction is determined by the appropriate statute of the state in which the voting firms are organized. For instance, if the company being acquired is incorporated in the state of Delaware, the merger must be approved by more than a majority of those shares voting. When the required number of votes is received, the merger may be completed by filing the required forms with the states involved in the transaction. Arbitrageurs must diligently research each individual transaction in order to be in a position to predict the outcome of the announced merger transaction.

Tender Offers

A second type of transaction that arbitrageurs analyze is called a tender offer. Tender offers can be either friendly or hostile. The acquiring company is simply using a different structure to initiate the acquisition of another company. It is a two-step process. In the first step of a tender offer, an ad is placed in *The Wall Street Journal* and local newspapers to inform the target company's shareholders that there is a formal offer to buy their stock. This offer is made directly to the shareholders of the company being acquired and does not require a shareholder vote. The tender offer's consideration may be cash, securities, or a combination of the two. A cash tender offer can theoretically be executed in a relatively short period of time (approximately 20 business days). However, tender offers involving the issuance of securities to target company shareholders require a registration process similar to the one used for mergers. These offers that involve securities are also known as "exchange offers." We will deal with them later in the chapter.

The prime reason for using a tender offer rather than a merger is speed. A cash tender offer allows the acquiring company to acquire a majority of the shares of the target company within a very short period of time. This also assumes that the proper waiting period under the Hart–Scott–Rodino (HSR) Act is fully complied with. The HSR Act, passed in 1976, requires companies involved in mergers and acquisitions to file certain information regarding their plans and their respective businesses with both the Justice Department and the Federal Trade Commission. The HSR Act requires the companies to adhere to various minimum waiting periods prior to closing their transactions. The HSR statute and waiting periods will be examined in later chapters.

When the acquiring company holds a majority of the target's shares through the tender offer, the companies follow the tender offer with SEC filings to complete the merger of the two firms. This process is known as the second-step transaction.

One of the most important uses of the tender offer is in a contested takeover situation. Not all takeovers and mergers are friendly. Many times, when an acquiring company approaches a target company for negotiations, the negotiations may be refused or may be unsuccessful. To pressure the target company, the offering company may start a hostile tender offer. As with friendly tender offers, advertisements are placed in *The Wall Street Journal* and local newspapers, and the clock starts running on the offer. The target company must respond to the tender offer within a short period of time and must tell its shareholders what action its board of directors is recommending to shareholders. (The actual document that the target company must file with the SEC is called a "14-d-9." It must be filed with the SEC within 10 days of the commencement of the offer.)

The board of directors can recommend that the company's shareholders accept or reject the offer or wait for further recommendations.

Many boards initially recommend that shareholders take no action and wait for further instructions. In hostile situations, the target company usually pursues various defenses to prevent a complete takeover, or it tries to find a "white knight."—a company that enters the bidding as the favored merger partner of the target company. The white knight may be a company that approaches the target company to help keep it from being taken over by the hostile bidder, or it may be a company that is solicited by the target company or the target's investment bankers. These situations are the stuff that arbitrageurs' dreams are made of.

Notes from the File ══════════════════════════════

Whenever a hostile tender offer is announced, an arbitraquer should drop everything else and work on the hostile tender! Hostile tenders can develop quickly, and they frequently represent arbitrageurs' most attractive investment opportunities. Profits from hostile tenders can be quite large (especially when white knights enter the bidding), and the situations can develop very quickly. The arbitrageur usually has many days or weeks to analyze merger transactions. However, hostile tenders require immediate attention!

A white knight's entry into the bidding can touch off a bidding war. If the arbitrageur gets involved in the situation prior to the white knight's entry, the bidding war could provide the arbitrageur and his or her investors with significant profits. Furthermore, these profits may be realized over a very short period of time.

Hostile tender offers have had an interesting place in corporate takeover history, and their presence is predicted to continue in future years. However, developments over the past 10 years or so have made hostile offers more difficult to accomplish. We will deal with these developments and their effect on hostile offers in later sections of this book.

Hostile tender offers may become friendly transactions. By topping a white knight's bid, or through an eventual accommodation or agreed-on transaction with the target company, a hostile situation may be transformed into a friendly transaction. Once it turns friendly, the transaction may continue in its tender offer form or it may actually change its structure—usually becoming a typical merger transaction.

Hostile bids are generally the takeover situations that receive the most coverage in the press. They are potentially the most lucrative situations analyzed by the arbitrage community.

Exchange Offers

Exchange offers are tender offers in which the consideration being offered has a non-cash element such as stocks or bonds. Because these securities must go through the registration process, an exchange offer may not be completed as quickly as its cash tender offer counterpart. All securities issued under the exchange offer must go through the same registration process that exists for mergers. However, because there is no required vote of shareholders of the target company, the exchange offer may theoretically be completed faster than a transaction structured as a statutory merger. During the time when the acquiring company is going through the registration process, the issuer is able to satisfy other requirements such as the HSR Act and any legal or regulatory hurdles.

Exchange offers may be friendly or hostile transactions. Like tender offers, exchange offers are made directly to the target company's shareholders.

The main advantage of using an exchange offer, as opposed to a statutory merger, is that a shareholder vote of the target company is not required. As with a tender offer, the acquiring company can obtain a majority stake in the target company without a stockholders' vote. An exchange offer is usually followed by a statutory merger as a second-step transaction. Because the issuer may already hold a large percentage of the target company's voting shares at this point, the vote is usually a foregone conclusion.

As in tender offers, the arbitrageur is generally purchasing securities that are subject to the exchange offer. These securities are usually common stock of the target company but may include debt securities of the target company.

Spin-Offs

Spin-offs are a relatively recent phenomenon to risk arbitrageurs. Over the past 20 years, there has been a proliferation of this type of transaction in the marketplace. In a spin-off transaction, a company decides to split its businesses into separate units. Each new and separate unit may then be distributed to the current holders of the issuer's stock. As evidence of ownership, the issuer's holders receive additional shares of stock of the new company. Arbitrageurs will receive these new shares as long as they hold the parent company's stock on the record date of the spin-off. Sometimes, however, the issuer distributes the shares directly to shareholders or sells the shares through a public offering to establish a market value for the new entity. At a later date, the issuer may distribute the remaining shares of the spun-off unit to shareholders, to complete the divestiture of the operation.

For years, it was assumed that no matter how a company split up its businesses, the total value for shareholders would be the same. This assumption was based on the existing investment teachings in the field of finance. However, practical experience with spin-offs has called those theories into question. In most situations where companies have spun off businesses to their shareholders, the total value of all the securities held after the spin-off has exceeded pre-spin-off valuations. Analysts and academicians have suggested a number of reasons for this phenomenon.

By simplifying the corporate structure, spin-offs allow analysts on Wall Street to analyze the individual businesses in depth, as opposed to grouping them together as a whole. Many conglomerates have been able to create value for their shareholders by breaking up into several distinct companies and distributing the shares of these individual companies to their shareholders.

By simplifying the corporate structure, these spin-offs have also made it easier for Wall Street analysts to follow the company. Analysts may not have felt qualified to analyze the conglomerate, but additional research coverage can be created for the individually traded companies.

When a business is broken down into more understandable elements, it may become clear that some of the operations have growth and earnings characteristics that are quite different from those of the parent company. These growth and earnings characteristics may cause Wall Street to put a higher valuation on these businesses, and investors may be willing to pay a premium price for them. Therefore, it could be in the parent's best interest to spin off these operations in order to create value for shareholders.

Risk arbitrageurs have found that their financial analysis skills can be readily applied to spin-off transactions. Because arbitrageurs frequently have to study and value securities that are to be received in arbitrage transactions but do not have a current trading market value, they are in a good position to be able to value a security created by a spin-off transaction.

Spin-off transactions do carry additional risk that the arbitrageur does not generally encounter in a merger or tender offer transaction. Spin-offs result in trading of a new security in the marketplace. As a result, initiating a position causes the arbitrageur to assume equity market risk. Because the security is new, the arbitrageur is unable to hedge the purchase that creates the new unit. For instance, the arbitrageur may estimate that the spin-off security is worth $10, given the existing marketplace when he or she buys the issuers' shares. However, spin-offs are also required to go through the registration process. Because this process commonly takes 60 to 90 days, the overall pricing framework of the equity market may change the valuations in the stock market. During this period of time, no security that represents the spin-off operation is being traded. Moves in the equity market may cause the arbitrageur's initial $10 estimate to be inaccurate. The arbitrageur may either accept this market risk or look to hedge off this risk through the use of futures or some other financial instrument that can be predicted to react like the new security. When the registration process is complete and the new security trades in the marketplace, the arbitrageur can look to unwind the artificial hedge and then sell off the security being spun off to shareholders. In either case, the spin-off transaction represents an interesting opportunity for arbitrageurs to create value in their portfolios.

Recapitalizations

Recapitalizations are similar to spin-off situations in that the arbitrageur is usually faced with valuing a security before it trades in the marketplace. With recapitalization transactions, shareholders of the issuing corporation are generally receiving securities or a combination of securities and cash. A typical transaction might be structured so that current shareholders receive a $15 cash dividend and a new share in the reorganized company. The arbitrageur must (1) try to estimate the value of the new shares and (2) determine the likelihood of the transaction's actually occurring. This valuation process is very similar to what financial analysts do at brokerage firms when they advise clients on their investments. The analysis involves looking at cash flows, earnings, price/earnings multiples, and the issuing firm's balance sheet and credit rating. After the arbitrageur arrives at the estimates of recapitalization values, the next step is to determine what potential problems could occur that would affect the likelihood of the transaction's occurring.

Many recapitalization transactions present attractive opportunities to the arbitrage community and the general investment community. In a later chapter, we will analyze some specific examples to show the profit potential as well as the valuation framework.

Speculative Situations

Over the past 10 years, there has been a trend toward accelerated disclosure of corporate plans. Formerly, if two companies were considering a merger or if a company was considering selling out, negotiations were conducted in private. If an agreement was reached, a public announcement was made and the arbitrageur's investment process would commence. However, possibly due to an increased sensitivity to leaks in the marketplace, some companies actually disclose that they are in talks or discussions on possible corporate transactions that would affect their shares and the securities' value. An early disclosure of merger talks may significantly affect the prices of the underlying securities and could present an additional type of transaction for the arbitrageur to consider. However, investors must realize that these situations do *not* qualify as arbitrage. They are merely speculative transactions, and they are much more difficult to predict than actual arbitrage opportunities. The speculative situations are exciting and potentially lucrative, but they are too premature and contain too much uncertainty for most arbitrageurs to consider.

Notes from the File ━━━━━━━━━━━━━━━━━━━━━━━━━━━

Speculative situations are not *true arbitrage. They are closer to gambling at a casino than any other situation an arbitrageur might consider for investment. Arbitrageurs should avoid these types of transactions! They are a loser's game! During 1989, a large number of companies publicly announced that they were putting themselves up for sale. The investment community and arbitrageurs alike attempted to predict whether the targets would receive a bid and what consideration might be offered for the individual companies. Subsequently, many of these companies announced that because they had not received adequate bids, they were removing themselves from the auction block and returning to business as usual. Prices of the stocks of these companies declined, and 1989 became a very difficult year for the risk arbitrage community to generate acceptable returns.*

Speculative situations are exciting and tempting to investors and arbitrageurs alike. It is relatively easy to formulate overly optimistic forecasts for speculative situations. Too much uncertainty exists in these transactions for arbitrageurs to get an analytical handle on them. Accurate predictions of value and of the possible outcomes are virtually impossible. If these situations are "played," they should be restricted to a quite low percentage (5 to 10% in the aggregate) of the overall portfolio.

Thus far, we have seen that many types of transactions can be considered for an arbitrage portfolio. Table 2.1 summarizes the basic features of the numerous risk arbitrage opportunities. Each of these transactions requires a different type of analysis. Chapter 3 delves into how these various analyses are achieved.

Table 2.1 Types of Arbitrage Transactions

Type of Transaction	Nature of Transaction	SEC Filing	Shareholder Vote	Typical Timing
Merger	Consentual	Proxy and/or registration statement	Target company and both target and acquiring company may be required	90–120 days (except mergers involving regulated industries)
Tender offers	Consentual or hostile	14-d-9	Not required	Friendly 30–45 days, unfriendly 60–365 days
Exchange offers	Consentual or hostile	Registration statement	May be required	Friendly 60–90 days, unfriendly 90–365 days
Spin-off	Friendly (consentual)	Proxy and registration statement	Usually required	90–180 days
Recapitalization	Friendly	Proxy and registration statement	Usually required	90–180 days
Speculative situations	Either friendly or hostile	Registration may be required	May be required	90–180 days

Chapter 3

The Risk Arbitrage Industry

When I first became involved in risk arbitrage, in the 1970s, there were very few competitors. The business was characterized as being performed under a cloak of silence by a limited number of firms. Generally, the participants in the business operated as an arbitrage department within the auspices of a brokerage firm. When I first started, only 10 to 15 firms were involved in risk arbitrage.

Over time, however, the business developed and additional people began to participate in various ways. This additional participation came from two directions. Brokerage firms began to establish arbitrage departments by hiring experienced arbitrage personnel who worked at other brokerage firms. The newly formed departments were generally centered in the capital markets areas of the firms. Figure 3.1 shows the structure and the typical line of reporting within a brokerage firm.

The second form of participation developed during the 1970s: An entirely new firm was formed to participate in risk arbitrage. Using a limited partnership format, some arbitrageurs formed their own firms and raised money from outside investors. These investors became limited partners and their capital was funneled into a limited partnership where it was utilized to invest in risk arbitrage situations. The partnership was compensated based on the investment return generated for the limited partners. In the typical fee structure, an incentive fee was charged based on the return earned on the limited partnership's portfolio. This limited partnership form is illustrated in Figure 3.2.

In some cases, the fee was based on the incremental return over a minimal hurdle rate set in the limited partnership agreement. A typical fee arrangement in a limited partnership would have the manager receiving (1) a management fee based on assets under management and (2) an incentive fee based on investment returns generated to limited partners. These fees varied from arbitrage boutique to arbitrage boutique. In fact, the incentive percentage ranged from 20 percent in

Figure 3.1 Typical Arbitrage Structure within a Brokerage Firm

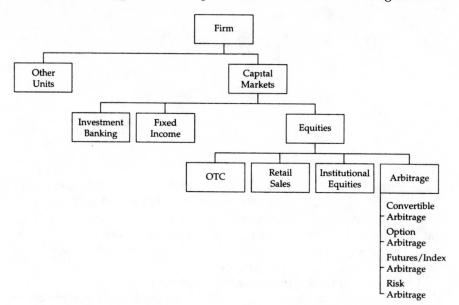

Figure 3.2 Structure of Limited Partnership

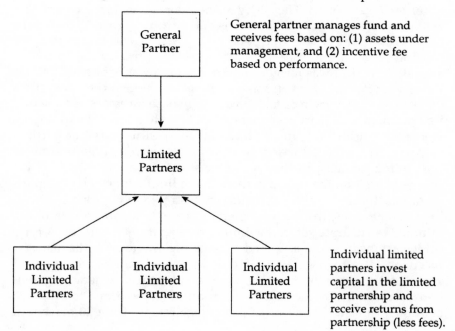

some boutiques to more than 50 percent in others where the arbitrageur received over half the return and the limited partners received the balance. Today, the typical arbitrage boutique firm incorporates a fee structure of a 1 percent fee on assets plus a 20 percent incentive fee based on performance.

The development of the arbitrage boutiques changed the arbitrage business forever. The boutiques funneled additional investment capital into the arbitrage area. Previously, because only a small number of firms were participating with a limited capital base, much higher spreads and returns were possible. Raising the additional capital from outside investors created competition for participating in the transactions, which ultimately put pressure on deal spreads. Over time, as the capital in the industry increased dramatically, the spreads in the industry narrowed.

Over the past 10 years, additional participants have entered the risk arbitrage business. Many hedge funds that were set up in a format similar to the risk arbitrage boutique but were applying investors' money to trading in the overall equity market began to participate in the risk arbitrage business. Generally, this occurred when the hedge funds had excess resources that were not being applied to the equity market. In other cases, the hedge fund may have allocated a specific amount of its capital to arbitrage transactions. The amount of capital being applied to the arbitrage business increased, placing further pressure on investment returns.

Pension funds have also become participants in the business over the past decade or so. Pension funds used to be sellers of target companies as they became subject to takeover attempts and mergers. Pension fund managers had been holding these securities as long-term investment vehicles. Once the arbitrage transactions were announced, pension managers usually cashed out. Arbitrageurs were generally the beneficiaries of these sales because they were able to purchase the target's securities at lower prices. Now that a number of pension funds have hired arbitrageurs to take over the investment decisions on securities subject to takeover attempts, the supply of stock upon the deal's announcement has dwindled, causing further pressure on spreads and returns.

Despite the pressure on spreads and returns, returns in the risk arbitrage business remain attractive to many types of investors. Spreads have declined, but attractive returns can still be realized, and these returns usually show a low correlation with overall equity market returns.

The overall size of the arbitrage business has been difficult to quantify. Recently, however, *Fortune* estimated that over 200 firms are

Figure 3.3   Risk Arbitrage

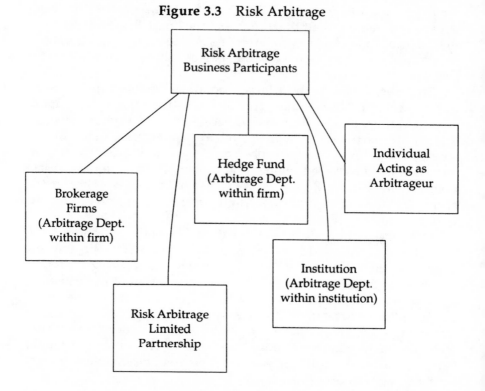

participating in the arbitrage business. These firms are estimated to control over $30 billion of investment capital.[1]

Because of the increased level of publicity and an explosion in deal volume, individual investors have also become participants in the arbitrage business (Figure 3.3). These investors have not had much impact on deal spreads, but they have contributed to the increased level of competition. Individual investors face a difficult task in competing with the professional arbitrageurs in the arbitrage business; the professionals usually have greater financial resources as well as more experience. Individuals, however, if they maintain discipline and perform solid analysis with these transactions, have historically been able to generate substantial returns. As a result, the risk arbitrage business offers an attractive alternative for individual investors seeking to supplement their investments in typical equity and debt market instruments. This book is designed to aid these investors in their use of risk arbitrage as an investment technique.

---

[1] *Fortune* Magazine, August 3, 1998, pp. 270–272.

The risk arbitrage business exhibits an important characteristic that sets it apart from the general investment business: the degree of interaction among arbitrageurs. Even though they compete with one another every day in analyzing their information flows and assembling their portfolios, there is a high degree of cooperation among arbitrageurs.

It is quite common for an arbitrageur to interact with numerous other arbitrageurs who are involved in the marketplace every day. The cooperation among arbitrageurs is usually dependent on each individual arbitrageur's relationships. The more arbitrageurs know and respect one another, the closer their relationships and their sharing of information and ideas.

Because the universe of potential arbitrage transactions is usually quite large, each arbitrageur tends to realize that he or she can be knowledgeable about and analyze only so many transactions at any given time. Additionally, there is always room for a supplementary interpretation. As a result, it is common for an arbitrageur to consult with other arbitrageurs regarding their feelings toward an individual deal or a group of transactions, and their estimates of the potential outcomes. In this way, many arbitrageurs are actually collaborating on their research efforts! This is rarely done in other areas of equity or debt investments.

The relationships developed by arbitrageurs depend on the level of trust they establish with other arbitrageurs with whom they deal. Some arbitrageurs prefer to go it alone. Recently, at a luncheon with an arbitrageur who has been involved in the business for over 40 years, the arbitrageur mentioned to me that although he knows that other arbitrageurs consult with one another, he feels that he operates best on his own. The general reason for his lack of interest in cooperating with other arbitrageurs was that he would find it surprising if an arbitrageur were to tell him the whole truth regarding his or her feelings about a transaction. He thought the competing arbitrageur would hold back important information and not necessarily share it. One might conclude that the veteran arbitrageur would keep information to himself, to profit from it, but I have always found that view too cynical. Over time, I have been able to develop relationships with a small group of arbitrageurs whom I trust greatly. These relationships were built gradually and have stood the test of time.

Notes from the File

Some of my most cherished friendships have been developed through meeting other arbitrageurs. I have met these people through various trips and functions that I have attended while covering various deals for the firms for which I have worked. There have been instances where I have spent a week or more in a courtroom, contending with these professionals. Later, we would have dinner and socialize together. These types of experiences have led to close relationships during my career of 25 years or so. The friendships have been unexpected byproducts of doing risk arbitrage, and I am very fortunate to have had these experiences.

Developing these good relationships has added to the information flow and the analysis flow in my decision process. Experienced arbitrageurs select deals that they feel are worthwhile and avoid deals that they feel are too risky. Similarly, they develop relationships with people who can be trusted and they minimize relationships with people who make them feel uncomfortable.

This process of consulting with other arbitrageurs on a daily and continual basis sets the arbitrage business apart from other investment businesses. In the next four chapters, we will examine the key elements of the risk arbitrage business and how these elements are combined in the risk arbitrage decision process.

Chapter **4**

Return

Investors are always keenly interested in what they can potentially earn on their investment. Arbitrageurs are no different. In fact, an analysis of an arbitrage transaction generally results in a more quantitative estimate of return than is achieved through a traditional analysis of a stock or bond position. Security analysts usually come up with a range of values for a given equity security. These estimates are generally the basis for their recommendation to buy, hold, or sell. Risk arbitrage analysis yields a more defined value of a security, based on the arbitrageur's estimate of "deal value"—the first step toward an estimate of return on a risk arbitrage position. This return becomes the initial key element in the arbitrageur's analysis framework.

Simple Deals

Some deals are simple transactions on which it is easy to calculate return. For instance, we will assume that Company A is purchasing Company T in a friendly cash tender offer. The tender-offer price is $20. This means that the acquiring company, Company A, is paying $20 for each share of stock of the target company, Company T. The deal price is $20, and we will assume that the transaction will close in approximately one month (30 days). If Company T's stock is trading at $19.50 per share, we may calculate the return on the deal as follows:

$$ER_{UL} = GS/I; GS = DP - SP_t$$

where ER_{UL} = expected return (unleveraged)
GS = gross spread
DP = deal price
SP_t = target company's stock price
I = arbitrageur's investment in the transaction (in this case, $I = SP_t$)

Because the transaction is for cash and the only transaction the arbitrageur must enter into is the purchase of Company T's stock at $19.50 (no short sale is involved), the arbitrageur's investment is $19.50 per share. It is assumed that the arbitrageur purchases the shares for cash and is not utilizing any debt financing in the transaction. Substituting dollar amounts:

$$GS = \$20 - \$19.50$$
$$= \$.50 \text{ per Company T share}$$
$$ER_{UL} = \$.50/\$19.50$$
$$= 2.56 \text{ percent}$$

As long as we expect the transaction to be completed on the announced terms, we must convert the unannualized expected return to an annualized expected return. Arbitrageurs will always use this annualized expected return to analyze arbitrage positions and to compare various arbitrage opportunities.

$$ER_{UL} = (GS/I) \times (365/P)$$

where ER_{UL} = expected return on an annualized basis
GS = gross spread
I = investment
P = estimated investment period
= estimated closing date − initial investment date

For our example, the expected annual return can be found as follows:

$$ER_{UL} = (\$.50/\$19.50) \times (365/30)$$
$$= 31.2 \text{ percent}$$

If the transaction occurs on the expected terms within the expected time horizon, the arbitrageur expects to earn a 31.2 percent return on an annualized basis. The arbitrageur assumes that, at the closing of the deal, the proceeds will be reinvested in another risk arbitrage opportunity.

In the above example, it was assumed that the $20 deal price was the only form of proceeds received in the transaction. If the company paid a dividend during the period when the arbitrageur held the stock, the dividend would enhance the return the arbitrageur would earn. Similarly, if the security held by the arbitrageur was a bond, the interest received on the bond would have to be accounted for in the spread calculations. For instance, if Company T in the prior example paid a $.05 dividend per share within the 30 days the arbitrageur held the stock, the spread would increase from $.50 to $.55 and the annualized return would increase from 31.2 percent to 34.3 percent. The equation would again be:

$$ER_{UL} = (NS/I) \times (365/P)$$

where NS = net spread (gross spread plus all other cash flows on investment during investment period P).

In our example, the expected return calculation using the net spread would be as follows:

$$
\begin{aligned}
NS &= GS + D_t \\
&= \$.50 + \$.05 \\
&= \$.55
\end{aligned}
$$

where D_t = dividend paid by target company
$$
\begin{aligned}
ER_{UL} &= (NS/I) \times (365/P) \\
&= (\$.55/\$19.50) \times (365/30) \\
&= 34.3 \text{ percent}
\end{aligned}
$$

If the security purchased in the arbitrage transaction is a bond, the interest earned would be added to the net spread.

Again, it should be emphasized that the annualized expected return is used by the arbitrage community to compare the deal's spread to (1) other opportunities available in the universe of arbitrage situations and (2) the arbitrageur's cost of capital. In this way, the arbitrageur's decision is no different than a typical capital budgeting decision made by a corporation's managers when they compare their cost of capital to the expected return on various investment projects. Logically, it may be assumed that an arbitrageur will not invest capital in a transaction for which the expected return is less than the required rate of return. In fact, the arbitrageur most likely will require a premium over the minimum expected return in order to compensate for the risk involved in the transaction. We will analyze this aspect of the arbitrageur's decision later in the book.

Before we examine more complicated transactions, it may be useful to walk through an actual transaction that had various components of a spread calculation.

On February 25, 1997, Fina (FI) agreed to be acquired by its parent company, Petrofina SA (FIN). FIN, which previously owned 60 percent of FI, agreed to pay each shareholder of FI $60 in cash plus one warrant for each share of FI stock. Each warrant was to give its holder the right to buy .9 FIN share at $42.25 for approximately 5 years after the closing of the transaction, which was expected to occur on June 30, 1998.

If the warrant had been currently trading in the marketplace, the arbitrageur would have been able to use its current market price to calculate its value in the spread calculation. However, because this was a newly created warrant that would not trade until the transaction was about to close, the arbitrageur needed to utilize a financial model to calculate the probable market value of the warrant if it were trading currently. Arbitrageurs may develop their own models or they may use models developed by others and sold by various services and vendors. At the time this transaction was announced, a number of arbitrageurs who analyzed the proposed FI transaction estimated that the warrant would be worth approximately $4.15 when the transaction closed.

The annualized return could be calculated as follows:

$$ER_{UL} = (NS/I) \times (365/P); \; NS = (C + W + D_t) - SP_t$$

where   C = cash portion of deal value ($60)
W = warrant value ($4.15)
D_t = dividend to be paid on FI stock during investment period (P)
= $.80 (on 3/4/98) + $.80 (on 6/4/98)
= $1.60
P = investment period (assumes an analysis date of 3/1/98 and an expected closing date of 6/30/98)
= 122 days
SP_t = $63.25

Substituting dollar amounts:

$$ER_{UL} = \{[(\$60 + \$4.15 + \$1.60) - \$63.25]/\$63.25\} \times (365/122)$$
$$= [(\$65.75 - \$63.25)/\$63.25] \times (365/122)$$
$$= (\$2.50/\$63.25) \times (2.99)$$
$$= 11.83 \text{ percent (on an annualized basis)}$$

Assuming that the arbitrageur's estimates of warrant value, dividends, and closing date were correct, the arbitrageur expected to earn an annualized return of 11.8 percent on the FI deal. We introduced a form of consideration in addition to cash (the FI warrant). Many transactions require additional estimates to determine expected rates of return.

STOCK-FOR-STOCK DEALS

In today's merger market, many of the transactions being announced in the marketplace are known as *stock-for-stock transactions:* Two companies announce their plan to merge, and the medium of exchange is shares of the acquiring company. On August 19, 1997, Texaco and Monterey Resources jointly announced that they had agreed to merge in a stock-for-stock transaction. Monterey Resources had previously been owned by Santa Fe Energy and had been recently been spun off to Santa Fe shareholders. Monterey owned significant heavy-oil reserves, primarily in California, and Texaco was looking to add to its significant oil reserves. Shareholders of Monterey were to receive $21 in Texaco stock for each share of Monterey held. Texaco would issue the stock based on a 10-day average price formula. Because the merger consideration (deal price) was fixed at $21, the spread calculation was similar to that of a cash transaction:

$$\text{Monterey Resources common stock price} = \$\ 20.375$$
$$\text{Texaco common stock price} = \$111.50$$

$$GS = (\$21 - \$20.375)$$
$$= \$.625$$

$$NS = GS + D_t$$
$$= \$.625 + \$0.00$$

$$ER_{UL} = (NS/I) \times (365/P)$$
$$= (\$.625/\$20.375) \times (365/90)$$
$$= 12.4 \text{ percent}$$

Monterey's stock was not paying a dividend during the expected holding period, and the merger was expected to close in approximately 90 days.

Unlike the Monterey–Texaco deal, where the stock-for-stock value was a fixed amount of dollars, most stock-for-stock transactions involve a fixed exchange ratio. For instance, on July 17, 1997, Louisiana Land & Exploration (LLX) and Burlington Resources (BR) announced their plans to merge in a stock-for-stock transaction. Both of these companies, like Texaco and Monterey, were producers of hydrocarbons. Each stockholder of LLX was to receive 1.525 shares of BR for each LLX share held. This transaction required a different type of calculation to determine investment return. The deal price was not fixed; it depended on both the stock exchange ratio and the acquiring company's stock price. With the exchange ratio fixed, the deal price would rise if the underlying stock price rose. Conversely, if the underlying stock price declined, the per-share consideration would decline.

In the LLX/BR deal, we would calculate the deal price (DP) as follows:

$$DP = R \times SP_a$$
$$= 1.525 \times \$44.375$$
$$= \$67.67$$

where   R = ratio of the acquiring company's shares to be received for each target company share
SP_a = the acquiring company's stock price

In the LLX/BR merger, if the price of BR common stock declined from \$44.375 to \$40, the deal value declined from \$67.67 (1.525 shares × \$44.375 per BR share) to \$61 (1.525 × \$40). If the arbitrageur did not hedge off the BR shares he or she expected to receive in the transaction, the spread of the deal would have declined in relation to the BR common stock price decline. If the price of BR shares rose instead, the deal value would also have been impacted. The deal value and spread would have increased as the price of the underlying stock increased.

At this point, it should be noted that, in stock-for-stock deals, arbitrageurs commonly utilize a hedging process that allows them to lock in a deal value and a spread so that these important values no longer are dependent on the acquiring company's stock price. In this hedging process, once the terms of the transaction become known and the arbitrageur decides to initiate a position, he or she hedges off the purchase of the target's common stock by selling short the underlying shares of the acquiring company's stock that are expected to be received in the transaction. The process of selling short is initiated when the arbitrageur has a broker or clearing firm borrow shares of the stock being sold short. An order is then placed to sell the shares "short." If the order is executed, the arbitrageur is "short" the shares. If the price of the shares rises, the arbitrageur is losing money on a mark-to market basis. Conversely, if the underlying shares decline in value, the arbitrageur is making money on a mark-to-market basis. Ultimately, the arbitrageur will close out the short position by either purchasing the shares in the open market or by delivering shares of the acquiring company that are received after the consummation of the merger.

In our LLX/BR example, it may be useful to go through the math and show how the arbitrageur's spread is locked-in, no matter what the acquiring company's stock price does, if the arbitrageur uses the short selling process. Previously, we calculated that if BR's stock price declined from $44.375 to $40, the deal price then dropped from $67.67 to $61. Had the arbitrageur sold 1.525 shares of BR short at $44.375 when he or she bought a share of LLX at $65.50, the following spread would have been created:

$$DP = R \times SP_a$$
$$= 1.525 \times \$44.375$$
$$= \$67.67$$

$$GS = DP - SP_t$$
$$= \$67.67 - \$65.50$$
$$= \$2.17$$

If the BR price drops to $40, even though the deal price drops $6.67 per LLX share, the arbitrageur's gross spread remains $2.17 per share:

Long one share of LLX at $65.50:
    At deal closing, one share is worth 1.525 × $40
    Loss on long position ($61 − $65.50) $−4.50

Short 1.525 shares of BR at $44.375:
    At deal closing, 1.525 shares trade at $40
    Gain on short position ($44.375 − $40) × 1.525 shares   <u>$+6.67</u>
                                                    $+2.17

On the other hand, had BR's stock price risen to $50, the arbitrageur's gross spread would remain at $2.17:

Long one share of LLX at $65.50:
    At deal closing, one share is worth 1.525 × $50
    Gain on long position ($76.25 − $65.50) $+10.75

Short 1.525 shares of BR at $44.375:
    At deal closing, 1.525 shares trade at $50
    Loss on short position ($44.375 − $50) × 1.525 shares   <u>$ −8.58</u>
                                                    $ +2.17

As long as the arbitrageur hedged off the long position by shorting the exact amount of underlying shares that would be received when the transaction was completed, the gross spread was fixed, regardless of how the acquiring company's stock moved.

When an arbitrageur utilizes the short-selling technique to lock in a spread, several additional cash flows are created that must be considered when calculating the net spread and net returns. If the shares of the acquiring company pay a dividend and this dividend is paid during the time the arbitrageur is short, the arbitrageur must pay the dividend to the person from whom the shares were borrowed. The dividend on the short share becomes an expense for the arbitrageur; as a result, this cash flow reduces the net spread the arbitrageur receives. Additionally, the short sale of securities creates a credit balance for the arbitrageur. For example, if the arbitrageur sells 100 shares of Burlington Resources (BR) short at $44.375 per share, proceeds of $4,437.50 ($44.375 × 100) will be created in the arbitrageur's short account. Professional arbitrageurs (as well as many individual investors) are able to receive interest on these short proceeds. The interest rate received is less than the amount an individual brokerage firm charges for borrowings because additional fees are paid out in the process of borrowing the securities.

The creation of the short proceeds, which we will call the *short interest credit*, becomes an additional cash flow that must be accounted for in our return calculation.

The return on the LLX/BR transaction can then be viewed as follows:

$$GS = DP - SP_t$$
$$= (\$44.375 \times 1.525) - \$65.50$$
$$NS = GS + D_t - (D_a \times R) + SI$$

where D_t = dividend on target company
  D_a = dividend on acquiring company
  R = ratio of acquiring company's shares received and shorted
  SI = short interest credit
  $SI = SIP \times IS; SIP = R \times SP_a$

$$SIP = 1.525 \times \$44.375$$
$$= \$67.67$$

$$SI = \$67.67 \times .04^* \times \frac{90}{365}$$
$$= \$.67$$

where SIP = short proceeds
  IS = interest received on short proceeds
  = short interest rate × period of time short is outstanding

---

*Note: 4% is the interest rate the arbitrageur receives on the short proceeds.

The net spread on the LLX/BR deal is calculated as follows:

$$NS = GS + D_t - (D_a \times R) + SI$$
$$= \$2.17 + \$0.06 - (\$0.14 \times 1.525) + .67$$
$$= \$2.17 + \$0.06 - \$0.21 + 0.67$$
$$= \$2.69$$

We assume that the transaction will close in 90 days and the arbitrageur will receive 4 percent on the short proceeds. The next step is to calculate the arbitrageur's annualized return on investment:

$$ER_{UL} = (NS/I) \times (365/P)$$
$$= (\$2.69/\$65.50) \times (365/90)$$
$$= 16.61 \text{ percent}$$

This calculation also assumes that the arbitrageur has adequate margin available to enter into the short sale transaction. If adequate margin does not currently exist in the arbitrageur's account, additional funds must be deposited, and this would change the return-on-investment calculation. Later in the chapter, we will see that arbitrageurs generally utilize leverage in executing their trades. So far, we have assumed no leverage in our examples. When leverage is introduced, the return cash flows are affected, as are the return calculations.

Collars on Stock-for-Stock Transactions

Many stock-for-stock deals have built-in safeguards, or "collars," that are designed to protect either the acquiring or the target company. Collars usually take one of two different forms. If the stock bid is fixed in price (e.g., $20 worth of the acquiring company's stock), the acquiring company may set minimum and maximum exchange ratios to protect its shareholders against major moves in the acquiring company's stock price. The acquiring company may be concerned that after negotiating and announcing the agreement, its common stock price could drop significantly. If the deal price is defined in terms of a fixed-dollar consideration of the acquiring company's stock, the actual exchange ratio is generally determined by a formula. A typical method would involve taking an average of the acquiring company's closing stock price (on the exchange on which it trades) for a specific number of days prior to the transaction's closing. If the acquiring company's stock declines dramatically, the divisor declines and more shares must be issued to give the target company's shareholders the set dollar amount of stock.

Example 1

Facts:　Deal price set at $20 in acquiring company's stock.

Acquiring company's stock trades at $40 when the deal is announced.

As the deal approaches consummation, acquiring company's stock price has declined to $20 per share.

The acquiring company thought it would be issuing approximately .5 share of its stock to the target company, but, because of the price decline, the acquiring company must issue one share at the closing, to keep the deal value at $20.* Issuing twice as many shares of stock could very well change the economics of the transaction for the acquiring company and its shareholders.

With this type of collar, arbitrageurs must be careful of the actual minimum and maximum exchange ratios that the acquiring company stipulates—for two reasons. First, with most collar deals, the parties may have the right to terminate the transaction if the acquiring company's stock price exceeds the parameters of the collar. The target company usually has the right to walk away from the transaction if the acquiring company's stock price drops below the minimum price level stipulated in the agreement. The decline in the acquiring company's stock price, combined with a fixed exchange ratio, results in the target company's shareholders receiving less than the agreed-on deal price. In Example 1, we can illustrate the point by assuming that in addition to setting the deal price at $20 in stock, the companies agreed that the acquiring company would not be obligated to issue more than .75 share and not less than .25 share. With that specific collar, if the acquiring company's stock price declined to $20, the new deal price would be only $15 ($20 × .75) instead of the original $20.

Example 1 also illustrates the second reason why arbitrageurs must pay close attention to collars. The deal price used to determine the return on the transaction may change if the price of the acquiring company's stock exceeds the stipulated collar range.

A second type of collar usually comes about when the merging parties state a particular exchange ratio in the initial definitive agreement. To protect themselves, the parties may also set up a range over which the exchange ratio is valid. The parties usually stipulate a minimum and maximum range of stock prices over which the exchange

---

*Number of shares issued equals deal price divided by acquiring company's stock price ($20÷40=.5).

ratio will hold. If the companies set a fixed exchange ratio of .75 share for the acquiring company's shares, the companies will commonly state that the transaction can be terminated if the acquiring company's stock price either exceeds an upper price level or declines below a minimum price level.

Example 2

Facts: Fixed exchange ratio of .75 share.

Acquiring company's shares trade at $40 when deal is announced.

Maximum acquiring company stock price is $55.

Minimum acquiring company stock price is $35.

If the acquiring company's stock price exceeds $55, the acquiring company may feel that it is paying too high a price (in the aggregate) for the target company's shares. This could result in the acquiring company's backing out of the transaction. Conversely, if the acquiring company's stock price declines below the $35 limit, the target company and its shareholders may feel that they are not receiving enough consideration for their shares. For instance, if the acquiring company's shares decline to $30 per share, the target company's shareholders would be receiving only $22.50 (.75 × $30) in value, as opposed to the originally expected $30 per share (.75 × $40). The arbitrageur in this case must substitute the minimum-dollar deal value instead of the fixed (.75 share) exchange ratio in the spread calculations.

In all transactions involving collars, the arbitrageur must carefully study and analyze the definitive agreement to determine how underlying stock price moves may affect the spread and, thus, the return on the transaction. How the arbitrageur actually hedges transactions that involve collars will be covered in Chapter 10.

COMPLEX DEALS

As mentioned earlier, many deals are more complicated than those we described as being cash or stock-for-stock arrangements. It is quite common to have merger transactions include a combination of cash and securities. These transactions require additional steps to calculate the deal value and the resulting spreads. Each piece must be valued separately, and the arbitrageur must take into account how much of each piece will be received upon consummation of the transaction. Usually, the acquiring company will limit how much of each piece of consideration can be received by each target company shareholder. This is necessary because when there are two different forms of consideration, one part may be worth more than the other, even if the transaction was designed to give equal weight to the individual pieces.

This problem can be best illustrated by a recent example that occurred in the merger and acquisition market. On March 31, 1997, Astoria Financial Corporation agreed to acquire the Greater New York Savings Bank, which was serving the communities of Brooklyn, Queens, and Long Island. Astoria, a bank specializing in single-family residential mortgage lending, operated more than 40 offices in the New York metropolitan area and in some upstate New York counties. The companies agreed that Greater New York shareholders would receive a combination of cash and common shares of Astoria's stock. Greater New York shareholders would receive $19 in cash for up to 25 percent of their shares. For each remaining share, they would receive .5 share of Astoria's stock. The stock element of the transaction was limited to 75 percent. At the time the transaction was announced, Greater New York's shares were trading at $17.25 per share, and Astoria was trading at $36 per share.

The gross spread calculation for the deal price (DP) was as follows:

$$DP = (p_1 \times C_1) + (p_2 \times C_2)$$

where p_1 = percentage of first type of consideration to be received
p_2 = percentage of second type of consideration to be received
C_1 = value of first type of consideration
C_2 = value of second type of consideration

In the Greater New York/Astoria deal, we would apply the formula as follows:

$$DP = (.25 \times \$19) + [.75 \times (.5 \times \$36)]$$
$$= \$4.75 + \$13.50$$
$$= \$18.25$$

The spread and return calculations would then be:

$$GS = DP - SP_t$$
$$= \$18.25 - \$17.25$$
$$= \$1.00$$

$$NS = GS + D_t - (D_a \times R \times p_2) + SI$$
$$= \$1.00 + (2 \times .05) - [(2 \times .11) \times .5 \times .75] + \{[(.5 \times \$36) \times .75] \times .04 \times 180/365\}$$
$$= \$1.2835$$

The calculation is clearer if we break it down into its individual elements:

D_1 = .05 per share × 2 (since we expect two dividends to be paid out during the six months we estimate the transaction will take)
= $.10

D_2 = .11 per share × 2 (since we expect the Acquiring Company to also pay two dividends during the time we are short the stock)
= $.22 (but remember: we are shorting only .5 share on only 75 percent of the Greater New York position)

$$SI = SIP \times IS$$

where SIP = short proceeds
= (.5 × $36) × .75 (since we will short .5 share of Astoria on only 75 percent of the entire position)
= $13.50
IS = .04
SI = $13.50 × .04 × (180/365) (since we are assuming we receive 4 percent short interest credit for 180 days on the net short proceeds created). This 4 percent rate varies according to changes in the interest rate market.
= $0.266
NS = GS + D_t – (D_a × R × p_2) + SI
= $1.00 + $0.10 – $0.0825 + $0.266
= $1.2835
and ER_{UL} = (NS/I) × (365/P)
= ($1.2835/$17.25) × (365/180)
= 15.08 percent

It should be noted that the individual portions of consideration to be received were worth different amounts. With Astoria trading at $36, the stock portion was worth $18 per Greater New York share, or $1 less than the cash consideration of $19. Greater New York shareholders would have preferred to receive $19 in cash for all their shares, but that arrangement would have forced Astoria to pay cash for virtually all the Greater New York shares. Precisely for this reason, Astoria set a limit of 25 percent as the total number of shares that could receive cash. Astoria did not want to pay cash for more than 25 percent of Greater New York's shares. Had Astoria's stock price risen dramatically prior to the consummation of the deal, an alternative problem would have occurred. In fact, over the next several months *after* the transaction was announced, Astoria's shares rose to the high 40s.

On August 8, 1997, a much different spread calculation existed for the prices of the securities:

Greater New York stock price: $22.50
Astoria Financial stock price: $48.75

$$DP = (.25 \times \$19) + [.75 \times (.5 \times \$48.75)]$$
$$= \$4.75 + \$18.28$$
$$= \$23.03$$

(The deal price increased from $18.25 to $23.03 due to the rise in Astoria's share price from $36 to $48.75.)

$$GS = DP - SP_t$$
$$= \$23.03 - \$22.50$$
$$= \$0.53$$

$$NS = GS + D_t - (D_a \times R \times p_2) + SI$$

where $D_t = \$0.05$ (only one dividend is now anticipated prior to the transaction's closing)

$D_a = \$0.11$ (only one dividend is anticipated to be lost on the short side)

$SI = (.5 \times \$48.75 \times .75) \times .04 \times 53/365$ (it is now August 8, 1997, so there are only 53 days to the estimated closing date)
$= \$0.106$

$NS = \$0.53 + \$0.05 - (\$0.11 \times .5 \times .75) + \$0.106$
$= \$0.53 + \$0.05 - \$0.041 + \$0.106$
$= \$0.645$

$ER_{UL} = (NS/I) \times (365/P)$
$= (\$0.645/\$22.50) \times (365/53)$
$= 19.74$ percent

When Astoria's stock price rose from $36 to $48.75, holders of Greater New York would much rather have received Astoria stock for *all* their Greater New York shares. The deal value would then have been $24.375 instead of the weighted deal price of $22.84. This, however, would have caused Astoria to issue more shares than was planned. By setting a maximum ratio of 75 percent, Astoria eliminated the possibility of issuing too many shares.

At the time of closing, the target company's shareholders must fill out a form requesting the form of consideration that they would like to receive. After all these forms are submitted, the acquiring company and its advisers total up the number of shares requested and the amount of cash requested. If either of these totals exceeds the limits set in the definitive agreement, the amount of cash and securities to be received is prorated so as not to violate the limits of the transaction. Arbitrageurs must be very careful to calculate the proration factors correctly, because they ultimately determine how much of each consideration will be received. Spreads and expected returns will be affected by these proration factors.

LEVERAGE

Until now, we have assumed that the arbitrageur uses only capital to invest in transactions. All our expected return calculations have assumed no use of leverage. This approach is fine for some investors, but most arbitrageurs utilize leverage in their operations. The use of leverage affects the return that the arbitrageur receives in any transaction. Because this book is directed toward individual investors, we will assume that arbitrage investors utilize typical Regulation T leverage: Purchases are financed by putting up capital for 50 percent of the purchase and borrowing up to the remaining 50 percent from the arbitrageur's broker or clearing firm. Borrowing the remaining 50 percent of the purchase cost creates an additional expense because all brokerage firms charge investors for this privilege. To calculate the cost of borrowing—also known as the *cost of carrying (COC) the position*—we will use the following formula:

$$COC = [(N \times SP_t) \times MR \times i_d] \times (P/365)$$

where N = number of shares purchased
MR = current Regulation T margin rate (at present 50 percent)
i_d = interest rate charged by broker on customer debit balance

Arbitrageurs may actually use additional leverage that may not be available to individual investors. If an arbitrageur is investing money in these transactions through an entity that is a registered broker/dealer, he or she is able to use broker/dealer financing, which can be far more aggressive than typical Regulation T leverage. Typically, the broker/dealer may be able to borrow up to 85 percent of the cost of the securities on the long side. However, because individuals do not have access to broker/dealer financing, we will assume that Regulation T leverage applies.

To illustrate the use of leverage in arbitrage and the effects it has on expected return, we employ the original set of calculations at the beginning of the chapter. Company A is acquiring Company T for $20 a share in cash. The $20 cash tender offer was expected to be completed in 30 days. With Company T's stock trading at $19.50, we can calculate a leveraged rate of return as follows:

$$ER_L = [(NS - COC)/I_L] \times (365/P)$$

where ER_L = expected leveraged return
NS = net spread
COC = cost of carry
I_L = investment (leveraged)
P = estimated investment period

To calculate the cost of carry, we use:

$$COC = [(N \times SP_t) \times MR \times i_d] \times (P/365)$$

where N = number of shares of target company purchased
SP_t = target company's stock price
MR = margin rate
i_d = interest cost on debit balance (interest on money borrowed)

Substituting calculations, we have:

$$COC = [(1.0 \times \$19.50) \times .50 \times .06] \times (30/365)$$
$$= (\$19.50 \times .50 \times .06) \times (365/30)$$
$$= \$0.585 \times .0821$$
$$= \$0.048$$

and
$$I_L = SP_t \times MR$$
$$= \$19.50 \times .50$$
$$= \$9.75$$
$$ER_L = [(NS - COC)/I_L] \times (365/P)$$
$$= [(\$0.50 - \$0.048)/\$9.75] \times (365/30)$$
$$= (\$0.452/\$9.75) \times (365/30)$$
$$= 56.40 \text{ percent}$$

In this case, the unleveraged annualized return of 31.2 percent became a leveraged annualized return of 56.40 percent by allowing the arbitrageur to finance the purchase of Company T's shares with 50 percent capital and 50 percent borrowings. As can be expected, the introduction of leverage will also cause the arbitrageur's losses to increase on a percentage basis.

Leveraged Returns on Stock-for-Stock Transactions

With stock-for-stock transactions, we must recognize that brokers require the investor/arbitrageur to have adequate capital for both the long position and the short position. The investor must put up capital equal to the long position times the current margin rate and the margin rate times the short proceeds in the account. Total investment when the arbitrageur sells short the proper ratio of the acquiring company's shares is therefore increased and must be accounted for in the return calculations.

In the following example, we will assume that Company A is offering to acquire Company T by issuing 1.5 shares of Company A stock for each share of Company T.

Company T's stock price	$28.50
Company A's stock price	$20.00
Exchange ratio	1.5 shares
Dividends	Neither company pays a dividend
Estimated investment period	90 days
Interest on debit balance	7 percent
Interest on short proceeds	6 percent

The return on this stock-for-stock transaction on a leveraged basis would be calculated as follows:

$$
\begin{aligned}
ER_L &= [(NS - COC)/I_L] \times (365/P) \\
&= [(\$1.94 - \$.25)/\$29.25] \times (365/90) \\
&= (\$1.69/\$29.25) \times (365/90) \\
&= 23.4 \text{ percent}
\end{aligned}
$$

The values for the respective terms are arrived at as follows:

$$
\begin{aligned}
GS &= (\$20 \times 1.5) - \$28.50 \\
&= \$30 - \$28.50 \\
&= \$1.50
\end{aligned}
$$

and
$$\begin{aligned}
SI &= SIP \times IS \\
&= (\$20 \times 1.5) \times .06 \times (90/365) \\
&= \$.44 \\
NS &= GS + SI \\
&= \$1.50 + \$.44 \\
&= \$1.94
\end{aligned}$$

because
$$\begin{aligned}
COC &= [(N \times SP_t) \times MR \times i_d] \times (P/365) \\
&= [(1 \times \$28.50) \times .50 \times .07] \times (90/365) \\
&= (\$.9975) \times (.2465) \\
&= \$.25 \\
I_L &= (SP_t \times MR) + [(SP_a \times R) \times MR] \\
&= (\$28.50 \times .50) + [(\$20 \times 1.5) \times .50] \\
&= \$14.25 + \$15.00 \\
&= \$29.25
\end{aligned}$$

The return is lowered significantly because of the requirement to put up 50 percent of the short side in addition to 50 percent of the long side.

The investor must realize that although these stock-for-stock transactions represent attractive risk arbitrage opportunities, they will impact the amount of available capital.

SPREAD BEHAVIOR OVER TIME

One might expect that, in theory, the spread in a deal will steadily decline because of the time value of money and the passage of time. It might also be assumed that the passage of time will continually diminish the risk associated with the deal. In other words, as time goes on, it becomes more and more likely that the transaction will be completed. This simplified expected relationship is illustrated in Figure 4.1.

This relationship may generally fit a number of simple transactions in which no problems arise. However, some transactions do not exhibit a straight-line relationship to closing, and others develop variations because of supply-and-demand factors. Overall, almost all transactions have variations in spread in terms of dollars and percentage of expected return. Figure 4.2 depicts the expected net spread in dollars for a transaction that develops an unexpected antitrust problem months after the public announcement. An actual case involving Lockheed-Martin Corporation's planned purchase of Northrop-Grumman Corporation will be further explored in Chapter 5.

Arbitrageurs must continually monitor the universe of transactions they follow, and they must update their estimates of expected return

Figure 4.1 Simple Transaction with No Unexpected Developments

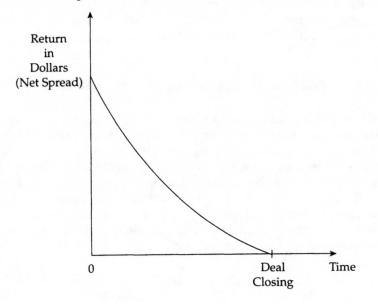

Figure 4.2 Complex Transaction—Antitrust Problem

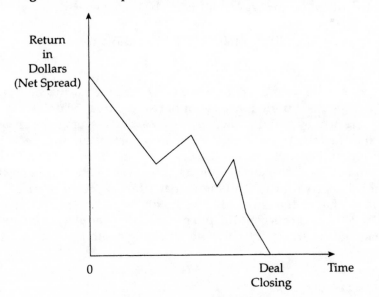

over time. From this perspective, an arbitrageur's investment process is very dynamic.

Timing of transactions also must be continually monitored, to maintain an accurate estimate of expected return.

TIMING OF RISK ARBITRAGE TRANSACTIONS

After determining the gross and net spreads on any given risk arbitrage transaction, the arbitrageur must accurately determine how long each transaction will take to complete. This estimate of timing has a direct impact on the arbitrageur's expected rate of return. For instance, in the simple cash tender-offer example, the expected return would drop dramatically if the arbitrageur's original 30-day investment period were lengthened to 60 days because an additional regulatory step needed to be completed prior to the transaction's closing. The expected return would be calculated as follows:

$$\begin{aligned}
ER_{UL} &= (GS/I) \times (365/P) \\
&= (\$0.50/\$19.50) \times (365/60) \\
&= 15.6 \text{ percent}
\end{aligned}$$

This expected return is exactly half of the expected return when the investment period was expected to be only 30 days:

$$\begin{aligned}
ER_{UL} &= (\$0.50/\$19.50) \times (365/30) \\
&= 31.2 \text{ percent}
\end{aligned}$$

In a simple unleveraged cash transaction, increasing the estimate of the investment period by a factor of two reduces the unleveraged expected return by half. If, however, we consider a leveraged transaction, varying the investment period estimate affects various aspects of the transaction. For instance, in the Greater New York/Astoria cash and stock-for-stock transaction, altering the investment period estimate would change various calculations that affect expected return.

If we change the estimated investment period in this example from 180 to 240 days (this could happen because of regulatory delays), the spread and return calculations would change as follows:

$$\begin{aligned}
GS &= DP - SP_t \\
&= \$18.25 - 17.25 \\
&= \$1.00
\end{aligned}$$

$$NS = GS + D_t - (D_a \times R \times p_2) + SI$$
$$= \$1.00 + (3 \times .05) - [(3 \times .11) \times .5 \times .75] + \{[(.5 \times \$36) \times .75] \times .04 \times$$
$$240/365\}$$
$$= \$1.3813$$

D_t = .05 per share × 3 (Three dividends are to be paid out during
the estimated 240 days we expect the transaction to take.)
= \$.15

D_a = .11 per share × 3 (We expect the acquiring company to also pay
three dividends during the time we are short the stock.)
= \$.33 (But remember: We are shorting only .5 share on only 75
percent of the Greater New York position):

$$p_2 = .75$$
$$SI = SIP \times IS$$

where SIP = short proceeds
= (.5 × \$36) × .75 (We will short .5 share of Astoria on only
75 percent of the entire position.)
= \$13.50

IS = .04

SI = \$13.50 × .04 × (240/365) (We are assuming we will receive
4 percent short interest credit for 180 days on the net
short proceeds created.)
= \$0.355

$$NS = GS + D_t - (D_a \times R \times p_2) + SI$$
$$= \$1.00 + \$0.15 - \$0.1237 + \$0.355$$
$$= \$1.3813$$

Also ER_{UL} = (NS/I) × (365/P)
= (\$1.3813/\$17.25) × (365/240)
= 12.17 percent

By lengthening the timing estimate from 180 to 240 days, the two
dividend cash flows, the short interest credit, and the annualization
factor are all affected. The net result is that the unleveraged expected
return drops from 15.08 percent to 12.17 percent. Because this deal involves more complex calculations than were needed in our previous

simple example, the decrease in annualized spread is not directly proportional to the lengthening of the timing estimate. We increased the investment period by 33 percent (60 days), but the annualized spread dropped only 19.3 percent (2.91/15.08).

Timing has a very important impact on the arbitrageur's rate of return calculations.

ESTIMATING TIMING IN MERGER TRANSACTIONS

Chapter 2 presented a general description of the steps that occur in the merger transaction process. The merging companies sometimes have an initial agreement in principle. They then enter into a process of due diligence that includes inspecting each other's books, records, and physical assets. This process can take anywhere from several weeks to several months. As we pointed out earlier, in most of today's mergers, this process is completed prior to any public announcement. The first public announcement of a merger generally occurs after the two companies reach a definitive agreement. When the definitive agreement has been executed, the lawyers for the respective firms work on any of the regulatory filings that are required under the law. If the merger involves a stock-for-stock exchange, a registration statement must be filed and declared effective by the Securities and Exchange Commission (SEC). If, however, the transaction involves only cash, a filing must be made with the SEC to allow the target company's shareholders to vote on the transaction. The companies must also file with both the Justice Department and the Federal Trade Commission (FTC) under the Hart–Scott–Rodino (HSR) Act, to comply with the federal government's requirement for documentation and information on the transaction. When the companies are deemed to be in compliance with their initial filings, the federal government has a 30-day period in which it may request additional information from the companies. After the companies provide the requested information to both the Department of Justice and the FTC, there is an additional 20-day waiting period. The companies must not close their transaction until the federal government either grants approval or decides to ask a federal court to halt the transaction because an antitrust violation has been revealed.

A request for additional information under the HSR Act tends to lengthen the time it takes for a transaction to close. During this waiting period, the companies may continue to perform any additional steps needed to complete the transaction. For instance, shareholders of

Figure 4.3 Merger Timing

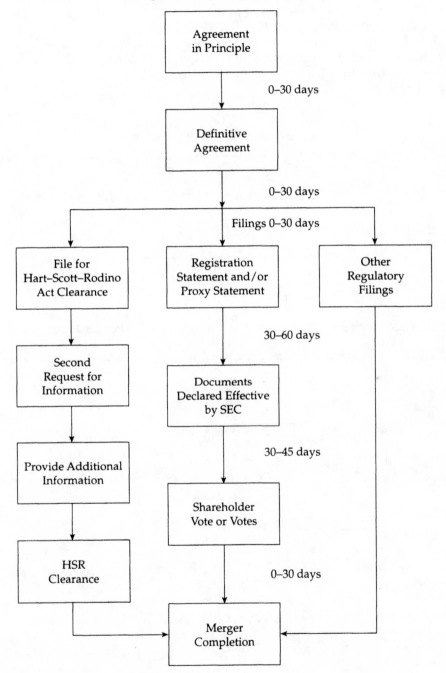

either company may vote on the merger while they wait for the HSR Act waiting period to expire.

The entire timing process is illustrated in Figure 4.3. All mergers should be analyzed on a case-by-case basis. The arbitrageur should be cautious about assuming that any merger transaction will be completed within the 90 days typically estimated.

Figure 4.4   Tender Offer Timing

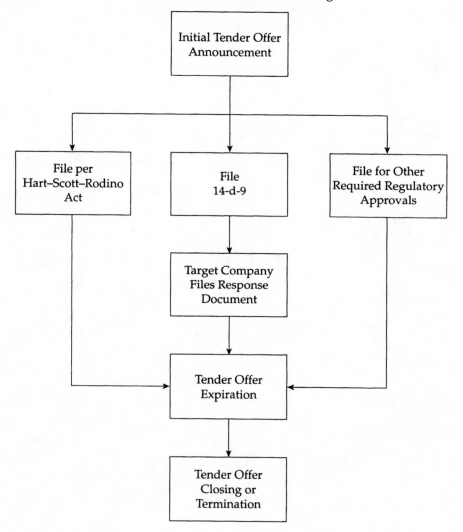

ESTIMATING TIMING IN TENDER OFFER TRANSACTIONS

The timing of a tender offer mostly depends on whether the transaction is friendly or hostile. Friendly tender offers that are endorsed by the target company's Board of Directors can be completed within a month, provided there are no regulatory or antitrust issues. Hostile takeovers can take significantly long time periods to complete. There is no way to generalize the time it takes to complete a hostile tender offer, but it is not unusual to have a 6-month battle, and battles that lasted more than a year have occurred in the recent past.

Like mergers, tender offers must comply with the Hart–Scott–Rodino Antitrust Act (HSR Act). When an acquiring company files the tender offer documents with the Securities and Exchange Commission, it will usually file simultaneously with both the Department of Justice and the Federal Trade Commission. For tender offers, the government waiting periods are different than for mergers. The initial waiting period during which the government may request additional information is only 20 days. If the government requests additional information, the companies cannot close the tender offer until 10 days after they have provided the government with the requested information.

Antitrust aspects of the tender offer, as well as other regulatory issues, may also affect the length of time it takes to complete a tender offer.

Figure 4.4 represents the individual steps needed to complete a tender offer.

Now that we have explored the calculation of spreads and the arbitrageur's estimates of expected returns, we can turn our attention to the risks involved in risk arbitrage transactions.

Chapter 5

Risk

In Chapter 1, I explained why the term *risk* is linked to arbitrage. In the Office Depot/Staples deal, arbitrageurs suffered large losses because the Federal Trade Commission succeeded in blocking the proposed friendly merger. After a preliminary injunction was issued by the court, arbitrageurs rushed to sell their shares. The results were: a sharp decline in the price of Office Depot, and large losses of capital for all Office Depot shareholders. Arbitrageurs must estimate and continually monitor the risks they assume when they invest in any risk arbitrage transaction.

The risk estimation process begins with the initial announcement of the deal. Simultaneously with their initial estimate of return, arbitrageurs begin the process of determining what their losses might be if the transaction does not close as planned.

The initial step in analyzing a deal's risk is usually an examination of the trading history of the target company's securities. The arbitrageur generally asks the following questions:

- Where was the target company's stock (or other related securities subject to the takeover) trading prior to announcement of the transaction?
- Was there an information leak that generated insider trading prior to the announcement? Did the stock price rise several days or weeks prior to announcement of the transaction?

If the target company's stock moved up significantly prior to announcement of the deal, and no fundamental reason or explanation could be found in the general equity market activity, the price level that existed just prior to the announcement would not be a good initial guide for determining the arbitrageur's risk. A stock price jump may indicate a possible leak in the negotiations. The arbitrageur must then go back to the stock's trading price before any inside information was available. This price becomes the estimate for the initial downside price. If the negotiations break off within a short period of time, in the absence of any other information, the target company's stock may trade back down to this level.

Figures 5.1 and 5.2 illustrate downside estimates without and with inside information. In Figure 5.1, no inside information was leaking into the marketplace, and therefore no jump in the price of the target company's stock occurred prior to the announcement of a merger deal. The downside estimate of the target company's stock is clear. The security was trading within a narrow band of prices prior to the announcement of the deal.

In contrast, Figure 5.2 tracks the stock price of a target company involved in a transaction where there was a leak in the negotiations. The price of the target company stock rose prior to the announcement of the deal, and significant volume was traded prior to the deal announcement. This pattern generally indicates that a leak in the negotiations occurred, and information filtered into the marketplace and forced price to rise. Arbitrageurs always take into account the possibility of

Figure 5.1   Downside Estimate—No Leaks of Information

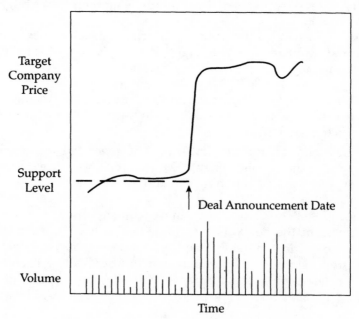

Figure 5.2   Downside Estimate—Information
Leaks during Negotiations

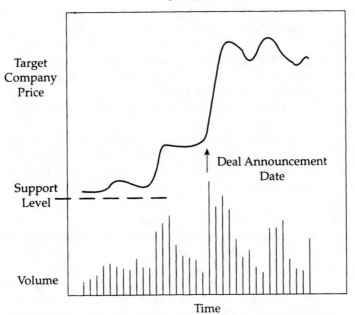

inside information leaks when they estimate a company's downside risk. Not taking into account the effects of inside information leaks could cause an understatement of the downside risk and could contribute to an erroneous analysis of the deal.

The arbitrageur's estimates of downside risks can be compared to a technical analyst's estimate of support levels. Technicians often estimate where securities will receive support on the downside.

Additional factors must be considered when trying to determine the downside risk in any given transaction. If the transaction is terminated within a few weeks after it was announced, the arbitrageur usually does not have to worry about fundamental factors that would affect the target company's stock price. If, however, a rather lengthy period of time passes between the deal's initial announcement and the arbitrageur's efforts to estimate risk, the arbitrageur must consider any fundamental changes that have occurred at the target company and judge whether they are good or bad. If the company's earnings outlook has improved, that would be a reason for potentially increasing the estimate of the downside price. However, if there has been deterioration in the fundamentals at the target company, the arbitrageur would have to consider lowering the estimate of the downside price. These considerations become more and more difficult as the length of time from the announcement of the deal increases.

If the target company's fundamentals have deteriorated since the initial transaction was announced, the arbitrageur is faced with the worst possible situation. Not only has the deal broken, causing losses on the arbitrageur's long position, but the original downside price estimate has almost surely become overstated, causing the arbitrageur's losses to exceed the prior estimates. Especially in today's capital markets, companies' common stocks can be severely affected by unfavorable fundamental developments.

Other factors also must be considered. When a transaction actually breaks apart, supply and demand factors come into play because the arbitrage community usually has a substantial position in the underlying security of the target company. Depending on the particular transaction, the arbitrage community could have a cumulative position of 20 to 40 percent of the target company's outstanding shares. Arbitrageurs are generally short-term investors who have no interest in taking any long-term investment positions, so they tend to work out of their positions by selling them into the marketplace at the earliest possible time. Some arbitrageurs operate under policies that require them to sell out positions in any securities that are not involved in active transactions. The result can be an oversupply of the target company's stock in the marketplace when the transaction initially terminates. The oversupply may cause the target company's stock to sell below its normal trading level for a number of days or weeks, or until the arbitrageurs work out of their arbitrage positions. This type of situation is illustrated in Figure 5.3. Ultimately, the target company's security will trade at the level that the general investment community regards as its correct value. The typical investment valuation framework will then control the level at which the target company's stock trades.

The arbitrageur must consider why a transaction actually broke. If government intervention or a private suit caused something "out of the blue" to terminate the transaction, the adjustments needed in the initial estimate of downside risk may not be indicated. If, however, the transaction terminates because of the underlying fundamentals of the target company's business, the arbitrageur's initial estimate of downside risk could be substantially understated. The price was determined in the marketplace when the investment community expected certain results from the target company. If the target company's fundamentals have declined, the odds are that the price of the underlying stock will also trade lower than expected.

Occasionally, when a deal breaks up, the effects may not be as bad as some arbitrageurs might expect. If a company terminates a transaction

Figure 5.3 Target Company Stock Trading below Downside Price
Estimate after Transaction Termination

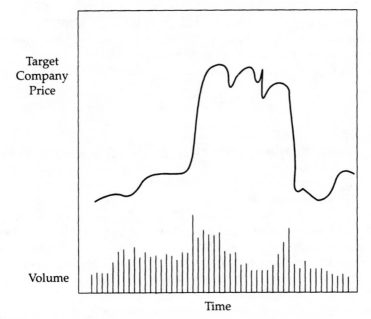

and the target company leaves the door open to other potential transactions, a premium will be assigned to the target company's underlying stock price because of the possibility that another transaction will take place. When the deal breaks up, instead of trading at the arbitrageur's downside estimate, the stock will trade at some price above that initial estimate. Similarly, if the company announces, after terminating a transaction, that it has hired investment bankers to explore additional opportunities and potential transactions that can improve shareholder value, this announcement would also create a premium for the arbitrageur's downside risk estimate.

The actual calculation of downside risk can be determined by this formula:

$$DR = SP_t - TD$$

where DR = downside risk
SP_t = target company's current stock price
TD = arbitrageur's estimate of the target's downside price

In a stock-for-stock transaction, or a deal involving a security that the arbitrageur sells short in order to hedge the transaction, we must also estimate what can be lost on the short side of the transaction if the deal breaks up. In other words, unlike a one-sided deal, this hedging transaction creates a two-sided deal, and the arbitrageur potentially has risks on both the long side and the short side.

We find the risk on the short side by using the following formula:

$$UR = (AU - SP_a) \times R$$

where UR = upside risk
AU = arbitrageur's estimate of acquiring company's upside price
SP_a = acquiring company's current stock price
R = exchange ratio

This formula also assumes that the arbitrageur has fully hedged his or her position by selling short the exact number of the acquiring company's shares that will be received upon consummation of the transaction. Should the arbitrageur not be fully hedged, upside risk can be calculated using this formula:

$$UR = (AU - SP_a) \times (AS / TT)$$

where AS = number of acquiring company's shares sold short
TT = number of target company's shares owned

Both of the above formulas calculate upside risk in terms of the number of shares held in the target company's stock. This is important because when arbitrageurs calculate return, they want to have the proper comparative calculation for risk. If an arbitrageur believes a gain of $2.50 per share in net spread in the target company is possible, he or she also wants to know how much can be lost per target company share.

At this point, an analysis of an actual merger may be useful to illustrate how the risk estimates are calculated. On April 10, 1998, Star Banc Corporation agreed to acquire Trans Financial Incorporated in exchange for common stock. Trans Financial shareholders were to receive .9003 share of Star Banc for each share of Trans Financial owned. Charts of Trans Financial (TRFI) and Star Banc (STB) are shown in Figures 5.4 and 5.5, respectively.

As can be seen in Figure 5.4, Trans Financial stock had been trading in the range of $47 per share prior to the deal's announcement. But

Figure 5.4   Daily Price Chart of Trans Financial

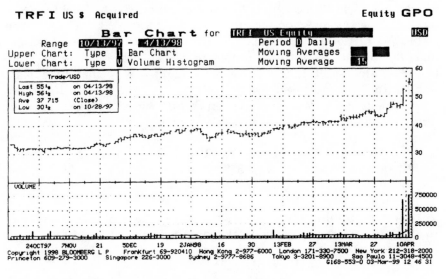

Figure 5.5   Daily Price Chart of Firstar Corporation
Composite Trading Record

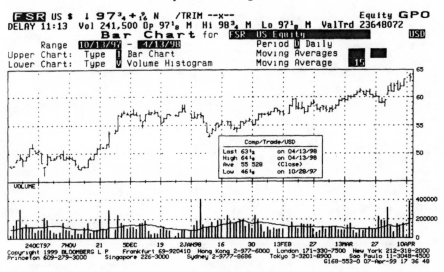

note the market action in the two weeks prior to the announcement: The shares of TRFI moved up to $47 from the $42–$43 level (see Figure 5.6). The key question for the arbitrageur was: Was the move from $42 to $47 related to the fundamentals of TRFI and the overall equity market movements, or did it represent a leak in the merger negotiations? Quite possibly, the price movement was related to a leak. Volume in TRFI increased dramatically during the week prior to announcement of the transaction. Given this information, the arbitrageur might estimate the downside risk as follows:

$$
\begin{aligned}
DR &= SP_t - TD \\
&= \$55.125 - \$42 \\
&= \$13.125
\end{aligned}
$$

After examining the table on the price action of Star Banc (Figure 5.7), the arbitrageur would calculate the upside risk as follows:

$$
\begin{aligned}
UR &= (AU - SP_a) \times R \\
&= (\$62 - \$63.5) \times .9003 \\
&= -\$1.35 \text{ per TRFI share}
\end{aligned}
$$

Figure 5.6   Trans Financial (TRFI)

Page						DG15 **Equity** G P O		
Hit <MENU> to return to graph or <PAGE> to continue.								
P R I C E T A B L E W / M O V A V E & V O L						PAGE 1 OF 9		

T R F I   U S ⠀⠀⠀⠀⠀⠀⠀⠀⠀⠀⠀⠀⠀⠀⠀⠀⠀⠀⠀⠀⠀⠀⠀⠀⠀⠀⠀⠀USD
  THIS PAGE: 4/13/98 TO: 3/30/98

DATE	OPEN	HIGH	LOW	CLOSE	MA1	MA2	VOL	VAVE
F								
T								
W								
T								
M 4/13	55	$56^1{}_2$	$54^1{}_4$	$55^1{}_8$			756700	138533
F 4/10								
T 4/ 9	$47^1{}_4$	$52^3{}_4$	$46^5{}_8$	$52^5{}_8$			667100	89587
W 4/ 8	$46^5{}_8$	$47^1{}_4$	46	$47^1{}_4$			94600	47247
T 4/ 7	$47^5{}_8$	$47^5{}_8$	$46^1{}_8$	$46^5{}_8$			24700	43853
M 4/ 6	$47^1{}_8$	$47^3{}_4$	$47^1{}_8$	$47^5{}_{16}$			89900	43293
F 4/ 3	$46^1{}_8$	$47^3{}_4$	$46^1{}_8$	$46^1{}_2$			102800	40460
T 4/ 2	$44^1{}_8$	$45^7{}_8$	$44^1{}_8$	$45^3{}_4$			57100	36347
W 4/ 1	43	44	43	44			41100	38587
T 3/31	43	$43^3{}_8$	43	$43^1{}_4$			17200	40100
M 3/30	$43^3{}_8$	$43^3{}_8$	43	43			28800	42027

Copyright 1998 BLOOMBERG L P   Frankfurt 69-920410 Hong Kong 2-977-6000 London 171-330-7500 New York 212-318-2000
Princeton 609-279-3000   Singapore 226-3000   Sydney 2-9777-8686   Tokyo 3-3201-8900   Sao Paulo 11-3048-4500
G168-553-0 03-Mar-99 12:50 04

Figure 5.7 Firstar Corporation (FSR)

```
F S R    U S                                                      USD
   THIS PAGE: 4/13/98 TO: 3/30/98
```

DATE	OPEN	HIGH	LOW	CLOSE	MA1	MA2	VOL	VAVE
F								
T								
W								
T								
M 4/13	$63^7{}_8$	$64^1{}_8$	$62^{13}{}_{16}$	$63^1{}_2$			379700	156053
F 4/10								
T 4/ 9	62	$63^5{}_{16}$	$61^{15}{}_{16}$	$63^5{}_{16}$			153700	136060
W 4/ 8	$61^7{}_{16}$	$62^7{}_{16}$	$61^7{}_{16}$	62			129700	129400
T 4/ 7	$62^5{}_{16}$	$62^7{}_8$	$61^5{}_{16}$	$61^5{}_{16}$			146800	125647
M 4/ 6	$61^1{}_{16}$	$62^5{}_8$	$61^1{}_{16}$	$62^1{}_8$			64800	126053
F 4/ 3	$62^1{}_8$	$62^5{}_8$	$60^{15}{}_{16}$	$61^1{}_8$			115100	130660
T 4/ 2	$60^1{}_2$	62	$60^\cdot{}_2$	$61^1{}_8$			312000	128367
W 4/ 1	$59^1{}_8$	$59^9{}_{16}$	$58^5{}_{16}$	$59^9{}_{16}$			174300	113073
T 3/31	$58^7{}_8$	$59^{15}{}_{16}$	$58^7{}_8$	$59^1{}_8$			184200	106640
M 3/30	$60^1{}_{16}$	$60^3{}_{16}$	$58^7{}_8$	59			225700	101680

Source: © 1999 Bloomberg L.P. All rights reserved.

This estimate of upside risk would have been considered unusual in the past. It means that if the deal were to break up, the arbitrageur would actually realize a gain on reversing his or her short position.

For many years, in a stock-for-stock transaction, it was common for the acquiring company's stock price to drop after a proposed merger was announced. It was assumed that when the transaction was terminated, the acquiring company's shares would most likely rise to their previous level, barring any additional information on the security. In recent years, however, we have been witnessing a totally different price reaction in the acquiring company's shares. In today's merger market, in many instances, the shares of the acquiring company have increased in value after the transaction announcement, and sometimes the increase has been significantly large. This may be a result of the investment community's concluding that by combining the companies, their earnings outlook or their growth rate has improved; or, the investment community may be expecting additional benefits from the combination of the firms. Whatever the reason, this situation can change the dynamics of a two-sided deal. Before, an upside risk would occur if the transaction was terminated and arbitrageurs sought to cover their short sales. Now, the acquiring company's shares may fall if the transaction is called off, because the investment community may roll back its viewpoint on the acquiring company's shares. The arbitrageurs had bought shares and increased the price of the acquiring company's shares based on some positive influence. If the transaction is terminated, they will only purchase the securities of the acquiring company at the previous level—the price when no positive changes were expected.

If the acquiring company's share price increases after the announcement, the arbitrageur may actually be estimating a gain on the short side of the transaction if the deal breaks up. This estimated gain may partially or fully offset whatever loss the arbitrageur may sustain on the long side of the transaction. Figures 5.8 and 5.9 show the price action of the acquiring company's share price over a period of time that includes the announcement and its aftermath. In Figure 5.8, the acquiring company's stock declines after the merger announcement, but Figure 5.9 shows the price of the acquiring company's stock rising after the announcement. The investment community's optimism results in the acquiring company's stock price rising after the announcement.

Figure 5.8   Acquiring Company's Stock Behavior after Deal Termination (Acquiring Company Stock Declines)

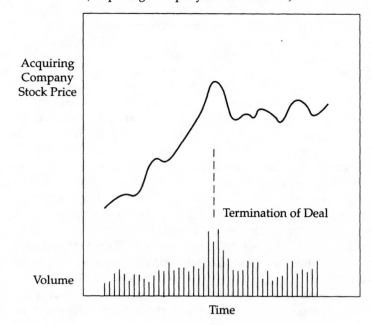

Figure 5.9 Acquiring Company's Stock Behavior after Deal Termination (Acquiring Company Stock Increases)

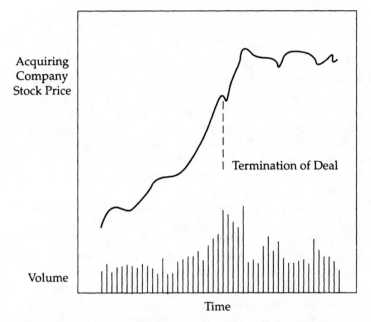

We must remember that, in a stock-for-stock transaction, when figuring the estimates of risk (or gain, in some cases) for the short position, we must also incorporate the exchange ratio that we have used to set up the hedged position. For example, if we estimate that a stock that we shorted could go up by 2 points if the transaction broke up, our risk estimate on the short side would be 2 points × the number of shares that we have actually shorted. In other words, if the transaction called for shorting half a share of the acquiring company for each share of the target company's stock, our risk estimate on the short side would be the 2 points of upside risk × the .5 exchange ratio, or only $1.00 worth of upside risk.

TOTAL RISK

When we have an estimate of risk on the long side and on the short side of a transaction, we refer to the concept of *total risk*. Total risk is simply the amount of long side risk plus the amount of risk that we have on the short side of the transaction. The formula for total risk is:

$$TR = DR + UR$$

where   TR = total risk
          DR = downside risk
          UR = upside risk

Total risk, along with other inputs, will be used by the arbitrageur in the decision process to determine whether he or she should take a position in any given arbitrage transaction. However, other considerations must be acknowledged when discussing risk in the transaction. First, risk arbitrage is a dynamic process. We may initially calculate our risk estimates based on the day when the deal is announced, and these estimates may hold for a certain period of time. If, however, it takes a while for the transaction to close, it is advisable for an arbitrageur to continually reassess the risk estimates.

The easiest way to update risk estimates over time is to adjust the initial estimates of risk (when the transaction was announced) for general moves in the equity market. This is usually done through the use of a computer. When a deal is announced, the arbitrageur inputs his or her estimates of risk as well as the date and an index—let's say the Standard & Poor's 500 Index—on the day the transaction is initiated. As time goes on, the arbitrageur will use a change in the S&P 500 Index (or some other market index) to measure a change in the overall equity market, and will apply it to the initial estimate of risk in the target company and the acquiring company. This activity can be shown by these formulas:

$$DR = \left\{ SP_t - \left[TD \times \left(1 + \left(\frac{SNP_c}{SNP_o} - 1 \right) \right) \right] \right\}$$

and

$$UR = \left\{ AU \times \left[1 + \left(\frac{SNP_c}{SNP_o} - 1 \right) - SP_a \right] \right\} \times R$$

where   DR = adjusted downside risk
          UR = adjusted upside risk
        SNP_c = current Standard & Poor's 500 Index
        SNP_o = Standard & Poor's 500 Index when deal was announced

These formulas may also incorporate a "beta" or sensitivity measure for each individual security, to basically improve the arbitrageur's estimate of risk. If the arbitrageur is able to measure how sensitive each security is to general overall market moves, he or she may gain improved accuracy by utilizing this sensitivity measure. The formulas for incorporating sensitivity are:

$$DR = \left\{ SP_t - \left[TD \times \left(1 + \left(\left(\frac{SNP_c}{SNP_o} - 1 \right) \times B_t \right) \right) \right] \right\}$$

and

$$UR = \left\{ AU \times \left[\left(1 + \left(\frac{SNP_c}{SNP_o} - 1 \right) \times B_a \right) - SP_a \right] \right\} \times R$$

where B_t = adjusted downside risk
B_a = adjusted upside risk

To illustrate the calculations for using the change in the Standard & Poor's 500 Index and their effect on the arbitrageur's estimates of upside and downside risk, we will assume the following:

Target Company	Factor	Acquiring Company
$20	Current stock price	$35
$15	Downside price	—
—	Upside price	$37
1.1	Beta	.9

We will also assume that because the deal was announced, the Standard & Poor's 500 Index increased from 915 to 960, and the acquiring company is issuing 1.2 shares for each target company share.

$$DR = \left\{ \$20 - \left[\$15 \times \left(1 + \left(\frac{960}{915} - 1 \right) \times 1.1 \right) \right] \right\}$$

$$= (\$20 - \$15.81)$$

$$= \$4.19 \text{ (vs. original downside risk of \$5)}$$

$$UR = \left\{ \$37 \times \left[1 + \left(\left(\frac{960}{915} - 1 \right) \times .9 \right) \right] - 35 \right\} \times 1.2$$

$$= \left[(\$37 \times 1.0442) - \$35 \right] \times 1.2$$

$$= (\$38.63 - \$35) \times 1.2$$

$$= (-3.63) \times 1.2$$

$$= \$4.36 \text{ (vs. original upside risk of \$2.40)}$$

In many instances, it is advisable for the arbitrageur to take a fresh look at the underlying securities involved in a transaction. If a long period of time has elapsed since the deal was announced, it is generally advisable to look at the target company's and acquiring company's individual industries and be able to forecast what would happen to their underlying stock prices. An arbitrageur does this by first assembling a list of securities from companies within the target company's industry group which seem to compare well with the target company. The arbitrageur will also assemble a group of companies that compare well with the acquiring company and are within its industry group. The next step is to look at what these comparative companies' stock prices have done during the period of time that is being analyzed in the deal. Arbitrageurs generally construct a table and go back to the initial date on which they estimated the upside and downside risk in the transaction. They assemble the prices of the comparative securities, and compare them (and the price changes) to the current-day prices of the same securities. In this way, arbitrageurs are able to construct their own index of comparative securities and arrive at a better estimate of the downside and upside risks.

This type of calculation gained attention when the Justice Department challenged a transaction in which Lockheed-Martin is trying to acquire Northrop-Grumman. This transaction was announced on July 2, 1997, and it was expected that it would occur within a 3- or 4-month period. For each share of Northrop-Grumman, shareholders were to receive 1.1923 shares of Lockheed-Martin. However, the Justice Department's investigation of the antitrust aspects of the transaction has significantly delayed the transfer of shares. In May 1998, the Justice Department filed suit and asked for Federal District Court in Washington, DC, to issue a preliminary injunction against the merger. The case was due to go to trial in September 1998.* This injunction has presented a number of challenges to the arbitrageur. The most difficult challenge is to estimate the likelihood that the merger will ever occur, but the arbitrageur's job of estimating the total risk in the transaction has also been significantly complicated. By examining the data on Northrop-Grumman and Lockheed-Martin (Figures 5.10–5.13), the arbitrageur could have developed the following initial risk estimates:

---

*This transaction was ultimately terminated by Lockheed-Martin on July 17, 1998, due to the government's objection to the merger.

$$DR = SP_t - TD$$
$$= \$110 - \$88$$
$$= \$22$$

$$UR = (AU - SP_a) \times R$$
$$= (\$104 - 99.125) \times 1.1923$$
$$= \$5.81$$

$$TR = DR + UR$$
$$= \$22 + \$5.81$$
$$= \$27.8$$

The LMT stock split 2 for 1 on January 4, 1999 causing the prices to be half of what they would have been at the time of the deal.

These estimates might have been accurate if used by the arbitrageur on July 3, 1997. However, to calculate total risk as of May 13, 1998, the arbitrageur must use a different method.

The arbitrageur may have formulated a good estimate for the downside and upside risk at the time the transaction was first announced, but a significant period of time has passed since then. The arbitrageur

Figure 5.10 Graph of Northrop-Grumman

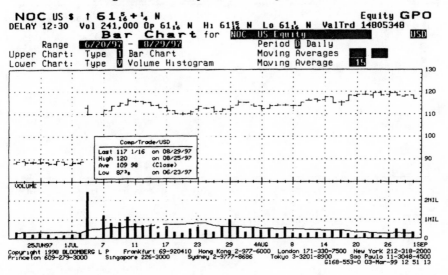

Source: © 1999 Bloomberg L.P. All rights reserved.

Figure 5.11 Price Volume Table of Northrop-Grumman

Page   DG15 **Equity** G P O
Hit <MENU> to return to graph or <PAGE> to continue.
P R I C E   T A B L E   W / M O V   A V E   &   V O L   PAGE 3 OF 4

N O C   U S   USD
THIS PAGE: 7/18/97 TO: 6/30/97

DATE		OPEN	HIGH	LOW	CLOSE	MA1	MA2	VOL	VAVE
F	7/18	$111\frac{3}{8}$	$111\frac{1}{2}$	110	$110\frac{3}{8}$			345600	729467
T	7/17	113	113	$115\frac{5}{16}$	$111\frac{7}{16}$			627100	719027
W	7/16	$113\frac{15}{16}$	$114\frac{7}{16}$	$112\frac{3}{4}$	$112\frac{15}{16}$			610300	693533
T	7/15	$115\frac{1}{8}$	$115\frac{1}{8}$	$113\frac{11}{16}$	$113\frac{7}{8}$			818900	666100
M	7/14	$115\frac{3}{4}$	$115\frac{11}{16}$	$114\frac{5}{8}$	115			658100	633407
F	7/11	$115\frac{3}{4}$	$116\frac{1}{4}$	$115\frac{3}{16}$	$115\frac{3}{4}$			764500	612527
T	7/10	$114\frac{1}{4}$	117	$114\frac{1}{4}$	116			1129300	608593
W	7/ 9	$113\frac{3}{4}$	$115\frac{1}{4}$	$113\frac{11}{16}$	$114\frac{11}{16}$			854300	557047
T	7/ 8	$115\frac{5}{8}$	$113\frac{3}{4}$	$111\frac{5}{8}$	$113\frac{11}{16}$			819600	534780
M	7/ 7	$110\frac{1}{8}$	$112\frac{1}{16}$	$109\frac{7}{8}$	$111\frac{3}{4}$			1216500	509213
F	7/ 4								
T	7/ 3	113	$114\frac{1}{4}$	$109\frac{1}{2}$	110			2440100	452233
W	7/ 2	$88\frac{1}{8}$	$88\frac{7}{8}$	88	$88\frac{7}{8}$			242500	306647
T	7/ 1	$87\frac{9}{16}$	89	$87\frac{1}{2}$	$88\frac{1}{8}$			177800	314747
M	6/30	$88\frac{3}{4}$	$88\frac{3}{4}$	$87\frac{7}{16}$	$87\frac{13}{16}$			128600	321520

Page   DG15 **Equity** G P O
Hit <MENU> to return to graph or <PAGE> to continue.
P R I C E   T A B L E   W / M O V   A V E   &   V O L   PAGE 4 OF 4

N O C   U S   USD
THIS PAGE: 6/27/97 TO: 6/20/97

DATE		OPEN	HIGH	LOW	CLOSE	MA1	MA2	VOL	VAVE
F	6/27	$87\frac{7}{8}$	$88\frac{15}{16}$	$87\frac{3}{4}$	$88\frac{15}{16}$			108800	326173
T	6/26	$88\frac{7}{16}$	$88\frac{1}{2}$	$87\frac{3}{4}$	$87\frac{11}{16}$			189000	332680
W	6/25	$88\frac{1}{4}$	$89\frac{3}{4}$	$88\frac{3}{16}$	$88\frac{7}{16}$			244700	334760
T	6/24	$88\frac{5}{8}$	$88\frac{15}{16}$	$87\frac{7}{8}$	$88\frac{1}{2}$			198800	326187
M	6/23	89	89	$87\frac{3}{8}$	$88\frac{1}{2}$			328500	322087
F	6/20	$88\frac{1}{4}$	89	88	$88\frac{7}{8}$			344900	305993

Source: © 1999 Bloomberg L.P. All rights reserved.

Figure 5.12   Graph of Lockheed-Martin

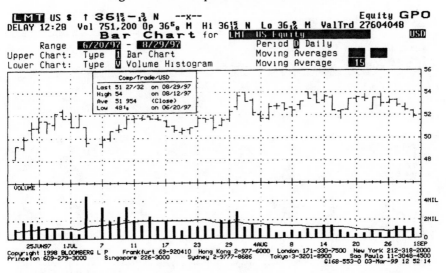

therefore must assemble a group of securities that are comparable to the Northrop-Grumann stock's activity in the marketplace, and calculate the price changes of those securities over the same period of time. The necessary calculations are shown in Table 5.1.

If we assume that the calculated industry average increase in stock price is applicable to both Northrop-Grumman's and Lockheed-Martin's stock prices, we would calculate the adjusted risks as follows:

$$DR = \{SP_t - [TD \times (1 + CI)]\}$$

where   CI = change in industry index
   $= (\$108.125 - (\$88 \times 1.1989)$
   $= (\$108.125 - \$105.50)$
   $= \$2.625$

and $UR = \{[AU \times (1 + CI)] - SP_a\} \times R$
   $= (\$104 \times 1.1989 - \$99.125) \times 1.1923$
   $= (\$124 - \$113.125) \times 1.1923$
   $= \$13.78$

   $TR = \$2.625 + \$13.78$
   $= \$16.405$

70 Risk

Figure 5.13 Price and Volume Table of Lockheed-Martin

L M T   U S   USD
THIS PAGE: 7/18/97 TO: 6/30/97

	DATE	OPEN	HIGH	LOW	CLOSE	MA1	MA2	VOL	VAVE
F	7/18	51^1_{32}	51^3_{32}	50^{15}_{32}	50^{21}_{32}			1287600	1929013
T	7/17	51^{17}_{32}	51^{19}_{32}	51	51			1834200	1926533
W	7/16	51^{11}_{16}	51^{27}_{32}	51^9_{16}	51^{21}_{32}			1320600	1894333
T	7/15	51^7_8	51^{15}_{16}	51^5_8	51^{11}_{16}			2347600	1920173
M	7/14	51^{25}_{32}	51^7_8	51^9_{16}	51^{11}_{16}			1415600	1879320
F	7/11	51^{11}_{16}	51^{15}_{16}	51^5_{16}	51^{25}_{32}			1968200	1855160
T	7/10	50^{29}_{32}	51^{15}_{16}	50^{13}_{16}	51^{11}_{16}			3401000	1765880
W	7/ 9	50^{23}_{32}	51^3_{16}	50^1_2	50^{25}_{32}			2316400	1603187
T	7/ 8	49^{31}_{32}	50^5_8	49^{25}_{32}	50^5_8			1793000	1536067
M	7/ 7	49^{17}_{32}	50^3_{16}	49^3_{16}	49^{27}_{32}			3402600	1497280
F	7/ 4								
T	7/ 3	51	51	49^1_4	49^9_{16}			4646600	1318160
W	7/ 2	51	52^1_8	51	52			554600	1050787
T	7/ 1	51^{25}_{32}	52^1_4	51	51			756800	1055360
M	6/30	52^3_8	52^5_8	51^3_4	51^{25}_{32}			861800	1065293

L M T   U S   USD
THIS PAGE: 6/27/97 TO: 6/20/97

	DATE	OPEN	HIGH	LOW	CLOSE	MA1	MA2	VOL	VAVE
F	6/27	51^3_{16}	52^1_4	50^{11}_{16}	52^1_8			1028600	1069867
T	6/26	51^1_2	51^1_2	50^1_2	51^5_{16}			1250400	1073427
W	6/25	50^7_8	51^{13}_{16}	50^9_{16}	51^1_2			1351200	1026000
T	6/24	50^{13}_{16}	51^7_{16}	50^1_{16}	50^7_8			1708200	970000
M	6/23	49^3_{16}	50^3_{16}	49^1_{16}	49^{15}_{16}			1734800	897933
F	6/20	48^1_8	49^1_4	48^1_8	49^1_4			1053200	828653

Source: © 1999 Bloomberg L.P. All rights reserved.

Table 5.1 Stock Price Performance in the Defense Industry from June 30, 1997, to May 13, 1998

Company Name	Symbol	Closing Price June 30, 1997	Closing Price May 13, 1998	Percentage Increase
Northrop-Grumman	NOC	$ 87.8125	$106.9735	
Lockheed-Martin	LMT	103.5625	113.00	
Boeing	BA	53.0625	49.875	−6.4%
Allied Signal	ALD	42.00	44.4375	5.8
Raytheon B	RTN'B	51.00	56.9735	11.7
Gulfstream Aerospace	GAC	29.25	43.125	47.4
Litton	LIT	48.3125	59.75	23.7
Cordant	CDD	35.00	53.25	52.1
Gencorp	GY	23.125	30.375	31.3
Average Price		40.25	48.255	19.8

As can be seen from these data, the arbitrageur's initial estimate of downside and upside risk has significantly changed because of the passage of time and the movement in the overall general equity market. Had the arbitrageur not updated the estimates of risk, the estimates used in the decision-making process would have been invalid.

The arbitrageur must always try to improve his or her ability to estimate risk on the long side and the short side of any transaction. It is a dynamic process, as we have previously discussed, and the arbitrageur must continually try to apply methods that will improve the estimates. Risk represents important input in any arbitrage transaction, and the arbitrageur will need estimates that are as accurate as possible.

Chapter **6**

Probability

It is very helpful for an arbitrageur to have estimates of both return and risk, but having these two elements does not give the arbitrageur a complete picture. The third and hardest element of the risk arbitrage decision process involves estimating the probability of a transaction's occurrence.

By taking several examples, an arbitrageur can estimate both return and risk on separate proposed transactions. As Table 6.1 illustrates, each transaction has its own return and risk. The dollar amounts vary from deal to deal. If we look at the two columns that show return and risk estimates, we realize that it is very difficult for an arbitrageur to determine which deal, if any, is worth an investment. Is it wise to invest in Deal ABC and earn $2.00 per share, or does it make more sense to invest in Deal GHI for a spread of only $0.375 per share? The amount of dollars at risk in these deals is almost the same. Why invest capital to earn only $0.375 per share?

In Table 6.2, we express return and risk in percentages. The return incorporates not only the required capital investment but also the time needed to earn the expected return. Because percentage calculations incorporate the element of timing, they are usually more useful than return and risk expressed in terms of absolute dollars. We can see that the expected return on Deal GHI (18%) is greater than on Deal ABC

Table 6.1   Risk and Return on Selected Deals (in terms of dollars)

Deal	Return ($)	Risk ($)
ABC	2.00	4.00
DEF	1.50	7.00
GHI	0.375	3.25
JKL	5.30	12.50

Table 6.2   **Risk and Return on Selected Deals (in terms of percent)**

Deal	Return (%)	Risk (%)
ABC	12	11
DEF	14	21
GHI	18	19
JKL	21	28

(12%), even though the absolute dollar return on Deal GHI is dramatically less than on Deal ABC. Comparing the two tables may offer the arbitrageur a better method for evaluating transactions, but further improvements can be added. Using either table, we can see the difficulty in trying to choose among the deals. Something still seems to be missing.

Arbitrageurs are in the business of predicting outcomes. Their success is only partly determined by the returns they can generate by investing in transactions; it is also directly linked to their ability to estimate the probability of any particular deal's occurrence. As deals are completed, the arbitrageurs' returns improve. If, however, an arbitrageur owns a deal that breaks up, losses are sustained. This chapter explores methods for arbitrageurs to maximize their returns and minimize their losses.

GATHERING INFORMATION

In today's merger-and-acquisition marketplace, arbitrageurs have a tremendous amount of information available. Their job is to gather relevant information and analyze it. Table 6.3 gives a partial listing of the information sources that arbitrageurs use when they analyze any given transaction. This listing is not all-inclusive. From time to time, arbitrageurs may need special information related to particular proposed transactions.

As shown in Table 6.3, the types of information that an arbitrageur studies are categorized as financial, legal, and tax and accounting information. Financial information generally consists of Annual Reports, Quarterly Reports, and 10-Ks, as well as reports done by analysts at brokerage firms on individual companies involved in transactions. The arbitrageur may also use reports prepared by analysts who have studied the industries in which these companies operate. These reports are secured either directly from the analysts or from various data services.

Table 6.3   Arbitrage Information

	Sources
Newspapers	*The Wall Street Journal*
	The New York Times
	Financial Times
	Investors Daily
	American Banker
	USA Today
	Local newspapers
Publications	*Business Week*
	Barron's
	Forbes
	Fortune
	Various newsletters related to arbitrage business
General News Services	Dow Jones News Ticker
	Reuters News Ticker
	Bloomberg News
	PR News Wire
	Fed Filings
	First Call
	News Edge
Databases	Newsnet
	Factset
	Dow Jones News Retrieval
	Nexis
	Lexis
	Various chart services (i.e., Bloomberg)
Pricing Services	Bloomberg
	ILX
	Track Data

	Types of Information
Financial Information	Annual reports
	Quarterly reports
	10-K statements
	Standard & Poor's reports
	Value Line
	Brokerage firms' research reports
	Registration statements
Legal Information	Antitrust Information:
	Relevant markets
	Market shares

(continued)

Table 6.3   (Continued)

	Litigation documents
	Definitive agreement
	Registration statement
	Tender offer documents
	Information from legal advisers
Tax and Accounting	
Information	Details of type of transaction (from documents filed by companies)
	Details of accounting treatment
	Internal Revenue Service Rulings
	Information from accounting advisers

The second type of information is generally legal information. Depending on the transaction and the companies involved, legal information may pertain to either the antitrust aspects of the two companies' combining or to regulatory issues. The arbitrageur also may have to gather tax and accounting information, such as how the transaction is structured and how the relevant government authorities will treat it. An important issue is whether the parties require a tax ruling from the Internal Revenue Service (IRS) or whether they need only an opinion of their counsel as to the taxability of the transaction.

The flow chart in Figure 6.1 shows the process that the arbitrageur uses in assembling and analyzing information. The sequence of steps in the process affords the arbitrageur the information needed to make an intelligent decision on what securities should be purchased or sold in the respective portfolios.

INITIAL RESEARCH

To determine the probability of a deal's occurrence, an arbitrageur must utilize all available information when formulating an estimate. The estimating process generally starts when the transaction is first announced. News of a transaction may appear initially in *The Wall Street Journal, The New York Times,* or some other widely circulated business publication, or it may be announced on either the Dow Jones or Reuters News Tape. Initially, the arbitrageur is most interested in getting a copy of the official press release in which the two companies announced their proposed transaction. This press release is important because it is the unedited version of what the companies are planning

Figure 6.1   Analyzing and Assembling Information

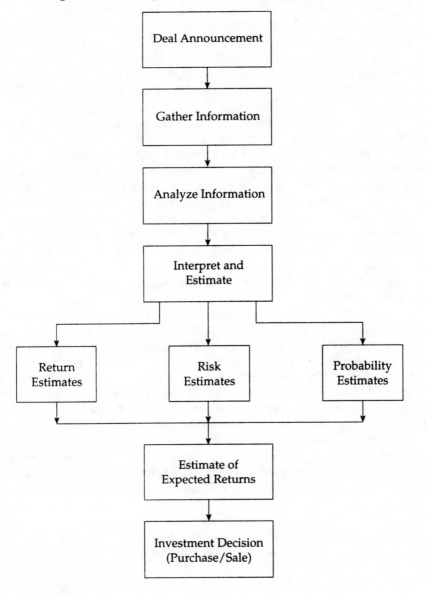

to do. Usually, the press release details the particular terms of the transaction as well as some background information that the arbitrageur may find helpful. Press releases are normally edited by the news agencies that receive them. The agencies choose what they want to report, and they often leave out certain aspects of the original press release. An account, in *The Wall Street Journal* or other newspapers, of a proposed arbitrage transaction may not have the level of detail available in the original press release.

After a deal is announced, the arbitrageur quickly tries to determine whether the two companies are planning a conference call in which they will announce their plans and generally address the Wall Street community. Analysts and shareholders alike are usually allowed to ask questions regarding transactions. A conference call or a meeting with analysts can give helpful insight about the background of the participants and the logic behind the transaction. Arbitrageurs generally attend and ask questions during the question-and-answer session, to obtain information that will be helpful in their decision process. Typical questions address the timing and legal aspects of the transaction, so the conference call becomes an important source of information for the arbitrageur.

During the period of time when the deal is outstanding, the arbitrageur may call either company and speak directly to officials who can supply particular information. Arbitrageurs usually speak with the investor relations manager or the treasurer of the corporation, or, in rare cases, with the President, Chairman of the Board, or members of the Board of Directors. In years past, it was a common practice for arbitrageurs to also contact the respective companies' advisers, including the investment bankers and the companies' legal counsel. However, since the Insider Trading Scandal in the 1980s, contacts with these outside advisers have been more limited. When contact with outside advisers is made, they disclose very little information because of their responsibility to the companies and the limitations imposed by the securities laws.

FINANCIAL INFORMATION

After a deal is announced, the arbitrageur tries to gather information on the transaction as quickly as possible. As previously stated, the first step may be to get copies of the companies' Annual Reports, Quarterly Reports, and 10-Ks describing their financial condition. The arbitrageur will also try to assemble any relevant research generated by brokerage firms on the two companies and the industries in which they compete. This process has been facilitated in recent years through the use of online databases and services such as First Call, which maintains a database of reports on companies and industries. An arbitrageur who subscribes to such a service can print out reports that have recently been generated by Wall Street analysts. These services have simplified a process that, years ago, required many hours of researching the analysts who had written reports on the various companies.

In addition to understanding the individual companies, the arbitrageur wants to gain insight into the industries in which each company operates, and to learn the logic behind the transaction. A transaction that makes good business sense not only is a good choice for a portfolio, but it holds more promise that the transaction will be completed. In the recent merger wave, a high percentage of the announced transactions have been based on solid business logic. Usually, one company purchases another company within the same industry to gain market share or geographic diversification. In the merger activity of the 1980s, financial buyers were purchasing companies and assets and utilizing sophisticated financial engineering to generate profits.

Because most of the deals in the late 1990s were based on very good business sense, there was a higher probability that these transactions would be completed. The completion rate is very important to an arbitrageur; it helps to determine his or her ultimate profitability.

It is important for the arbitrageur to analyze the individual parties and personalities involved in a transaction. The companies involved may have a past history of doing deals or initiating various types of transactions. If one or both of the companies has a history of completing similar transactions, the historical success rate will help the arbitrageur to predict whether the present transaction will become final. For instance, if the acquiring company has a history of announcing deals but completing only a low percentage of them, the arbitrageur would be forewarned to assign a lower probability to a current announced transaction. On the other hand, if the acquiring company has completed numerous similar transactions, it is highly likely that the current transaction will also close.

Besides researching the individual parties, the arbitrageur will examine the structure of the announced transaction. What type of deal is it, and what is the transaction's precise structure? Is it going to be accounted for as a pooling of interest or as a purchase? Is it a merger in which one company is taking over the other, or is it an amalgamation? Questions like these are relevant when the arbitrageur must determine the likely outcome of a transaction. It is also helpful if the arbitrageur understands exactly what has to be done in order to complete the transaction. Knowing the actual steps that need to be completed allows the arbitrageur to anticipate and complete each step in turn.

When a deal is based on only an agreement in principle, further due diligence is necessary before the companies can arrive at a definitive agreement. The need for additional due diligence may cause the arbitrageur to assign a lower probability to an ongoing transaction. As a general rule, the more legal work and due diligence performed by the companies, the higher the likelihood that the transaction will be completed. However, if the companies still have much work to be done—such as examining each other's books, records, and facilities—there is a great possibility that something could turn up that would upset the proposed transaction. Thus, the quantity of due diligence still needed in a transaction has a significant effect on the arbitrageur's estimate of probability.

Regarding financial information, in addition to examining the Annual Reports, Quarterly Reports, and 10-Ks issued by the companies, it is very important for the arbitrageur to read and analyze all the registration statements and tender offer documents that are related to the announced transaction. The information they contain will be very helpful to the arbitrageur's process of estimating the probability of the outcome. Appendix 1 shows how an arbitrageur actually evaluates these registration and tender offer documents. The "Points" interspersed in Appendix 1 call attention to information and responses that are extremely important when an arbitrageur is trying to determine whether a transaction will take place.

When they analyze the financial information included in all the above reports, arbitrageurs are particularly interested to know:

- What price is being paid for the target company?
- Is it a friendly merger or a tender offer? (Hostile transactions will be discussed in a later chapter.)
- How does the price relate to the company's earnings per share, cash flow, and other measures that the investment banking community generally refers to in a transaction?

If, in the eyes of the Wall Street community, the acquiring company is paying a high price as compared to other similar transactions, there is a higher likelihood that the transaction will not take place. An arbitrageur always hopes to determine that a transaction's price is within an acceptable range of values, thereby giving the Wall Street community a reason to support the transaction.

Arbitrageurs are also interested in determining whether there will be any dilution to the acquiring company. In today's equity market, dilution becomes a very important aspect of arbitrage transactions. Very few shareholders are interested in having their company acquire another company when the result will be a dilution of earnings. If dilution occurs, the acquiring company's stock will come under a great deal of selling pressure in the marketplace. If the acquiring company encounters a steep price decline in response to dilution resulting from a merger transaction, this factor would cause the arbitrageur to lower his or her estimate of the probability that this particular transaction will occur.

Notes from the File ══════════════════════════════

The arbitrageur must examine the relative size of the two companies involved in a transaction. If the acquiring company is much smaller than the company being acquired, the discrepancy is usually a tip-off for a potential problem. People will compare it to a minnow swallowing a whale. Because this type of transaction generally does not have a history of a high completion rate, the arbitrageur should be extra careful when such a situation occurs.

One of the first deals of this type that I was involved in occurred in the late 1970s. A relatively unknown company, APL Corporation, offered to acquire Pabst Brewing Company in a hostile transaction. Pabst had no interest in being taken over by anyone—particularly an unknown company that was much smaller than itself. Pabst pursued various takeover defenses, including a regulatory proceeding before the Wisconsin Securities Board. Ultimately, APL gave up the fight, and Pabst remained independent—at least for the time being. Many arbitrageurs lost money when APL gave up the fight for Pabst. Ever since that time, I have always been careful in transactions involving the purchase of a company by a smaller entity.

Another aspect that the arbitrageur must analyze is how the particular transaction is being financed. If the deal is a cash transaction, the arbitrageur will be quite interested in determining the sources of the acquiring company's required capital. Is it being borrowed from banks? Is it coming out of cash on hand? Or is there an unidentified source of the financing? Perhaps more importantly, what is the status of any required financing? If firm agreements are already in place for the borrowing of the required amount of money, the arbitrageur has an opportunity to assign a much higher probability to the deal's taking place.

Alternatively, if the acquiring company is still negotiating to borrow the required amount of money to complete the transaction, there is a higher degree of risk that the transaction will not occur. The registration statements and tender offer documents always contain a section on financing, and arbitrageurs refer to this section immediately upon receiving the documents. The financing and the degree of security of the financing are extremely important to the arbitrageur and his or her probability estimates.

The final step in analyzing the financials of the respective companies is to determine how the shares of the companies involved in the transaction are owned. The arbitrageur tries to determine how much stock is owned by the management team and by the entire Board of Directors. If management or the Board owns a significant amount of stock, this can be an important key in determining whether the transaction is likely to occur. If this is a friendly transaction, most of the stock will clearly be voted in favor of it. Institutional ownership is also important. The arbitrageur always wants to determine how much of the target company's or the acquiring company's stock is held by the institutions on Wall Street. These institutions can have a major say in whether a transaction will take place. Many of these institutions have been known to communicate with one another. Furthermore, there are organizations that analyze transactions and make recommendations as to how the institutions should vote. Arbitrageurs always try to anticipate how these organizations and institutions will vote.

The arbitrageur must find out how many votes are needed to approve a particular transaction. It is important to know whether a simple majority of the outstanding shares is enough to approve the transaction or whether a majority of the voting shares is needed. The difference can be very important. In some agreements, a percentage greater than a majority is needed. The required vote can be found in the company's Charter and By-Laws. In general, the higher the percentage needed, the harder it may be for the companies to get sufficient votes. As we have discussed previously, if the transaction is a cash transaction and is structured as a merger, usually only the shareholders of the target company need to approve the transaction. The position of the target company's ownership then will help the arbitrageur determine the likelihood of the transaction's taking place. If, however, this is a stock-for-stock transaction in which the acquiring company is issuing so many shares that its own shareholders, as well as the target company's shareholders, are required to vote, the arbitrageur must also estimate the likelihood of the acquiring company's shareholders approving the transaction. The arbitrageur analyzes how the acquiring company's shares are held in order to estimate the probability that the acquiring company's shareholders will approve the transaction.

If there is one particular control shareholder, that shareholder is also a key item for the arbitrageur to analyze. Control shareholders may or may not indicate ahead of time whether they support a given transaction. If they have not announced their intention to support the transaction, it is the arbitrageur's job to determine whether these shareholders are likely to vote in favor, or, in the case of a tender offer, whether they are likely to tender their shares under the tender offer.

There are many additional financial factors that the arbitrageur must consider from time to time, but those discussed here are most common to any given transaction. All the financial information is analyzed so that the arbitrageur may formulate an estimate of the probability that the transaction will occur. Financial characteristics frequently have a big influence on the possible outcomes of any given transaction. The better the information and analysis, the better the estimate of probability for the arbitrageur's decision process.

LEGAL INFORMATION

Next, the arbitrageur must assemble and analyze the legal aspects of the transaction. If the companies are involved in any type of litigation or if certain legal liabilities are disclosed in the notes to the financial statements, the arbitrageur must try to determine whether the transaction could be in danger if litigation came to a conclusion or verdict that would be detrimental to either of the companies. Usually, the arbitrageur will need to refer to the definitive merger agreement, the tender offer documents, or the additional documents and disclosures in the registration statements, to determine whether favorable resolution of the litigation is a condition that the companies will require in order to close the deal.

Another aspect of legal analysis usually involves antitrust theory. When a transaction is announced, the arbitrageur, as we stated earlier, always tries to learn about the industries in which each company operates. He or she is particularly interested in whether the two companies are actual competitors in the marketplace. If the two companies compete with one another, this is known in antitrust theory as a "horizontal merger." Horizontal mergers are frequently examined closely by both the Federal Trade Commission and the Justice Department under the previously discussed Hart–Scott–Rodino (HSR) Act.

In a horizontal merger, the arbitrageur will often try to determine what percentage of the particular market each company holds. This is the key element of antitrust analysis. The analysis starts by first determining the relevant product market, that is: What actual product market will the government utilize in trying to determine whether the two companies' combined market share will be unacceptable according to the federal antitrust laws? This relevant market determination is rarely easy. Sometimes, the government defines a narrow market in much broader terms. Antitrust analysis must also include any potential substitutes for the related goods and services being studied. If there are no (or very) few substitutes, the market shares within the narrow product market will be the basis for any legal antitrust determination.

After the arbitrageur determines the relevant product market, he or she must also ascertain where that product market exists geographically:

- Is it a regional market?
- Is it a national market within the United States?
- Or, as we have seen more frequently in today's advanced world economy, is it a worldwide market?

Depending on the answers to these questions, the arbitrageur tries to determine the sales of that particular product market within the defined geographic market. The arbitrageur attempts to determine: Who are all the individual competitors, and what are their relevant sizes within the marketplace? In the most ideal case, the arbitrageur would determine, in dollars of sales, how much each company sold in the relevant product market, and would then determine each company's respective share of the market. For example, if an arbitrageur found that there were only five competitors in the relevant product market, the market shares would be calculated as shown in Table 6.4.

The market shares were calculated by dividing each company's sales by the total industry sales.

If Company A and Company C are planning to merge, the two companies would have a combined market share of 42.7 percent (24.4% plus 18.3%). Table 6.5 shows the premerger and postmerger market shares.

Table 6.4   Competitors' Market Shares

Competitor	Sales ($ million)	Market Share (%)
Company A	$20	24.4%
Company B	40	48.8
Company C	15	18.3
Company D	5	6.1
Company E	2	2.4
Total industry sales	$82	100.0%

Table 6.5 Competitors' Premerger and Postmerger Market Shares

Competitor	Premerger Market Share	Postmerger Market Share
Company A (+ C)	24.4%	42.7%
Company B	48.8	48.8
Company C	18.3	0.0
Company D	6.1	6.1
Company E	2.4	2.4
Total	100.0%	100.0%

The combined market shares, plus the fact that only three other competitors are left in the market, would alert the arbitrageur to the likely possibility that either the Department of Justice or the Federal Trade Commission has serious concerns regarding the proposed combination. The arbitrageur would most likely retain the services of private antitrust attorneys who would study the transaction and render an opinion as to whether the government might challenge the transactions.

The antitrust analysis process is usually very difficult. It is quite common for arbitrageurs to retain outside counsel as consultants, to help them perform this analysis. The attorneys generally have knowledge from prior lawsuits or from relationships with clients within the industries, and they try to construct accurate tables that indicate market shares. Arbitrageurs may have to incur expensive fees to get this type of advice. An arbitrageur who pays outside attorneys is also seeking their opinion as to whether the government may challenge a particular transaction and, if so, whether the government might prevail in any proceeding before a federal or state court. In many cases, the government will actually file a motion requesting a court to issue what is called a "preliminary injunction," which is intended to prevent the merger of two companies. The government makes this request when it believes an antitrust violation is indicated. The accompanying complaint contains the reasons for seeking the preliminary injunction. The arbitrageur needs to obtain all the documents filed by the government and the respective parties. These documents will be critically analyzed so that the attorneys and the arbitrageur can gauge the likelihood of the government's success.

When a case is heard by a judge, it is common for an arbitrageur or the retained attorneys—or some times, both—to attend hearings before the court or the relevant commission from which the government is requesting a preliminary injunction. These proceedings can offer tremendous opportunities if the arbitrageur is able to predict accurately the outcome of the hearings and therefore the disposition of the transaction. (Recall, in Chapter 1, how the outcome of the Office Depot/Staples case substantially affected the arbitrageur's profitability.)

Notes from the File ═══════════════════════════════

Over the years, I have found that the most successful strategy in cases of litigation has been to personally attend all hearings on any matter, when the government or a private party is seeking an injunction against a particular transaction. I have had the best success when my outside counsel attended these hearings with me. Having our two independent opinions, plus the opportunity to consult with one another, has been the most successful approach that I have employed. Because I am not an attorney, I need interpretation and understanding of the many technical issues that affect the litigation process. The attorneys I retain are very familiar with these technicalities and are able to explain them to me. They are also in the best position to judge which side may have the better argument. I try to use my experience and common sense in formulating my own estimate of the outcome of the case before the judge or panel of judges rules. I continually consult with my attorneys and compare their opinion with mine. Historically, when we have been in agreement on the estimate of the outcome, we have rarely been wrong. This process greatly improves the chances of making money on the transaction.

I also find that, at the hearings, my viewpoint as an arbitrageur is invaluable. I know how other arbitrageurs will react to various information and developments at these proceedings. Frequently, trading opportunities surface and I am able to take advantage of them. For instance, if the judge appears to ask insightful and challenging questions of the government's attorneys in a case brought by the Federal Trade Commission or the Justice Department, arbitrageurs may feel that the odds are improved for the injunction request to be denied. They may then look to increase their position in the deal, and the stock of the target company may rise. The only way for me to spot these opportunities is to attend the hearings.

In all these cases, my attorneys and I are focused on trying to predict the decision of the judge or panel of judges prior to its issuance. I then try to set up a position in the securities, in order to profit from the ultimate decision.

═══

A court may issue or deny an injunction request from the government, but frequently it is not the court of final determination. The companies involved in the deal, or the government, may request an additional review by a court of appeals. A court proceeding at the appeals level becomes even more critical to the arbitrageur's difficult process of estimating the probability that the deal will be completed. Again, the arbitrageur and the outside counsel will attend the hearings before the Court of Appeals, to improve their chances of predicting the final outcome.

At this point, it may be helpful to review how the appeals process works. We will examine an actual case. In June 1976, Empire Gas, a large liquefied petroleum (LP) and gas company, was attempting to take over Pargas Incorporated, a smaller liquefied gas company. It was a hostile takeover, and Pargas was doing everything in its power to prevent it.

The attorneys retained by Pargas had filed for and were granted a preliminary injunction against Empire's tender offer in the Federal District Court in Maryland, on the grounds that the proposed merger could tend to create a monopoly in the LP/gas business in various regional markets. Empire's attorneys had then filed an appeal requesting that the U.S. District Court of Appeals for the Fourth Circuit vacate the lower court's decision so that the Empire tender offer could proceed.

Many arbitrageurs owned Pargas common stock. They were gambling that a three-judge panel would side with Empire Gas. The Empire tender offer was at a share price of $18.50 and Pargas's stock was trading at $16 per share, so the arbitrageurs were hoping to gain the spread between the two prices as profit.

Everything depended on the outcome of the proceeding before the Court of Appeals. Attorneys for Pargas were on their side of the courtroom, seated around a large conference table, and the Empire Gas attorneys sat around their corresponding table on the other side of the podium. The two groups took turns sending representatives to the lectern to present their technical and sophisticated legal arguments to the panel of three judges. As each speaker began a delivery, a green light became visible on the podium. At a certain timed interval during each argument, the light turned amber. The attorneys then spoke much faster, trying to get in every possible word before the light turned red and the judges cut off any unconcluded arguments. Hearings at a Court of Appeals are usually strictly timed to give each side an equal advantage.

After both sides progressed through the traffic-like cycle of lights and verbal arguments, the three-judge panel dismissed all parties and took the case under advisement. Meanwhile, on the floor of the New York Stock Exchange, Pargas common stock was trading at prices that represented a significant discount to the Empire Gas bid. The arbitrageurs had the task of figuring out—before the decision was handed down—what the Court of Appeals would decide.

If the Court found for Pargas and upheld the preliminary injunction, Empire Gas would be thwarted and Pargas's stock would fall. If the judges decided to reverse the lower court's decision, the Empire offer would be allowed to proceed. The price of Pargas's stock would soar to the tender offer price or might even trade right through the current $18.50 price if investors and arbitrageurs were counting on Pargas to try to negotiate a friendly deal at a higher price. This situation could create a bidding war if Pargas found a white knight.

Unfortunately for arbitrageurs who owned shares of Pargas, the Court of Appeals affirmed the lower court's decision in October 1976. Pargas's stock declined to $12 per share, and Empire Gas withdrew its offer.

Thus far, we have discussed only the horizontal type of acquisition, in which the companies are actually competing with one another by selling the same product or service. Another type of merger, known as a "vertical merger," involves a situation where the acquiring company seeks to take over a supplier of materials or services that are needed for a particular product or good that is marketed by the acquiring company. Transactions that aim to vertically integrate operations are much more infrequently challenged by the government. However, an arbitrageur must still respond to the possibility of such a suit. Recently, the federal government has taken a deeper interest in this type of transaction—perhaps in response to the current political environment. Historically, when the country has had a Democratic Administration in power, interest in antitrust enforcement has been heightened.

The government, usually represented by the Justice Department or the Federal Trade Commission, uses its own staff to analyze arbitrage transactions. Generally, when the analysis is completed, the staff recommends to either the full FTC or the Justice Department an opinion on whether the transaction should be challenged. In the analysis, the government's legal staff incorporates certain legal techniques, mirroring the arbitrageur's efforts to determine market shares. The government staff, however, has the advantage of access to large amounts of nonpublic information. Under the Hart–Scott–Rodino Act, the government may request, from the companies and other competitors in the marketplace, information to which the arbitrageur does not have access. Given this information, plus a computation of market shares, the government staff may frequently calculate what are known as "Herfandahl Indices." The Herfandahl Index (HI) has been developed, during recent years, to help the government determine which transactions should be challenged.

Usually, in a Herfandahl analysis, market shares are first individually determined for each of the competitors within the industry. These

Table 6.6   Market for Refrigerators

Company	Current Market Share	Premerger HI	Postmerger Market Share	Postmerger HHI
Company A	30%	900	30%	900
Company B	22	484	22	484
Company C	14	196	14	196
Company D	11	121	11	121
Company E	7	49	7	49
Company F	6	36	12 (F + G)	144
Company G	6	36	0	0
Company H	2	4	2	4
Company I	2	4	2	4
Total	100%	1,830	100%	1,902

market shares are then squared mathematically. This process is done two ways: on a premerger and a postmerger basis. The Herfandahl Index for the entire relevant product market is then added up. If the calculations of the combined total index (premerger and postmerger) change by a certain amount, the government follows preset guidelines for whether it will challenge a transaction.

Herfandahl calculations can best be explained with an example. Tables 6.6 and 6.7 show the hypothetical market shares of all the individual competitors in the market for refrigerators and freezers, respectively.

Tables 6.6 and 6.7 show the calculations for a proposed combination of Company F with Company G. The arbitrageur and antitrust attorneys could have constructed these tabulations by obtaining

Table 6.7   Market for Freezers

Company	Current Market Share	Premerger HI	Postmerger Market Share	Postmerger HHI
Company F	25%	625	35% (F + G)	1,225
Company B	24	576	24	576
Company E	17	289	17	289
Company D	15	225	15	225
Company G	10	100		
Company H	5	25	5	25
Company I	4	16	4	16
Total	100%	1,856	100%	2,356

information from industry reports or industry publications. In either case, market shares and Herfandahl Index (HI) numbers are shown both premerger and postmerger.

From Table 6.6, we can see that the combination of the two companies results in a market share of 12 percent in the market for refrigerators and a postmerger HI of 144. The total HI increased from 1,830 to 1,902. The government considers any market with a Herfandahl Index greater than 1,800 to be a concentrated market. Guidelines issued by the government indicate that the agencies involved are unlikely to challenge a merger in a concentrated market if the increase in the HI is less than 50. We have seen that, after the merger, the HI in the refrigerator market increased by 72 (1,902 less 1,830). This could indicate that the government would challenge the proposed transaction. However, because of other factors, the government agency may find that the merger does not significantly lessen competition. This is a case where input from experienced antitrust counsel is invaluable. This deal represents a tough call for the arbitrageur.

In the freezer market, the arbitrageur's calculation indicates a much more dangerous situation. The Herfendahl Index increased 500 points, from 1,856 to 2,356. The arbitrageur should be quite wary of taking a position in this merger because there is a high likelihood that the government will challenge the transaction.

There are other legal aspects that the arbitrageur must consider. If the companies involved in the transactions are in a regulated industry, it is the arbitrageur's job to determine what approvals are needed and what is the likelihood of getting them. Timing, and the individual steps needed in the process, can be important for the arbitrageur. Usually, the industries that request regulatory approvals include insurance companies, banks, gaming type companies, utilities, and telephone or telecommunications firms. In some industries, a specific governmental body must approve the transaction prior to its completion. The arbitrageur will try to identify the relevant governing body and will follow the transaction to gauge its chances of success. Frequently, analysis will center on:

- What past cases have passed before that regulatory agency;
- What transactions have been approved, and why;
- What transactions have been disapproved, and why.

Regulatory approvals generally lengthen the time it takes to complete a transaction. The individual merits of a deal may add more time to the approval process. For instance, bank deals typically take five to nine months to complete. Each deal must be analyzed, on a deal-by-deal basis, to estimate the timing and the likelihood of the outcome.

This legal analysis can be a very difficult part of the arbitrageur's job. Some arbitrageurs are also attorneys and have prior experience in the field. Over time, arbitrageurs with no legal background educate themselves on the specific legal aspects and possible outcomes of any given transaction. As mentioned above, it is common to employ outside counsel to advise the arbitrageur and to help in determining the probability that a transaction will be completed.

TAX AND ACCOUNTING INFORMATION

Another area that requires the arbitrageur's concern at times is the tax and accounting aspect of a given transaction. It is very important to determine whether a transaction will be treated by the companies on a "pooling-of-interest basis" or as a "purchase." If the companies are planning to use the pooling-of-interest method of accounting and a problem develops, the transaction may be canceled. The arbitrageur will draw on his or her own personal knowledge, as well as accountants' or attorneys' opinions, to help determine whether the structure of the transaction represents an impediment, thereby reducing the likelihood that the transaction will go through.

Tax aspects of the transaction may also be important. If the transaction is designed to be tax-free, specific rules must be followed to accomplish that objective. The firms may require an official tax ruling by the Internal Revenue Service, which can take four to seven months. Alternatively, the companies may elect to proceed with the transaction after receiving an opinion of counsel that the transaction will be treated as being tax-free. If the companies count on tax-free treatment and inform shareholders that there will be a tax-free exchange of shares, a later problem in receiving the required tax ruling, or an adverse opinion of counsel, can cause the transaction to be canceled. The arbitrageur must closely examine each transaction's structure as well as its individual merits and aspects.

By gathering all these types of information, the arbitrageur is trying to gauge the best estimate and the true probability of a transaction's occurrence. This information-gathering and analysis process is highly subjective, and it is very difficult to determine a precise probability estimate for any given transaction. For these reasons, the estimate of probability is the hardest element to determine in the risk arbitrage decision process. It is a factor that is not conducive to mathematical modeling. Subjective estimates are constantly required, and the arbitrageur can only devote a best effort to trying to determine what these estimates will be. The estimation of probabilities is much more an art than a science. No system has been developed to assemble all this information in a mathematical model or in mathematical algorithms that will generate an objective estimate of probability of occurrence. The arbitrageur can only analyze all available information and submit his or her best estimate of probability.

After the arbitrageur estimates the probability that any given transaction will succeed, he or she can input this information into the decision process, along with the completed estimates of expected return and risk. When the arbitrageur considers the elements, he or she tries to determine which securities to purchase for the portfolio.

In the next chapter, we will examine how the arbitrageur combines the three elements of return, risk, and probability in the decision process, and we will show how the arbitrageur chooses securities for the arbitrage portfolio.

Chapter 7

The Risk Arbitrage Decision Process

Now that we've explored how the arbitrageur estimates the possible returns and risks, and the probability of any particular transaction's occurring, we will use these estimates to form a decision framework for the arbitrage investment process.

In Chapter 6, we saw that the arbitrageur had estimates of return and risk on four separate deals. The probabilities of those deals, expressed as percentages, are shown in Tables 7.1 and 7.2.

We can now use the three estimates in each deal to calculate the risk-adjusted expected return on each transaction, as follows:

$$RAR = \frac{(P_1 \times EP) + (P_2 \times EL)}{I} \times \frac{365}{P}$$

where RAR = risk-adjusted return
P_1 = probability of deal closing
EP = expected profit (net spread)
P_2 = probability of deal's breaking up
= $1 - P_1$
EL = expected loss (total risk)
I = total investment
P = estimated investment period

Table 7.1 Risk Arbitrage: Returns, Risks, and Probability (in Dollars)

Deal	Return (in $)	Risk (in $)	Probability (in %)
ABC	2.00	4.00	85
DEF	1.50	7.00	90
GHI	0.375	3.25	95
JKL	5.30	21.25	70

Table 7.2   Risk Arbitrage: Returns, Risks, and Probability (in Percentages)

Deal	Return (in %)	Risk (in %)	Probability of Deal Closing (in %)
ABC	12	11	85
DEF	14	21	90
GHI	18	19	95
JKL	21	28	70

All the returns we have used in the above calculations are unleveraged returns. If we were to assume the arbitrageur utilizes leverage, these returns would be affected accordingly.

We are assuming that any of these given transactions have only two possible outcomes (see Figure 7.1):

1. Completion of the deal.
2. Break-up of the deal.

When we have the probability estimate of the deal's occurring, we can easily calculate the probability of the deal's breaking up.

In a later section of this chapter, we will discuss other types of transactions in which the arbitrageur estimates the probability of various outcomes. These situations may typically include hostile takeovers and similar challenges for which the arbitrageur will frequently use a "decision tree" in calculating the risk-adjusted return.

In our simplified decision model, we must have estimates for the amount the arbitrageur expects to earn if the deal closes, the amount that will be lost if the transaction is called off, and the probability that the deal will actually occur. If the arbitrageur estimates an 85 percent probability of occurrence, the probability of cancellation is then only

Figure 7.1   Possible Outcomes and Probability

Deal Announced

Deal Completion (P_1)

Deal Breaks ($1 - P_1$)

15 percent (see Figure 7.1, Deal ABC). Using the estimates in Table 7.1, we would calculate each risk-adjusted return (RAR) to be as follows:

$$RAR_{Deal\ ABC} = \left[\frac{(.85 \times \$2.00) + [.15 \times (-\$4.00)]}{35} \right] \times \frac{365}{100}$$

$$= \frac{(\$1.70 - \$.60)}{35} \times \frac{365}{100}$$

$$= 11.5\ percent$$

$$RAR_{Deal\ DEF} = \left[\frac{(.90 \times \$1.50) + [.10 \times (-\$7.00)]}{42} \right] \times \frac{365}{90}$$

$$= \frac{(\$1.35 - \$.70)}{42} \times \frac{365}{90}$$

$$= 6.3\ percent$$

$$RAR_{Deal\ GHI} = \left[\frac{(.95 \times \$.375) + [.05 \times (-\$3.25)]}{17} \right] \times \frac{365}{45}$$

$$= \frac{(\$.35625 - \$.1625)}{17} \times \frac{365}{45}$$

$$= 9.2\ percent$$

$$RAR_{Deal\ JKL} = \left[\frac{(.70 \times \$5.30) + [.30 \times (-\$21.25)]}{76} \right] \times \frac{365}{120}$$

$$= \frac{(\$3.71 - \$6.375)}{76} \times \frac{365}{120}$$

$$= -10.7\ percent$$

If the arbitrageur's estimates are accurate, investing in Deal ABC makes more sense than investing in Deal DEF. As shown in Table 7.3, Deal ABC's risk-adjusted return is 11.5 percent, or 5.2 percent higher than Deal DEF's return. Deal GHI also has a significant positive un-leveraged risk-adjusted return of 9.2 percent. This contrasts greatly with Deal JKL, which has a negative expected risk-adjusted return. This negative return suggests that, according to the arbitrageur's esti-mates of probability, this transaction is actually expected to lose money if the arbitrageur invests in it.

The use of risk-adjusted returns gives the arbitrageur the ability to rank the investment alternatives. Many arbitrageurs, however, do not

Table 7.3   Risk Arbitrage Decision Matrix

Deal	Return (in $)	Risk (in $)	Probability (in %)	Risk-Adjusted Return (in %)
ABC	2.00	4.00	85	11.5
DEF	1.50	7.00	90	6.3
GHI	0.375	3.25	95	9.2
JKL	5.30	21.25	70	−10.7

go the full route of calculating risk-adjusted returns. Instead, they base their investment decision on information in the form of, say, Table 7.1. Using this information, and relying on their experience, they select their investment alternatives and assemble their portfolios. They rely on a "gut feeling" rather than the use of probability to quantify risk-adjusted returns.

Some arbitrageurs choose not to go the full route of calculating risk-adjusted returns because these returns can be dramatically affected by the subjective probabilities assigned by the arbitrageur. We can illustrate this effect by varying the probability estimates for one of the above examples.

In Deal ABC, if we were to change the arbitrageur's estimate of probability from 85 percent to 80 percent, and then from 85 percent to 90 percent, we could calculate what the risk-adjusted return would be in all three cases. Here are the calculations:

$$RAR_{ABC\,80\%} = \left[\frac{(.8 \times \$2.00) + [\$.2 \times (-\$4.00)]}{35}\right] \times \frac{365}{100}$$

$$= \frac{(\$1.60 - \$.80)}{35} \times \frac{365}{100}$$

$$= 8.3 \text{ percent}$$

$$RAR_{ABC\,90\%} = \left[\frac{(.9 \times \$2.00) + [\$.1 \times (-\$4.00)]}{35}\right] \times \frac{365}{100}$$

$$= \frac{(\$1.80 - \$.40)}{35} \times \frac{365}{100}$$

$$= 14.6 \text{ percent}$$

We can see that by varying the probability estimate, the risk-adjusted return changes dramatically. As we decrease the estimate from 85 percent to 80 percent, the risk-adjusted return drops from 11.5 percent to 8.3 percent. However, when we increase the probability estimate from 85 percent to 90 percent, indicating more optimism that the transaction will take place, our risk-adjusted return increases from 11.5 percent to 14.6 percent. When the unleveraged risk-adjusted return is 14.6 percent, the arbitrageur may very well want to invest part of the available capital in this transaction. If, however, the proper probability estimate is 80 percent, the arbitrageur would certainly find this transaction less attractive. Thus, we can see that the probability estimates can have a profound effect on the risk-adjusted return and the arbitrageur's decision process.

It may be difficult to quantify the estimates, but an arbitrageur armed with the risk-adjusted return calculation will find it much easier to compare investment alternatives. The risk-adjusted return calculation takes into account all the important aspects of the risk arbitrage decision process and melds them into one calculation.

DYNAMIC ASPECT OF RISK ARBITRAGE ANALYSIS

The risk arbitrage decision process is dynamic. The arbitrageur may analyze each deal when it is announced, and may calculate risks, rewards, and probability, but the job of the arbitrageur does not end there. As each day passes, information and conditions change. The arbitrageur must continually reassess his or her estimates of risk, reward, and probability to reflect the changes in the marketplace. When any of these elements is affected, the entire picture may change from the perspective of the arbitrageur. A deal that initially seemed quite promising may become unattractive if the arbitrageur must adjust the probability estimates to account for some adverse legal or regulatory development that may cause the transaction to fail. Conversely, a deal that seemed unattractive when it was initially announced may develop into a very attractive investment, and the arbitrageur may become more and more comfortable with the likelihood of the deal's being completed.

EVEN-MONEY PROBABILITY—A TOOL FOR RISK ARBITRAGE DECISION MAKING

As we mentioned in the previous chapter, many arbitrageurs find it difficult to estimate a precise probability for a deal's outcome. They rely on their experience instead of quantifying the probability to get a risk-adjusted return. One way to utilize the risk-adjusted return framework so that it assists the arbitrageur in estimating probability is to work backward from the market inputs. The arbitrageur can use his or her estimates of return and risk, along with the market values of the securities, to calculate a probability estimate that would make the deal an even-money proposition. Using market prices, we can work backward and find a probability that would make the expected rate of return zero. If the probability of the deal's occurring is greater than this even-money probability, the expected return would turn positive. Conversely, if the arbitrageur's estimate of the probability of the deal's closing is less than the even-money probability, the expected risk-adjusted return would become negative.

Some arbitrageurs may find it useful to calculate this probability and use it as a basis for comparison with their own estimates and those of others in the marketplace. In other words, for arbitrageurs who find it difficult to quantify the probability estimate, using market prices to infer probabilities may be an aid. If market prices infer a break-even probability of 90 percent, the arbitrageur must reflect on this question: "Do I think the probability of this deal's closing is greater or less than the 90 percent?" This process may spur the arbitrageur to improve his or her decision process.

EVEN-MONEY PROBABILITY FORMULA

The even-money probability may be calculated as follows:

$$\left(P_E \times EP\right) + \left(P_2 \times EL\right) = 0$$

so:

$$P_E = \frac{-\left[P_2 \times EL\right]}{EP}$$

$$= \frac{-\left[\left(1 - P_E\right) \times EL\right]}{EP}$$

where P_E = even-money probability
    = probability of the deal's occurring
  EP = expected profit (not spread) if the deal closes
  P_2 = probability of the deal's breaking up
    = $1 - P_E$
  EL = expected loss if the deal breaks up

Using Deal ABC from Table 7.1, ER = $2.00 and EL = −$4.00, so we have:

$$(P_E \times \$2.00) + (P_2 \times -\$4.00) = 0$$

where
$$P_E = \left[\frac{-(1 - P_E) \times EL}{EP} \right]$$

$$= \left[\frac{-(1 - P_E) \times -\$4.00}{\$2.00} \right]$$

$$= 2(1 - P_E)$$

$$= 2 - 2P_E$$

$$3P_E = 2$$

$$P_E = 66.6 \text{ percent}$$

CALCULATING COMPLEX RISK-ADJUSTED RETURNS

Thus far, in calculating risk-adjusted return, we have used a model that assumes only two possible outcomes: (1) the deal is completed or (2) the deal breaks up. Many deals cannot be adequately analyzed by using this simplified model. More specifically, a particular group of transactions can have more than two possible outcomes. A hostile takeover is the prime example of an arbitrage transaction that frequently has more than two possible deal outcomes. Hostile takeovers will be explored in depth in the next chapter. Here, we will examine the possibility of having more than two potential outcomes.

Assume that Company B is trading at $35 per share, and Company A has made a hostile cash tender offer for Company B at a price of $50 per share. We can foresee several possible outcomes:

1. Company A could ultimately buy Company B for $50 per share.
2. Company B could defend against Company A's offer. If Company B ultimately succeeds in fending off Company A, Company B's shares could return to their predeal level of $35 per share.
3. Company Z, coming forward as a "white knight" to save Company B from Company A, could buy Company B for $60 per share.

4. Company B could do a recapitalization to fight off Company A's hostile offer. Assume that shareholders of Company B would receive total consideration of $52 per share in the recapitalization.

Our simple model for calculating risk-adjusted return in cases such as this can be expanded. The general formula for *multiple potential outcomes* is as follows:

$$
\text{RAR} = \left[\frac{(P_1 \times R_1) + (P_2 \times R_2) + K\ (P_i \times R_i)}{I} \right] \times \frac{365}{P}
$$

$$
= \sum \frac{(P_i \times R_i)}{I}
$$

As shown in Table 7.4, the arbitrageur must estimate the probability of each of the possible outcomes.

By weighting each possible outcome according to the arbitrageur's estimate of probability, we get an expected rate of return on this deal of 10.42 percent.

To make the process even more accurate, we could use each possible outcome's annualized expected return instead of the unannualized percentage of return. This approach will take into account different timing elements for each potential outcome.

Table 7.5 shows that the probability weighted estimated return is 53.22 percent. This would be a very attractive deal for any arbitrageur.

Table 7.4   Probability Estimates

Possible Outcomes	Outcome in Terms of Price of Company B*	Expected Return (R_i)	Estimate of Probability (P_i)	$R_i \times P_i$
1. Successful hostile tender offer	$50	4.2%	25%	1.05%
2. Deal breaks up	35	−27.1	10	−2.71
3. White knight wins	60	25.0	40	10.00
4. Recapitalization effected by Company B	52	8.3	25	2.08
			100%	10.42%

*Company B's common stock was trading at $48 per share in the marketplace.

Table 7.5   Probability Weighted Estimated Returns

Possible Outcomes	Expected Time Hostile (days)	Unannualized Expected Return (R_i)	Annualized Expected Return	Estimate of Probability	$P_i \times R_i$
1. Successful hostile tender offer	90	4.2	17.0	25%	4.25%
2. Deal breaks up	120	−27.1	−82.4	10	−8.24
3. White knight wins	70	25.0	130.4	40	52.16
4. Recapitalization effected by Company B	150	8.3	20.2	25	5.05
				100%	53.22%

The 53.22 percent was derived by weighting each potential outcome in terms of its probable annualized rate of return. Summed up, the total return is estimated at 53.22 percent.

The decision trees shown in Tables 7.4 and 7.5 can be very useful in the risk arbitrage decision process. By using this method, the arbitrageur has the flexibility needed to adapt a decision model to any possible deal structure. Through the calculation of risk-adjusted return, which utilizes the arbitrageur's estimates of return, risk, and probability, the arbitrageur is able to make informed decisions in a dynamic marketplace.

Chapter 8

Contested Takeovers

Contested takeovers are among the most exciting arbitrage transactions. They are also the most challenging and, potentially, the most profitable, but an arbitrageur who makes a wrong call in a contested takeover can lose a great deal of money. Contested takeovers have brought great publicity and media attention to the risk arbitrage business. Specialty publications usually pick up on any contested takeover and write numerous stories regarding the transactions involved.

Contested takeovers also have a critical time factor from the arbitrageur's point of view. When mergers are announced, the arbitrageur does not need to drop everything and analyze the brand new merger transaction. Mergers tend to take three to five months to complete, and it is not necessary for the arbitrageur to complete an analysis on the very first day. Contested takeovers, however, are a different situation. Developments tend to occur quickly. It is imperative that the arbitrageur drop everything else when a new contested takeover is announced. He or she must try to analyze everything possible about this transaction.

DIFFERENCES BETWEEN CONTESTED
AND UNCONTESTED TAKEOVERS

What makes contested takeovers different from other transactions? They are unnegotiated; that is, the acquiring company has set its price, but the amount has not been mutually agreed to by the acquiring company and the target company. In mergers, two companies come out with either an agreement in principle or a definitive agreement; the two companies agree to the consideration being offered. In contested takeovers, the initial takeover price *can* be fair, but most likely it is not. The initial price is usually the price at which the acquiring company has started its bidding. In most hostile takeover attempts, the bidders won't make their best bid initially. Why? They want the opportunity to sweeten their bid as a way of getting the target company's Board of Directors to approve the transaction. In fact, most arbitrageurs assume that acquiring companies have regarded 5 to 10 percent of their initial bid price as the sweetener that will get them a friendly transaction.

Hostile takeovers usually begin with a cash tender offer. The tender offer is announced in a press release, and advertisements are placed in *The Wall Street Journal*, *The New York Times*, or local newspapers, to inform the target company's shareholders of the impending offer. Some hostile takeovers take the form of an exchange offer. Instead of cash, the acquiring company is offering securities. The offshoot of these types of transactions is that the acquiring company actually makes an offer public but does not formally launch a tender or exchange offer. They make the offer through press releases and directly to the company. The decision on whether the offer is made directly to shareholders depends on how the offer is handled. Lately, because of various takeover defenses, a few offers have stayed in a nonformal format for many months prior to the acquiring company's making a bid.

An acquiring company would always like to get the target company to agree to the takeover at the initial price, but many other things can happen in these transactions. The target company could search for and find a "white knight"—a company that will come to its aid by outbidding the acquiring company's initial offer. The white knight is usually a suitor of choice for the target company—a sought-after protector against being taken over by an undesirable entity.

The target company could also do some type of recapitalization or reorganization. This may involve buying back stock, at a premium, from its shareholders. The target company could also bargain with the acquiring company and come to some resolution—usually, a higher takeover price. Or, the target company could fight the hostile takeover, and this is what the arbitrageur worries about. If a target company fights, the arbitrageur must make a determination. Is the fight's only purpose to stall for time until a white knight is found or a better deal is negotiated? Is the target company sincere? Does it simply want to remain independent and not sell out to anyone?

TAKEOVER DEFENSES

In hostile takeovers, the target company's defenses become a very important aspect of the arbitrageur's analysis. Initially, when the bid is made public, the arbitrageur must analyze a separate set of potential defensive strategies. The first situation that the arbitrageur looks at is how the target company's Board of Directors is structured. Many companies today have what are called "staggered Boards of Directors." The companies put directors on the board with a period of time attached to their tenure. Instead of electing all board members in the same year, companies may stagger the terms of their directors so that only a portion of the Board is put up for reelection each year. For a Board consisting of twelve members, usually only three of the members would be elected each year. Election of the entire board would be spread over a four-year period. Staggered boards are utilized to discourage outsiders or hostile bidders from believing that they can get control of a Board over a short period of time. For example, it would take at least two years, electing three members a year, to gain control of a twelve-member Board. If a target company does not have a staggered Board, it will be viewed as being vulnerable to a hostile takeover attempt. If an arbitrageur finds that a target company does not have a staggered Board, the company, initially at least, will be regarded as not easily able to defend successfully against a hostile takeover.

Poison Pills

Another widespread takeover defense is the use of what is called a "poison pill." Many years ago, poison pills were designed by attorneys and instituted by the Boards of Directors of corporations to give them an additional defense against hostile takeover attempts. This is how a poison pill may work. Someone, or some entity, purchases a certain percentage (usually, a majority or an amount in excess of the majority) of the outstanding securities of a target company. The poison pill gives shareholders the right to purchase additional shares at a significant discount to the trading price in the marketplace. When it does this, the target company's Board is trying to discourage any assumption that someone could actually take over the company without prior Board approval. If the Board does not approve the transaction and the acquiring company gains the percentage of shares that triggers the poison pill, significant dilution would occur. In almost all such plans, the majority holder that triggers the pill is not able to participate in the discounted stock purchases that follow.

Poison pills have been challenged legally over the years. For a period of time, several of these pills were found to be unconstitutional. The attorneys then went back to the drafting table, read the court decisions, and essentially recrafted their remedy so that the court decisions would not hold up use of the new pills. They essentially corrected the defects that the courts had found in the prior version. Recently, there have been very few successful challenges of poison pills instituted by target companies' Boards. In the end, it is usually up to the Board of Directors of the target company to decide whether they are going to "pull the pill" prior to the tender offer's closing. The Board generally has the right to rescind the pill so that the dilution will not take place. Poison pills, however, are almost always mentioned as a significant incentive for an acquiring company to bring its hostile takeover attempt to a close. The pill must be resolved, one way or another, prior to the acquiring company's purchasing shares.

DEFENSES BASED ON BYLAWS

The set of corporate bylaws is very important to the arbitrageur during hostile takeover attempts. The arbitrageur should analyze the bylaws very carefully. For example, does a shareholder have the right to call a special meeting of shareholders to elect an entire slate of directors? This right would give a tremendous advantage to an acquiring company making a hostile bid. The target company's Board would be at a distinct disadvantage. When faced with a threat to have the entire Board unseated, most Boards of Directors look to sell the company.

Other types of bylaws must also be examined by the arbitrageur because they apply to various aspects of the way the corporation is governed. It is important for the arbitrageur to get a copy of the bylaws and to read them carefully and analyze their important aspects.

PRIVATE LAWSUITS

Lawsuits are the primary defense that most target companies erect in order to avoid a hostile takeover attempt. Antitrust issues are the primary focus of both the arbitrageur and the target companies. If an antitrust issue exists, the target company will do everything in its power to utilize it as a defense against a hostile takeover attempt. As we discussed in a prior chapter, the arbitrageur must analyze the transaction in an effort to identify the business overlaps between the two companies. If the two companies sell or manufacture the same product, or operate in the same business segments, there is a danger in employing this defense. The arbitrageur must then also estimate the chances that this defense will be successful.

When an antitrust issue is involved, the one difference in hostile takeovers, as compared with friendly transactions, is that the nature of the litigation is different. When an agreed-to transaction gets involved in an antitrust litigation, the Justice Department or the Federal Trade Commission is usually trying to block the companies' transaction. In hostile takeover attempts, however, the target company can hire the best legal counsel that money can buy. Private attorneys often square off against private attorneys for the acquiring company, and few costs are spared. In other types of antitrust cases, the government pursues its argument via government employees, and, in my experience, they are either new to actual litigation or, for their own reasons, perhaps reflecting an over-supply of new members of the bar, they may choose to remain employed by the Federal Trade Commission or the Justice Department. Usually, new lawyers get jobs with these agencies to gain experience. After sufficient training and performance, they are commonly snapped up by private law firms. In numerous cases, the two sides have seemed unfairly endowed. Private attorneys representing the companies have endless assets at their disposal; the government attorneys, in comparison, have very few resources. Hostile takeovers summon attorneys who meet on a level playing field.

Arbitrageurs are mostly concerned with horizontal transactions in which the two companies actually compete against one another in the marketplace. Will the judge enter a preliminary injunction against the transaction on antitrust grounds? Is there a potential solution to the competition problem? The acquiring company may be willing to divest itself of a certain amount of the competing operation in order to complete the transaction. Many judges are open to suggested settlements that will avoid the need to enter a preliminary injunction against the transaction. This trend has also been noticed in antitrust enforcement. The Justice Department and the Federal Trade Commission have moved toward trying to settle potential antitrust problems in conference with the parties.

Other violations that must be analyzed by the arbitrageur include vertical types of transactions, and potential competition arguments. Neither of these has had a high probability of success in the courts. All antitrust issues must be examined in depth, to determine the likelihood of the transaction's being blocked. The arbitrageur must anticipate any troublesome aspects of the transaction, as part of estimating the probability that a takeover will eventually occur.

STATE TAKEOVER LAWS

Historically, takeover laws have been instituted by the individual states as a means of attracting target companies to incorporate (or to remain incorporated) within their boarders. Generally, takeover laws are drafted to give the target company's Board of Directors an ability to defend against hostile takeover attempts. Each state's laws generally incorporate some common issues, but there are also proprietary twists on how target companies can defend themselves. When these laws were initially instituted, many challenges were brought by acquiring companies seeking to declare the laws unconstitutional. A number of state courts held that various aspects of the state takeover laws were unconstitutional. Just as the attorneys redrafted poison pills so as to escape legally contesting them, legal practitioners have been able to counsel the states on ways to redraft their takeover laws to make them acceptable to the court system. Some original laws, held to be constitutional, are still in existence today.

The arbitrageur must examine the relevant laws of the state in which the target company is incorporated. (Usually, this state's takeover law is invoked in any takeover attempt.) The arbitrageur must determine whether any particular clauses might cause the probability estimate to be lowered. In other words: Will the law give the target company the ability to defend against a takeover? Usually, the success of a takeover attempt is not determined solely by state laws. Other valid takeover defenses have contributed to acquiring companies' not being able to succeed with their offer.

OTHER TYPES OF DEFENSES

Target companies may employ additional defensive strategies to block a hostile takeover attempt. Among the typical defenses companies use are: sell a block of stock or securities to a friendly party, or sell a segment of the business. These defenses are designed to make the target company less attractive to the hostile bidder. A sale of stock, if it represents a significant percentage of the outstanding shares of the target company during the pendancy of a hostile takeover attempt, is generally closely scrutinized by the courts. If a target company, at this stage, sells a significant number of shares to another company to block a takeover, it is highly unlikely that the sale would hold up in court. In the past, some companies have also tried to sell parts of their business or one of the most attractive assets that the acquiring company is interested in. Undoubtedly, this type of transaction would also be challenged in court by the acquiring company. Over the recent past, I have found it very unlikely that such a sale would succeed.

One defense tactic has succeeded on a number of occasions: the target companies' decision to buy back a significant amount of their own stock from current shareholders. They usually do this in conjunction with some type of recapitalization or reorganization attempt. A number of companies have used this strategy successfully.

Regulatory Defenses

The arbitrageur must also determine whether any regulatory defenses are built into any given transaction. If the target company or the acquiring company is involved in a business that is regulated by the U.S. Department of Transportation, a gambling commission, or the Interstate Commerce Commission, the arbitrageur also must analyze whether approval by these agencies is required for any particular transactions. If the target company is an insurance company, the arbitrageur must look to each individual state in which the company operates, and determine whether approval will be granted by each regulatory commission. If the business involves television or radio licenses, approval by the Federal Communications Commission (FCC) will probably be needed to complete the transaction.

Sometimes, regulatory defenses can be defused if the acquiring company offers to put any questioned assets or operations in a trust overseen by an administrator. The trust would be holding the assets, and the administrator would most likely sell or divest these assets or operations over a period of time. This type of arrangement frequently prevents use of the regulatory defense by the target company.

The "Just Say No" Defense

A defense that has been successfully utilized by several target companies has been what is known as the "Just say No" defense. Time-Life and Warner Communications successfully employed this defense to fend off a hostile takeover attempt by Paramount Communications in 1989. The Paramount Communications bid for Time-Life became a landmark case in the takeover business.

Time-Life had an agreement to merge with Warner Communications. Months after this agreement was announced, Paramount made an unfriendly cash tender offer for Time-Life. Until this time, there were very few, if any, instances where a target company's Board could just ignore an outstanding bid at a big premium to the current stock price and still remain independent. Time-Life, however, was in the process of a merger with Warner, it proposed to the Delaware court that it should be allowed to proceed with its own previously announced transaction rather than pursue a transaction with Paramount Communications. The two companies convinced the judge at the Delaware

Court of Chancery that because they had a defined business plan that made eminent sense for their shareholders over the long term, they should be able to proceed with their plan and not be taken over by Paramount. This defense became known as "Just say No."

A number of companies have since utilized the same defense or have tried to employ it in defending against hostile takeover attempts. It should be noted, however, that only recently have Time-Warner shareholders actually seen their stock price reach a level that represented a premium compared to what they would have received from Paramount Communications if its proposed transaction had gone forward as scheduled. Later in this chapter, we will be looking at another case that used the "Just say No" defense.

Responses to contested takeover attempts are not necessarily negative for the target company's shareholders. Until now, all the defenses that we have discussed in this chapter were generally employed to prevent a transaction from occurring. When this happens, the target company's stock usually declines. Many shareholders would prefer to have the target company's Board of Directors pursue some of the available options.

Recapitalization

One optional strategy is a recapitalization of the company. In a recapitalization, the target company may repurchase a significant number of shares at a premium compared to where the shares were selling prior to the contested takeover attempt. Often, management will then alter its business strategy to focus the operations, cut costs, or somehow generate a higher rate of return for current shareholders. Recapitalization programs have sometimes allowed target companies to fend off a hostile bid—usually, by driving the price of the stock up so that the hostile takeover attempt becomes unattractive. Recapitalizations can give shareholders of a target company (and arbitrageurs who own the stock) financial benefits by instituting the plan, but they are usually the weakest positive responses that a target company's Board can implement.

Sometimes, a target company will look to financial institutions to help it determine whether it could enter into a leveraged transaction or leveraged buyout. The target company borrows capital from these financial institutions and pays out significant cash—and sometimes securities—to its shareholders. Leveraged buyouts became quite popular in the 1980s and were frequently utilized by companies to fend off hostile takeover attempts. The rationale that is generally employed for these transactions is: If the hostile bidder is going to banks or institutions to borrow cash for the hostile bid to buy the target company, and the target company has adequate assets to support borrowing, management sometimes feels that the target's shareholders and management would be better off if the company borrowed against its assets and paid the money out to shareholders. This type of transaction can also benefit shareholders; they may be able to receive a premium over the stock's trading price prior to the hostile bid.

This type of defense, however, has become less utilized in recent years, probably because of the overall valuations given to equity securities in the marketplace. It has not been easy for corporations to execute a leveraged buyout in the face of these increased stock valuations. As we stated in earlier chapters, many of today's transactions are being carried out using an equity security or stock as a medium of exchange to accomplish the takeover. Current conditions may not be very conducive to utilizing the leveraged buyout defense, but, at some point in the future, it is likely to return as a possible method of defense against hostile takeover attempts.

Sale of the Target Company

Arbitrageurs and shareholders alike look for a target company to defend itself against a hostile bid with a strategy that will yield the highest possible rate of return on their investment. The available strategies could include the target company's putting itself up for sale and seeking to have other companies bid for the stock. The search for bidders is usually done secretly; for example, it is not disclosed publicly until after the process has come to a resolution. The target company generally hires an investment banker at first notice of a hostile bid. If the target company decides to seek other buyers, the investment banker will coordinate the process and search for firms that represent a sensible alliance *and* would be interested in making a bid. This defense by a target company is generally known as "seeking a white knight."

The white knight's role is to save a target company from an unwanted hostile takeover. The white knight strategy may be the most profitable alternative and is therefore the one that arbitrageurs hope the target company will pursue. By seeking other bids, it creates competition for the hostile bidder's effort to purchase the target company. Often, a bidding war results; two or more companies may bid against each other for the right to purchase the target company. When that happens, the target company's Board is generally able to maximize the value realized for the shareholders. (We will examine one of these transactions in depth later in this chapter.)

Predicting the Outcomes of Various Defensive Strategies

The arbitrageur's job, in hostile takeover attempts, is to try to determine which, if any, of the defensive strategies the target company's Board may employ successfully. To formulate correct estimates, an arbitrageur utilizes his or her experience in the field as well as input on the current transaction and any reliable advice received from outside advisers. Increasingly, the arbitrageur relies on the target company's Board to do "the right thing."

The Board has to balance two concepts: (1) the fairness of a transaction to shareholders, or what makes the most sense, and (2) ways of fighting the hostile takeover attempt so that shareholders will receive the best value. The Board may look at value as being short-term or long-term. Many Boards today are looking to maximize long-term value for their shareholders—or at least that is what they state when faced with a hostile takeover attempt. If the Board believes that the company's long-term value is far in excess of any short-term value that can be created through a hostile takeover attempt, it may elect to use some of the previously mentioned defenses, especially "Just say No," to try to beat back the hostile offer. On the other hand, if the Board balances the outcomes and decides that the outstanding bid makes sense for shareholders to receive, the Board may choose to negotiate and sell the company.

In years past, it was a foregone conclusion that a target company under attack for a hostile takeover would be sold. Today, with the numerous defenses that can be utilized, the outcome is not always that clear.

Two new aspects of hostile takeover attempts must be considered. One is the previously mentioned "Just say No" defense, which, on a number of occasions, has allowed target companies to avoid hostile takeovers. As a result of this avoidance, arbitrageurs and all shareholders of the target company have sustained losses on their holdings.

The second new aspect is that the time frame in which these transactions may be completed has lengthened dramatically. Staggered Boards, state takeover laws, and specialized defenses have been key factors. Many times, if a target company's Board is devoted to defending against a hostile bid, the hostile bidder may actually have to wait several years to overturn the target's defenses. The danger in this is that many things may change over that length of time. The hostile bidder may even change its decision to pursue the takeover.

In trying to determine the likelihood that a hostile bid will succeed, the arbitrageur analyzes numerous aspects of the target company's business and structure. The initial question the arbitrageur must ask is: "What are the likely defenses that the target company can employ?" If there is a clear overlap in business operations, the arbitrageur knows that he or she will have to determine how great that overlap is, and whether it might create an antitrust problem for the hostile bidder. The arbitrageur must determine, after figuring out what defenses are possible, whether these defenses will hold up in court. If a defense either stalls the transaction for a long period of time or becomes a potential stumbling block, this transaction can be a very dangerous one for the arbitrage community.

The arbitrageur must scrutinize the target company's Board of Directors. How many are inside directors and how many are from outside the company? Inside, or management, directors will tend to fight hostile takeover attempts more readily than outside directors will. If management or inside directors dominate the Board, the company is much more likely to try to defend against any hostile takeover attempts.

The arbitrageur must also look at how the target company's outstanding common stock is held. If management and the Board own a significant amount of stock, the arbitrageur knows that a defense pursued by the Board is more likely to succeed. If, however, management and the Board own a negligible amount of stock, their holdings will have no influence on the outcome of the transactions. If institutions own a high percentage of the outstanding shares of the target company, they could very well become the determining factor in how the target company's Board responds to a hostile takeover attempt. If the Board is concerned about falling into disfavor with these institutional holders if they successfully defend against a hostile takeover attempt, the Board may very well pursue some of the positive options that will generate short-term economic gain for their current shareholder base.

Perhaps the best way to examine the outcome of hostile takeovers is to look at some of these transactions in depth.

HOSTILE TAKEOVER CASES

Wallace Computer Services v. Moore Corporation Ltd.

On July 31, 1995, Moore Corporation announced its intention to commence a tender offer for all the shares of Wallace Computer Services (WCS) for $56 per share in cash. Moore had previously offered to purchase Wallace in an offer made directly to the Board of Directors of Wallace. Because the directors had rejected the proposal, Moore felt its only alternative was to go directly to Wallace shareholders with the tender offer.

The $56-per-share cash consideration represented an 84 percent premium over the price at which Wallace's shares were trading before Moore Corporation's first contact with Wallace, in February. The $56 price also represented a 42 percent premium over Wallace's most recent 30-day average closing price.

Wallace Computer Services is a manufacturer of business forms, commercial printing, and computer and office supplies. The company makes both standard and custom computer business forms, and has its own in-house software system to service the industry.

Moore Corporation manufactures a comprehensive line of business forms. They range from hand-written forms to various computer-based information systems. The company is also involved in selling form-based and form-related systems and services.

Just prior to the formal initiation of the cash tender, WCS's Board of Directors adopted, amended, and restated bylaws of the company that affected how a shareholder could bring an issue to a vote at a shareholder meeting. The Board apparently had anticipated that Moore Corporation would pursue a hostile takeover attempt, and had changed or amended the bylaws to help defend Wallace against this unwanted bid.

Also on July 31, Moore commenced an action in the U.S. District Court for the District of Delaware by filing a complaint against Wallace and the directors of Wallace. Moore's action asserted, among other things, that the use of certain antitakeover defenses and other defensive measures by the company was not proportionate nor within the range of reasonable responses to any offer. Therefore, these defenses were in breach of the directors' fiduciary duties to Wallace's shareholders. Specifically, Moore was seeking to have the court force Wallace's directors to redeem their poison pill and rights. In addition, the action sought to: (1) have the court restrict the Wallace Board from taking any further action to inhibit the proposed hostile offer; (2) have the court declare that Section 203 of the Delaware Takeover Law would not apply to the transaction; and (3) have various articles that were amended in Wallace's bylaws enjoined so as not to interfere with the offer.

Wallace responded on August 15, 1995, by filing its own complaint against Moore in the U.S. District Court in the Southern District of New York. Wallace asked the court to enjoin the Moore tender offer on the grounds that the combination of the two companies would substantially lessen competition in a relevant market and therefore violated Section 7 of the Clayton Act. Wallace also alleged that Moore had made numerous false and misleading statements of fact in connection with the offer, and therefore should be enjoined from proceeding with the bid.

As can be seen from Figure 8.1, Wallace's shares jumped dramatically on the news of the hostile takeover attempt. WCS had a 2 for 1 stock split on September 29, 1996. As a result, the price on the Y scale is actually one-half the number one would have seen at the time of the deal (i.e., 30 is 60). The common stock of Wallace rose from $44 to $58 after the offer was disclosed on July 31. Arbitrageurs and shareholders alike then had to ask themselves: How likely was it that Moore Corporation, or some other corporation, ultimately would take control of Wallace Computer Services through a hostile bid?

This case is interesting because it incorporates a great number of the potential takeover defenses we have previously discussed. The Wallace Board had altered the bylaws to strengthen its defense against an unwanted bid. It also had a poison pill rights plan in effect, and sought to use it as a major defense. And, the company was pursuing an antitrust argument in the federal court system to enjoin the offer. The arbitrageur's job was now to examine these defenses and determine whether any would work well enough to prevent a hostile takeover.

Figure 8.1 Wallace Computer Services (WCS) Trading Activity, March 1, 1995, to February 28, 1996

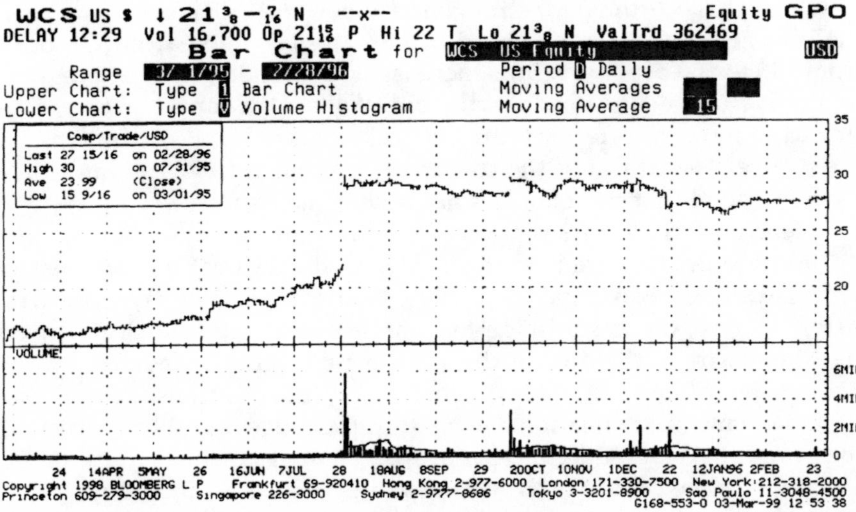

Source: © 1999 Bloomberg L.P. All rights reserved.

The battle waged on for a number of months. Wallace Computer Systems issued press releases, had meetings with shareholders, and conducted conference calls to indicate to its shareholders that this $56-per-share bid, while representing a premium over the price at which WCS shares had been trading, was much too low for the company or its shareholders to accept. The Wallace Board members trumpeted their growth strategy and how well it was working. They pointed out to shareholders that earnings per share were up significantly and the current growth looked like it would continue into the future. They also indicated that the Wallace Board was committed to delivering shareholder value but warned that this value sometimes takes time to develop and to be recognized by the market.

Moore Corporation was obviously on the other side of the fence. Moore urged shareholders to examine the Wallace Board of Directors' actions and ask some very basic questions. Where would Wallace's stock be without the Moore offer? Moore believed that it might return to the pre-offer level—the low $40s. If Wallace were to remain independent, when would its stock price reach the $56 per share that the shareholders were being offered now?

The two companies were clearly digging in for quite a battle. The site of the battle was to be Wallace's Annual Meeting, on December 8, 1995. Wallace, like many corporations, had previously instituted a staggered Board of Directors. Only three directors were due to be elected at the meeting. Moore Corporation was seeking to have three of its nominees elected to the Board instead of Wallace's nominees.

Prior to the Annual Meeting, on October 12, 1995, Moore increased the pressure on Wallace's Board of Directors by increasing the offer from $56 to $60 per share. This increase was intended to exert pressure on the Wallace Board to accept the bid. Wallace's Board, however, continued to fight the offer by telling shareholders of the Board's plans for the future. The health of the company was intact, they said, and they recommended that shareholders not tender their shares.

Hearings on Moore's motions for a preliminary injunction against the Wallace Board were held in the U.S. District Court for the District of Delaware, on November 7–9, 1995, before Judge Murray Schwartz. After hearing the case, Judge Schwartz was to make a decision on (1) Moore's request to have the poison pill rights redeemed by the Wallace Board and (2) Wallace's contention that the transaction represented an antitrust violation. Ultimately, the judge found that resisting the premium cash tender offer represented a reasonable and informed response to the Moore offer. Citing numerous cases, including Time-Warner, the judge found that Wallace's Board had made informed judgments about the future of the company and had responded properly to the Moore takeover bid.

Frequently, in hostile takeover cases, the courts have to interpret whether a company's Board has abided by what is known as "The Business Judgment Rule." Over the years, the courts have determined that, to comply with this rule, a Board must utilize all its efforts to perform an informed analysis of the situation under consideration. This usually requires the Board to retain outside advisers, including investment bankers and attorneys. If it is determined that the Board did utilize the proper effort to be informed in making its judgments, the courts have become increasingly less interested in exerting their judgment about any given transaction. In other words, shareholders must bear the increasing risk that courts will be less likely to overrule decisions by a target company's Board of Directors when the facts show informed judgments have been applied.

In this case, the court reviewed in depth each of the Wallace Board's actions with regard to the takeover. Ultimately, Judge Schwartz found that the Board had responded reasonably to the hostile bid that it was facing. He essentially believed the company's overall growth strategy, as well as the company's investment banker's financial projections for the future. Moore Corporation's request for an injunction to redeem the poison pill was denied.

Judge Schwartz, however, also denied Wallace's request to enjoin the takeover attempt based on antitrust consideration. Judge Schwartz analyzed the relevant markets as well as market shares and other data provided by numerous experts who testified at the hearings. He ultimately determined that Moore's case was the stronger one, and that there would be no violation of United States antitrust laws. This rejection of the antitrust claim was good for Wallace shareholders and arbitrageurs. The refusal to force the Wallace Board to redeem the poison pill and negotiate with Moore caused a dilemma. Moore Corporation's choices in their effort to take over Wallace Computer were then narrowed significantly. It seemed that the only way they could do it would be to elect their three Board nominees each year and ultimately hope to have a majority on the Board so that the companies could pursue a friendly merger. The poison pill, in this case, became an obstacle that could be overcome only over a long period of time. In the end, Moore Corporation withdrew its bid, and the shares of Wallace Computer declined. Figure 8.2 shows the market price action of the Wallace Computer Services stock over the time period in which the bid was outstanding.

The Wallace Computer case was an unfortunate experience for Wallace shareholders and for arbitrageurs at the time it occurred. This type of transaction shows why the arbitrageur must perform analysis that accurately indicates to him what will be the final outcome of the transaction.

Figure 8.2   Wallace Computer Services (WCS) Trading Activity, June 2, 1995, to October 10, 1997

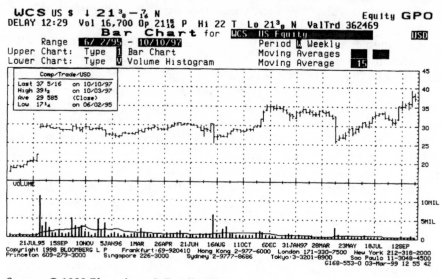

Appendix 2 contains the entire decision delivered by Judge Schwartz.

Echlin/SPX/Dana Corporation

On February 17, 1998, SPX Corporation (SPX) delivered a letter to the Board of Echlin Inc. The letter proposed a strategic business combination of Echlin with SPX. SPX was offering $12 in cash and 0.4796 share of SPX's common stock for each share of Echlin (ECH). SPX's common stock price was $36 at the time, so the offer had a total consideration of approximately $48 per share. Echlin's common stock had closed on the floor of the New York Stock Exchange at approximately $38⅞ prior to the offer to Echlin's Board. On the same date (2/17/98), SPX also filed with the Securities and Exchange Commission (SEC) a solicitation of demands from Echlin's shareholders and a call for a special meeting of the shareholders. At this meeting, SPX would propose, among other things, to remove the entire Board of Directors of Echlin and elect the SPX nominees as directors of the Echlin Board. After the offer was made, Echlin's Board met and decided to oppose the transaction. The Board also stated that Echlin was not for sale.

When the offer was made public, arbitrageurs analyzed Echlin's corporate bylaws and quickly determined that a special meeting to solicit votes from Echlin shareholders to essentially throw out the entire Board was a powerful weapon for SPX to pursue. It would be a difficult vote for Echlin to win. Echlin, however, had other plans. One of its defense strategies was a request to the Connecticut Legislature to alter the state's takeover laws so that it would be very difficult, if not impossible, for SPX to take over Echlin.

On March 4, 1998, a bill was introduced into the Connecticut House of Representatives which, if enacted, would amend the Connecticut Business Act to restrict the ability of shareholders of a public company to remove the company's directors. The bill would also require the approval of a majority of "continuing directors" rather than the approval of the Board of Directors. If enacted, the bill would refute SPX's ability to exercise the solicitation of Echlin shareholders. As a result, Echlin's Board would probably have a winning defense strategy whereby the hostile takeover could be prevented.

This strategy was somewhat new to most arbitrageurs. Instead of just predicting what a court or board of directors would do in the face of a defensive strategy, they now had to guess the probability of having a new law passed by the Connecticut Legislature. Arbitrageurs found this type of prediction much more difficult than in the typical case. Political aspects of transactions are much harder to track and predict for the arbitrage community.

Ultimately, the Connecticut Legislature, by a narrow vote, refused to pass the proposed bill. With its major defense against SPX nullified, Echlin had to evaluate what other strategies it would pursue. Unknown to the public, when the bill was voted down, Echlin's Board seemed to change the direction of its defense. Discussions with Dana Corporation (DCN) were initiated. They ultimately resulted in an agreement to merge Echlin with Dana Corporation for .9293 share of Dana common stock. This agreement was announced on May 4, 1998.

Normally, this would have been one of the better possible outcomes for shareholders of a target company. The target company's Board had dropped its defense and pursued another bidder. The bidder was found, and the new bid seemed to be offering shareholders increased value over the hostile takeover attempt. In this case, however, a decline in Dana Corporation's stock once the transaction was announced created a good news–bad news situation for the Echlin shareholders. The good news was that they got another bidder. The bad news was that the value of the transaction once Dana's stock declined was actually less than the value of SPX's proposed transaction. A few days later, SPX terminated its offer. Shareholders were left to accept the

Dana–Elchin merger. Figure 8.3 shows the stock price of Elchin during the period when the hostile offer was made. Figures 8.4 and 8.5 show, respectively, the activity of SPX and Dana Corporation during the relevant time period.

Elchin shareholders did not get the full benefit of a bidding war between the two companies, but the premium they received for their shares was over the amount at which the Echlin shares were trading prior to the commencememt of the hostile offer.

Notes from the File

Over time, I have found that when a situation involves multiple bidders, arbitrageurs can usually make significant returns. The arbitrageur must guard against overpaying for the target company's stock, but these situations represent extremely attractive opportunities for realizing large potential gains.

Whenever arbitrageurs come across a case of multiple bidders, they usually should go into an aggressive mode as long as they believe that they are not paying too high a premium. Arbitrageurs would probably desire full positions in these types of transactions.

Figure 8.3   Echlin, Inc. (ECH) Trading Activity,
December 1, 1997, to June 30, 1998

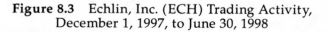

Source: © 1999 Bloomberg L.P. All rights reserved.

Figure 8.4   SPX Corporation (SPW) Trading Activity,
December 1, 1997, to June 30, 1998

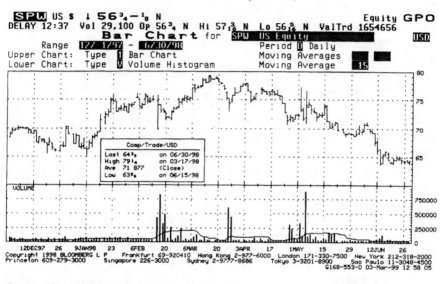

Figure 8.5   Dana Corporation (DCN) Trading Activity,
December 1, 1997, to June 30, 1998

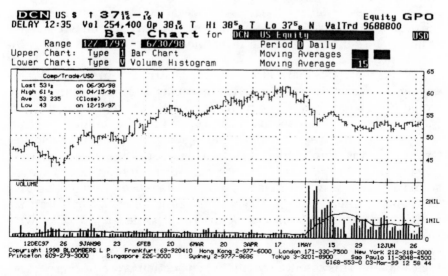

Grumman Corporation/Martin Marietta/Northrop

On March 7, 1994, Martin Marietta and Grumman Corporation agreed to merge. Martin Marietta was to pay Grumman shareholders $55 in cash for each Grumman share. Grumman Corporation is primarily an aerospace and electronics firm that designs and produces military aircraft, space systems, and commercial aircraft components and subassemblies. Grumman's electronics units design, manufacture, and integrate sophisticated electronics systems for aircraft, test equipment, and other defense-related products. Grumman also has an electronic data processing service for its affiliates and its customers, and it fabricates vehicles for the United States Postal Service and aluminum truck bodies. Martin Marietta, a diversified company, is principally engaged in the design and manufacture of advance technology products and services for the United States Government and private industry.

Both companies came to this friendly merger transaction after negotiating for a period of time. What makes this case different from others is that it ultimately evolved into a hostile takeover attempt.

After Grumman and Martin Marietta had agreed to Martin Marietta's $55-per-share cash tender offer, an interesting twist occurred. One of Grumman's competitors, the Northrop Corporation, had followed the Grumman–Martin Marietta situation closely. Three days after Martin's announcement of the $55 deal, Northrop made a cash tender offer to acquire Grumman for $60 a share. The offer was considered hostile at that time. Grumman Corporation's management and employees preferred to have Martin Marietta be the buyer. During the period of time when the offer was outstanding, despite Grumman's attempts to get Martin Marietta to increase its bid, Northrop ultimately prevailed.

When the $60-a-share offer was made, arbitrageurs were experiencing another "bidding war." The two-part question became: Who would ultimately buy Grumman Corporation, and at what price? Martin Marietta was insisting that Grumman had to enforce a standstill pact that the two companies had signed. Under the pact's terms, Grumman was bound to continue to support the agreement with Martin Marietta. However, because the Northrop bid was structured similarly and was worth $5 more, it would have been very difficult for Grumman's directors to justify pursuing the lower bid in a transaction. As a result, Grumman's Board finally opened up talks with Northrop Corporation. It was decided toward the end of March that Grumann was free of any commitment and was open to bidding for the company. This essentially created an auction process whereby any and all bidders could examine the books of Grumman and enter into a transaction.

Grumman clearly preferred to have Martin Marietta buy the company, but efforts to get Martin Marietta to raise the bid from $55 to $60 went for naught. Martin Marietta held to the $55 cash bid. Meanwhile, through negotiating with Northrop Corporation, Grumman was able to increase the hostile $60 bid to $62 per share. Grumman's Board at that point decided to support the $62-per-share bid, and Northrop ended up buying the company at $62 per share.

The shareholders of Grumman Corporation benefited from Northrop's hostile takeover attempt. They were able to realize an additional $7 per share. The arbitrageurs who had established positions based on the $55 Martin Marietta bid realized a tremendous rate of return over a very short period of time. Figure 8.6 shows the market action of Grumman's common stock price over the period.

USE OF DECISION TREES

In contested takeover situations, there are numerous potential outcomes. In friendly negotiated transactions, the deal is usually either completed or it breaks up for some reason. A two-outcome model does not usually work well in cases of contested takeovers. We therefore

Figure 8.6   Grumman (GQ) Trading Activity,
January 3, 1994, to April 15, 1994

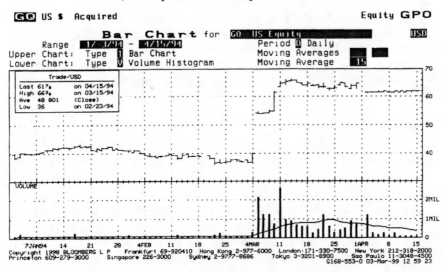

Source: © 1999 Bloomberg L.P. All rights reserved.

have to employ a more sophisticated method for estimating the likely outcomes of a transaction and the risk-adjusted return that will be realized.

Arbitrageurs identify all the potential outcomes of any hostile takeover transaction. After analyzing these potential outcomes, they try to determine two things:

1. The probability that a particular outcome will occur.
2. An estimate of what would happen to the target company's stock if a particular outcome occurs.

By having both the probability estimate and the estimate of what would happen to the target company's stock price, the arbitrageur is able to form a decision tree and apply the probabilities to the individual outcomes to determine the expected price of the target company in the transaction.

In Figure 8.7 on page 125, we show an example of how this is put to use by the arbitrageur. We have used an example involving Paramount Communications. In the fall of 1993, Paramount Communications had entered into a merger agreement with Viacom whereby Paramount would be merged into Viacom for a combination of cash and stock. After that merger agreement was executed, another company, QVC Network, Incorporated, made a competing offer for Paramount. QVC was also offering a combination of cash and stock. Paramount and Viacom were seeking to complete their merger in the face of a competing bid.

The takeover battle ended up in the Delaware Court system with the Delaware Chancery Court issuing an opinion forcing the Paramount Board of Directors to consider the competing QVC bid. Unlike the Paramount bid for Time-Life, the Delaware Court ruled that the prior court decision did not apply since Paramount was selling control to Viacom. The decision was appealed to the Delaware Supreme Court and the decision of that court would determine the outcome of the takeover battle.

We have included a decision tree that was prepared before the Delaware Supreme Court issued their decision on the Case. Figure 8.6 shows the potential outcomes as well as the arbitrageur's estimates of the probability and value for each of the outcomes.

By completing the analysis, we can see that the arbitrageur had an estimated expected value for Paramount of $86.85. In December 1993, the Delaware Supreme Court issued an opinion affirming the lower court's decision. Viacom ultimately prevailed in the takeover battle acquiring Paramount Communications. While the values received by

Figure 8.7 A Decision Tree Analysis of the Bids for Viacom by Paramount Communications and QVC Network

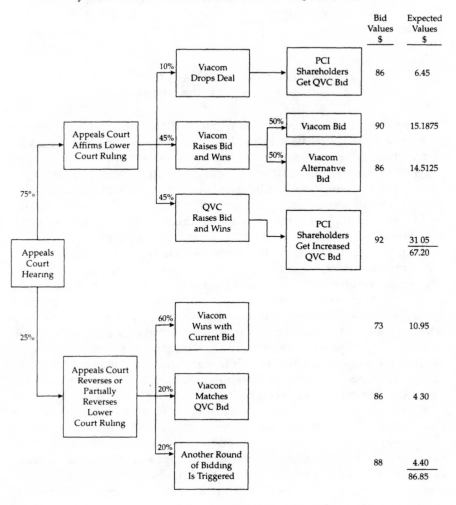

Paramount shareholders were different from the arbitrageur's $86.85 estimate in the decision tree, the decision tree provided a very important basis for the arbitrageur to participate and make money on the transaction.

ESTIMATION OF VALUE IN CONTESTED TAKEOVER ATTEMPTS

Because the price is agreed on in negotiated transactions, arbitrageurs have been able to calculate estimated returns based on the announced terms of such transactions. In hostile deals, however, the arbitrageur's job is more difficult. In addition to figuring out the target company's potential defenses and the likelihood of those defenses being successful, the arbitrageur must also try to determine the takeover price if the defenses do not work and the company is taken over. The price is influenced by the businesses that the target company has, the prices that have been paid recently in the company's particular industry, and the demand for the company's businesses among available buyers. The price is also influenced by whether a white knight is involved in the transaction.

To arrive at potential prices that could be paid in transactions, the arbitrageur has to estimate what a fair takeover value would be, and what value could be generated through a leveraged buyout or a recapitalization. This process requires the arbitrageur to spend a great deal of time with the financials of the target company. He or she must be able to analyze the financial statement and predict earnings and cash flows (or use other analysts' predictions) going into the future. Usually, an arbitrageur will take as many recent transactions as can be considered comparable to the subject transaction, and will determine the likely deal price and how it is related to the target company's earnings, cash flow, and asset values. This commonly means that the arbitrageur arrives at a range of estimates for deals done by companies of this caliber, expressed as, say, 15–20 times next year's earnings, or 7–9 times next year's cash flow, or something along those lines. The arbitrageur always tries to back up an analysis with facts from past cases.

Figure 8.8 (at the end of the chapter) is a sample analysis of Wallace Computer Services (WCS), done by an investment research firm shortly after the Moore Corporation's bid was announced. In this analysis, dated August 2, 1995, an analyst at Zimbalist-Smith and Oscar Gruss & Son arrived at a target merger value of $60.93 per WCS share, and a leveraged buyout value of $57 per share. Both of these prices exceeded the $56 proposed by Moore Corporation—an indication to the arbitrageur that there was upside potential in taking a position in WCS. As long as a transaction occurred, it would appear from this analysis that the arbitrageur could profit by purchasing WCS stock in the marketplace.

The target values arrived at by the analysts were dependent on various assumptions. These assumptions were applied to the company's operating information, expected revenues, and pretax income. The target estimates may have been quite accurate at the time, but, unfortunately, as we have seen, the outcome was much different. Still, this is a solid method to follow when analyzing the potential value of a target company in a hostile takeover attempt.

RISK ASSESSMENT

As in all other risk arbitrage transactions, the analyst or arbitrageur must analyze how much he or she risks by investing in a transaction. The arbitrageur must also estimate what can be lost in hostile takeover attempts, which, compared with friendly transactions, may cause the ultimate risk level to be adjusted. Sometimes, when a hostile takeover attempt does not go through and the price of the target company declines, the stock may not decline to the level at which it was traded prior to the deal's being announced. A premium sometimes develops; the stock of the target company may trade for a long period of time *above* its preannouncement level. The reason is that the target company's stock was trading at a low level when there was no public knowledge of a takeover situation. Once a takeover attempt is made, many shareholders feel that a transaction could occur in the future, and the investment community now knows that someone was willing to pay a premium for the stock. As a result, a takeover premium may be included in the amount new shareholders will pay for owning a share of the stock. The shareholders may feel that the hostile bidder may return and make an additional bid for the company, or they may expect that, ultimately, the target company will do something for its own shareholders so as to improve the value of the shares.

Initially, however, after a hostile transaction is defeated, the target company's stock declines. It may fall lower than the arbitrageur expects, simply because of supply and demand. If the transaction was outstanding for a long period of time and the arbitrage community established large positions in the marketplace, many arbitrageurs will be forced to sell—almost regardless of price—when the deal breaks up. If many positions were held and have to be sold, logic does not always prevail and prices may temporarily decline to bargain levels. This happens frequently in these types of transaction. Ultimately, the stock usually finds some equilibrium in trading—either close to the arbitrageur's estimate or somewhat above it, because of the aforementioned premium assigned to broken transactions.

SUMMARY

Hostile takeover transactions clearly represent a challenging and potentially lucrative opportunity for arbitrageurs. These types of transactions require the arbitrageur to engage in detailed analysis that involves many disciplines. Because these transactions can represent a large portion of an arbitrageur's profit over any given year, they should always be analyzed carefully.

Figure 8.8   Wallace Computer Services Report

Oscar Gruss & Son	*ZIMBALIST*
INCORPORATED	*/////SMITH*

74 Broad Street
New York, NY 10004
Phone: (212) 943-7610

125 MAIN STREET
WESTPORT, CT 06880
(203) 222-1515

SPECIAL SITUATIONS REPORT

WALLACE COMPUTER (WCS)

NYSE: $58.25

DJIA: 4690.14

MERGER VALUATION ANALYSIS

THE FOLLOWING MERGER VALUATION DETERMINES THE PRICE WHICH COULD
BE PAID FOR A TARGET COMPANY BY A QUALIFIED CORPORATE BUYER THE
LBO VALUATION ANALYSIS DETERMINES THE PRICE WHICH COULD BE PAID
BY AN INVESTOR GROUP BASED ON THE COMPANY'S ABILITY TO REPAY DEBT.
ADJUSTMENTS HAVE BEEN MADE FOR DIVESTITURES AND REDUCTIONS IN
CORPORATE AND CAPITAL EXPENDITURES

TRANSACTION SUMMARY

ON JULY 31, 1995, MOORE CORPORATION (MCL) ANNOUNCED ITS INTENTION TO
LAUNCH A HOSTILE TAKEOVER BID FOR WALLACE COMPUTER SERVICES (WCS)
FOR $56-PER-SHARE ($1 3 BIL) IN CASH

THE OFFER, SCHEDULED TO EXPIRE ON AUGUST 29, 1995, WAS PREDICATED BY
THE WCS BOARD'S CONTINUED REFUSAL TO DISCUSS A BUSINESS COMBINATION
WITH MCL MCL FIRST CONTACTED WCS ON FEBRUARY 24, 1995.

ON AUGUST 1, 1995 THE WCS BOARD STATED IT WOULD NEED A WEEK OR MORE TO
RESPOND TO THE MCL TAKEOVER BID

MCL HAS INITIATED A COURT ACTION TO INVALIDATE WCS' POISON PILL
ANTITAKEOVER DEFENCE

ON AUGUST 2, 1995 MCL ANNOUNCED IT HAD FILED FOR HART-SCOTT APPROVAL.
THE WAITING PERIOD WILL EXPIRE ON AUGUST 17, 1995

Figure 8.8   (Continued)

WALLACE COMPUTER (WCS)

($58.25 NYSE)

COMPANY

WALLACE COMPUTER SERVICES (WCS) MARKETS COMPUTER SERVICES AND
SUPPLIES, BUSINESS FORMS, LABELS, MACHINE RIBBONS, AND SOFTWARE.
WALLACE PRESS DOES COMMERCIAL PRINTING.

SUMMARY OF VALUES

	MERGER VALUE	LBO VALUE
	$60.93	$57 00
MULTIPLE TO:		
REVENUES.	1.98	1.85
OPERATING INCOME:	8.58	8.02
PRETAX CASH FLOW·	9.82	9.19
EBIT·	13.41	12.55
EARNINGS PER SHARE:*	21.01	19 66
BOOK VALUE.	3.06	2.86
INTEREST COVERAGE RATIO:	N.A.	1.31

FIRST CALL 1996 EARNINGS ESTIMATE

Figure 8.8   (Continued)

WALLACE COMPUTER
COMPANY STATISTICS-FISCAL 1995 ESTIMATES

OPERATING INFORMATION:	GROSS (MILL)	PER SHARE	AS PERCENT OF SALES
REVENUES	$695.0	$30 75	100.00%
OPERATING INCOME	160.5	7.10	23.10
DEPRECIATION	37.0	1.64	5 32
CORPORATE AND OTHER EXPENSE	20.9	0.92	3.00
EARNINGS BEFORE INTEREST & TAXES*	102 7	4.54	14 77
INTEREST EXPENSE–LONG TERM DEBT	1.4	0.06	0.20
INTEREST INCOME	1 9	0.08	0.27
TAX 36 50% TAX RATE	37 7	1.67	5 42
EARNINGS	65.5	2.90	9.43
NET PROFIT MARGIN			9.43
PRETAX CASH FLOW	140.2	6.20	20.17
AFTER TAX CASH FLOW	102.5	4.54	14.75
CAPITAL SPENDING	49.7	2.20	7.15
PRETAX FREE CASH FLOW	90.5	4.00	13 02

CAPITAL STRUCTURE:	GROSS (MILL)	PER SHARE	PERCENTAGE
LONG TERM DEBT	$25.0	$1.11	5.27%
BOOK VALUE	449.7	19 90	94.73
TOTAL	474.7	21.01	100.00

OWNERSHIP PROFILE:	SHARES	PERCENTAGE
PUBLIC SHARES	22.4	99.00%
INSIDER SHARES	0.2	1.00
TOTAL SHARES	22.6	100.00

First Call 1996 mean earnings estimate

Figure 8.8   (Continued)

WALLACE'COMPUTER
SCHEDULE A
ESTIMATED MERGER VALUE:

$60.93

	1995 (Mil)	ADJUST	PRO FORMA 1995
REVENUES	$695.0	$0.0	$695.0
OPERATING INCOME	160.5	0.0	160.5
CORPORATE AND OTHER EXPENSE	20.9	(3 1)	17.7
DEPRECIATION	37.0	0.0	37 0
EARNINGS B/INT. AND TAXES	102.7	3.1	105.8
INTEREST EXPENSE	1.4	0.0	1.4
PRETAX INCOME	101.3	3.1	104.4

PROFORMA NON-DILUTIVE MERGER VALUE:

CORPORATE BORROWING RATE	9.75%
PRETAX INCOME/CORP. BORROWING RATE	$1,071.2
PROFORMA NON-DILUTIVE MERGER VALUE PER SHARE	$47.40
MERGER PREMIUM PERCENTAGE	25.00%
MERGER VALUE BEFORE CASH ON HAND	$59.25
CASH ON HAND CREDIT PER SHARE	$1.68
ESTIMATED MERGER VALUE	$60.93

MERGER VALUE PREMIUM TO CURRENT PRICE:	5.28%

Figure 8.8   (Continued)

WALLACE COMPUTER
SCHEDULE B
ESTIMATED LBO VALUE: $57.00

FINANCING STRUCTURE:

FUNDS REQUIRED: (IN MILLIONS)

PURCHASE OF OUTSTANDING SHARES:	$1,288.2
EXISTING DEBT REPAYMENT.	25.0
TRANSACTION COSTS	38.6
TOTAL	$1,351.8

FUNDS PROVIDED BY:

EXCESS CASH ON HAND:	$37.9
ESTIMATED BANK DEBT:	657.0
ESTIMATED SUBORDINATED DEBT·	262.8
ESTIMATED EQUITY	394.2
TOTAL	$1,351.8

CAPITALIZATION AND INTEREST RATE ASSUMPTIONS:

	INTEREST RATES	CAPITALIZATION	
		MILLIONS	PERCENT
SENIOR DEBT·	9 75%	$657.0	50.00%
SUBORDINATED DEBT	13.75	262.8	20.00
EQUITY.	0.00	394.2	30.00
BLENDED TOTAL.	10 89%	$1,313 9	100.00%

Figure 8.8 (Continued)

WALLACE COMPUTER
LBO – FINANCIAL ANALYSIS:

PROFORMA INCOME STATEMENT:	Before LBO 1995	Adjustments	Proforma 1995	1996
	----------- Millions of Dollars-----------			
REVENUES	$695 0	$0.0	$695.0	$764.5
OPERATING INCOME	160.5	0.0	160.5	176.6
REORGANIZATION FEES	0.0	(7 7)	7 7	7 7
CORPORATE EXPENSES	20.9	(3.1)	17.7	17.7
DEPRECIATION	37.0	0 0	37.0	37.0
EARNINGS B/INT. AND TAXES	102.7	(4.6)	98.1	114.1
INTEREST EXPENSE	1.4	98.9	100.2	98.3
GAIN ON DIVESTITURE	0 0	0.0	0.0	0.0
PRETAX INCOME	101.3	(103.4)	(2.1)	15.8
INCOME TAXES	37 0	(37.7)	(0.8)	5.8
NET INCOME	64 3	(65.7)	(1.3)	10.0
PROFORMA CASH FLOW:				
SOURCES:				
NET INCOME	64.3	(65.7)	(1 3)	10.0
DEPRECIATION	37 0	0 0	37.0	37.0
BENEFIT OF NOL	0.0	0.0	0.0	0.0
AMORTIZATION OF FEES	0.0	7.7	7.7	7.7
BOOK VALUE DIVESTITURE	0.0	0 0	0 0	0.0
CASH FLOW	101 3	(57 9)	43 4	54.8
USES:				
CAPITAL SPENDING	49.7	(19.9)	29.8	29.8
REORGANIZATION FEES	0.0	0.0	0.0	0.0
FREE CASH FLOW/CASH AVAIL DEBT .	51.6	(38.1)	13.6	24.9
INTEREST COVERAGE RATIO:				
EARNINGS B/INT. AND TAXES	102.7	(4.6)	98.1	114.1
DEPRECIATION	37.0	0.0	37.0	37.0
BENEFIT OF NOL	0 0	0.0	0 0	0.0
AMORTIZATION OF FEES	0.0	7.7	7.7	7.7
BOOK VALUE DIVESTITURE	0 0	0.0	0 0	0.0
LESS: CAPITAL SPENDING	49.7	(19.9)	29.8	29 8
REORGANIZATION FEES	0.0	0 0	0.0	0.0
TOTAL	90.0	23.0	113 0	129.0
INTEREST EXPENSE	1.4	98.8	100.2	98.3
INTEREST COVERAGE RATIO	N A.		1.13	1.31

SEE NOTES TO LEVERAGED MODELS

Figure 8.8   (Continued)

WALLACE COMPUTER

NOTES TO LEVERAGED MODELS:

NOTE 1 - EARNINGS:

The estimated earnings are based on:
First Call mean estimate -   10.00%

NOTE 2 - CORPORATE EXPENSES AND CAPITAL SPENDING:

Corporate expenses and capital spending were reduced based upon
projected cost savings based on typical leveraged transactions:

Corporate expense reduction: 15.00%
Capital spending reduction: 40.00%

NOTE 3 - ADJUSTMENTS:

Adjustments have been made for reorganization fees and where
applicable, divestitures.

Source: Wallace Computer (WCS), Special Situations Report, August 2, 1995.
Used with permission.

Chapter **9**

Trading Tactics

When an arbitrageur takes a position in a particular arbitrage transaction, he or she must decide how to execute that decision and how to implement it with an overall portfolio strategy. In this chapter, we will explore the execution of trades and the tactics that arbitrageurs use to set up and unwind positions.

POSITION SIZE

An arbitrageur must initially set up a maximum position size in any given transaction. The maximum size will relate to either the overall equity capital that the arbitrageur is utilizing, or the risk in the individual position as it relates to this overall equity capital. In the next chapter, we will explore in depth the method by which arbitrageurs should limit their position size. If we assume at this point, however, that the arbitrageur has determined the maximum position size—for example, either 10 percent of the overall buying power in the portfolio, or a maximum loss of 5 percent of the portfolio's capital—the arbitrageur knows the dollar amount of that maximum position. This amount is considered by the arbitrageur to be a maximum or full position size. Rarely is a full position put on at one time. An arbitrageur will usually determine, when he or she is initially making hedges, whether to start by taking out ¼ of a position, ½ of a position, ¾ of a position, or a full position.

Notes from the File ═══════════════════════════════

I have always found it very helpful to view the positions described above: ¼, ½, or ¾. I happen to feel very strongly that a position should be held. For instance, in a contested takeover attempt where I believe that developments

137

will occur very quickly, I may very well take a full position as soon as feasible. However, in most deals, I (and other arbitrageurs) tend to work into the positions gradually by first setting up a small position and then gradually increasing it as I monitor the spreads.

EXECUTION OF TRANSACTIONS

Cash transactions that are set up by arbitrageurs are somewhat simpler than the complex transactions in which arbitrageurs have the short stock. In cash transactions, the arbitrageurs know what the targeted spreads are, so they can calculate, with relative ease, what the returns would be at any given stock level. Generally, an arbitrageur executes a trade by putting in a bid with a broker, at a level that provides an adequate return on the capital. These bids are generally given in *limit orders*—the arbitrageur limits the price at which he or she is willing to buy the stock. For instance, if the bid is a $20 cash tender offer, the arbitrageur may give the broker an order such as, "Buy 20,000 shares at $18½ or better."

This contrasts with the use of market orders. Market orders, such as "Buy 20,000 XYZ at the market," are utilized when the arbitrageur wants to own the securities without being sensitive to the price of execution. A market order is executed at the lowest level at which securities are offered on an exchange. Many arbitrage transactions offer arbitrageurs significant annualized *rates* of return, but they realize relatively small absolute dollar returns. Therefore, the use of limit orders can be a very important way to control the actual spread in any given transaction. As the absolute dollar spread gets smaller, the importance of utilizing limit orders grows proportionally.

Compared to cash transactions, stock-for-stock deals and complex transactions that involve the issuance of securities require much more intricacy in the execution of the orders and in setting up the position. Assume that securities are being used as a method of exchange in a transaction. To hedge the transaction, the arbitrageur must be shorting the anticipated securities to be received upon closing. This means that the arbitrageur needs an *up tick* in order to execute the short sale. With an up tick, the security has to trade on what is known as a "zero plus" or "plus tick"—the stock must trade at a higher price than the previous sale in the marketplace. A zero plus tick simply means that the price of the trade is the same as for a previously executed trade, and that previously executed trade was on a plus tick. The need to sell short on a plus tick can significantly restrict the arbitrageur's ability to set up a position. Additional trading skills may also be required to execute the trades needed to set up the position.

After an arbitrage trader decides to take a position in a stock-for-stock transaction, he or she must decide which side of the trade should be executed first. Usually, the arbitrageur will try to execute the short side of the transaction first and will follow that move with the purchase of the securities. The reason is: If the arbitrageur first purchases the securities to establish the long position and then does not get an up tick on the security in which he or she is trying to establish a short position, the result is a one-sided position that is unhedged. To avoid this situation, the arbitrageur may try to get the short sale off first. At times, the arbitrageur will depart from executing the short sale prior to the long purchase. Usually, these situations occur when the arbitrageur has a strong feeling that the underlying securities he or she needs to short will be rising during trading hours. The usual tactic is to take advantage of that increase by first establishing a long position. Later, the arbitrageur sells short the securities into the strength in the marketplace. Either way, the arbitrageur must make a call on which position to establish first. Because each security is traded separately, it is very difficult to execute what would be known as a "paired transaction."

Paired transactions can only be executed through a select number of brokers who are willing to take the risk of accepting orders on a paired basis. Some brokers will accept an arbitrageur's order to buy a certain number of shares and short a certain number of shares. The broker figures out how to execute those trades. The arbitrageur will receive a report of the trades only if both sides of the trade are executed.

The actual execution of the trades is done in various ways. A professional arbitrageur who has relationships with the brokers who operate on the individual trading floors has what are known as "direct lines" to the exchanges. An arbitrageur may have numerous direct wires to brokers on the floor of the New York Stock Exchange, Philadelphia Stock Exchange, Pacific Stock Exchange, and the Chicago Board of Options Exchange. The arbitrageur may also have a number of direct phone lines to other brokerage firms that handle the execution of orders in the over-the-counter, or NASDAQ, market.

Professional arbitrageurs also utilize various state-of-the-art systems to execute their trades. The primary system that is currently employed is Instinet, a computer-based trading system. Arbitrageurs work at a live terminal, and they may be able to enter their orders directly into the system. Bids and offers are posted on the screen and may be viewed by the operator. Communications can also be sent from one participant to another, being seen only by those two participants.

In other words, if an arbitrageur has an actual bid in Instinet for, say, 10,000 shares at a certain price, he or she may receive a communication from an active seller who offers the securities at a slightly higher price. The arbitrageur would then decide whether to purchase the securities at the seller's offering price, or to maintain the bid in the Instinet system.

The Instinet system has changed dramatically the execution of trades, especially trades of over-the-counter securities. Instead of having to execute trades through the dealer market and NASDAQ, an arbitrageur is able to post bids and offers on over-the-counter securities on the Instinet machine. Previously, the arbitrageur would have to look at a NASDAQ machine to get a market in a particular security. The machine would indicate what brokerage firms had the best bid and the best offer. The arbitrageur would either have to call those brokers to execute a trade at their advertised prices or go through a broker to make a bid for an offer in the machine. The spreads in these types of securities were generally very wide. The introduction of Instinet and its application to over-the-counter trading have had a profound effect on the spread between the bid and ask prices on over-the-counter securities. In general, the spreads have narrowed dramatically. As a result, it has become much more efficient to trade over-the-counter securities, especially in arbitrage-related transactions. Instinet charges a fee per share for the execution of trades. This machine is made available directly to securities firms that subscribe to this service. Only rather large operations can afford the cost of the subscription.

For an individual practicing the trade of risk arbitrage, it is incumbent to establish relationships and accounts at firms where trades may be executed quickly and reasonably. The choices for individuals vary. One of the highest growth areas for the execution of trades that need to be done is on the Internet. Many brokers have set up systems by which individuals may enter trades via the Internet and receive executions on a timely basis. This method has also brought down significantly the cost of executing these trades. Previously, individual investors paid relatively large commissions to establish positions. These commissions inhibited the rates of return that could otherwise have been realized by individuals in the arbitrage business. Today, readily available services allow individuals to execute trades at two cents per share—or less. Individual investors in the arbitrage business should carefully screen potential Internet-based brokers to determine whether they can properly service their accounts. Execution at fast speed and low cost is the most preferred option. The investor should also check out various other aspects of the relationship that can become quite important. What are the broker's charges on debit balances? Can an individual investor receive credit for cash balances and the execution of short sales? This business has been changing dramatically over very short periods of time, and the services the various brokers offer must be continually monitored.

Assuming that a relationship is established with an Internet-based firm, the execution of orders is similar to the procedure described above. Limit orders are generally used to establish positions that control the rates of return that will be realized by the arbitrageur. In two-sided deals, the arbitrageur must decide which side of the trade to execute first.

Notes from the File ═══════════════════════════════

Prior to entering a short order, the arbitrageur must make sure that the broker can borrow the security. The ability to locate the security to be shorted in the marketplace may be a determining factor for participation in any given transaction. Transactions in which the short side may be difficult to borrow usually carry greater-than-normal spreads, and this feature may entice many people to set up these positions. However, I have found that, over time, this can be a dangerous situation. If a security becomes tough to borrow and the arbitrageur is short, the arbitrageur many receive what is called a "buy-in notice" from the broker. In effect, the broker is forcing the arbitrageur to cover his or her short position. Generally, buy-ins do not occur for just one customer at one brokerage firm. They tend to spread throughout The Street. As a result, a "short squeeze" may develop; many people who have short positions will have to go out and cover their shorts. To do so and still remain hedged, they will have to sell out their long positions. As a result, the spreads in these types of situations may widen dramatically, and any widening of spreads results in losses for the arbitrageur. It simply does not pay to enter these types of transactions. It is much safer for arbitrageurs to focus their attention on deals based on securities that are readily available for borrowing and therefore will not subject them to these buy-in practices.

Individual arbitrageurs may also utilize traditional brokerage firms and pay their going rates of commissions on trades. This link is usually arranged because the arbitrageurs receive an additional service from the broker or brokerage firm—generally, some type of research the arbitrageurs need in their business. The fees paid to these brokers have decreased significantly over the past 10 years. An arbitrageur must decide whether the services received from the outside brokerage firm merit the payment of the incremental commission.

Only the arbitrageur can determine whether the tradeoff of the cost of execution is justified by the services that are received. Undoubtedly, lower commissions improve the arbitrageur's return on any given execution. But the arbitrageur cannot lose sight of the overall package of services received from any broker. The arbitrageur needs fast, efficient, and effective service at a low cost. Whether an arbitrageur takes an initial position of ¼, ½, ¾, or full position, he or she must continually monitor the position after it is set up. Initially, an arbitrageur is usually executing ¼ of the full position.

Increases in the position are accomplished in several ways. One reason to increase the position would be to react to a widening in the spread in the transaction. Suppose that there is no additional information that would cause the arbitrageur to adjust either the estimates of return and risk or the probability of the transaction's closing. The widening of the spread may then make it more attractive for the arbitrageur to make an additional trade in the securities so as to increase his or her position. A second way in which the arbitrageur may increase the position is to introduce new information into the decision process. When new information comes into the marketplace, whether through a press release, a new analysis, or some type of legal development, the arbitrageur may certainly want to adjust his or her position.

Note from the File

There are times in the arbitrage business when developments in a deal may cause the spread to widen dramatically. This usually happens when an unforeseen event occurs (e.g., a government agency may seek a preliminary injunction). At these times, the arbitrageur may be sustaining large losses on an unrealized basis. These losses can be quite painful. Sometimes, the pain gets so great that the arbitrageur may feel that he or she should "go to church" to pray for a better development. I have always found that when I get an urge to pray for a position, it is a signal that I should have sold it already!

While monitoring the markets in the individual securities and the spreads, the arbitrageur may find trading opportunities by liquidating positions. Some arbitrageurs emphasize the trading aspect of the business. They employ skilled traders who monitor the spreads in the transactions on a minute-to-minute basis. If the spread widens, they look to set up a position or increase a position already held in the portfolio. As the spread narrows, they tend to unwind positions. These types of arbitrageurs look to make money by trading the variations in the spreads in the marketplace.

Notes from the File ════════════════════════════════

I have always found that trading can augment an investment's returns, but in the risk arbitrage business, I believe that, over time, the main source of profit for the arbitrageur comes from good fundamental research. Concentrating one's efforts on analysis of the situation generally yields the best opportunity to make money. This may mean that the arbitrageur set up his or her positions too early from a trading point of view, but the spreads improved as time went on. However, I have found that the overall picture and the overall analysis of the outcome of the deal under study are usually the most important determinants of an arbitrageur's success.

In monitoring the spreads of the transactions, the arbitrageur may determine that because of the parameters chosen and his or her analysis of risk, return, and probability, a spread has declined to such a level that a position presently held in the portfolio should be unwound. The compensation received may not support the risk or the probability of the deal's breaking up, or the capital involved may be better employed by reinvesting the proceeds of the sale in other deals that have more attractive returns and attributes.

Sometimes, an arbitrageur does hold the established positions until the absolute closing of the transaction. In a cash transaction, the arbitrageur might receive cash proceeds in his or her account, in exchange for stock. In a two-sided arbitrage situation, if the arbitrageur holds the positions until closing, the long position will turn into the securities that are the medium of exchange. These securities are then generally exchanged against the already established short position, thereby canceling out both the long and short positions. No single generalization can predict or dictate whether the arbitrageur holds a position to its ultimate conclusion or unwinds the position prior to the deal's closing. Market forces will reveal to the arbitrageur the best method of operation.

TIMING OF EXECUTIONS

As stated elsewhere in this book, cash tender offers and contested hostile takeovers require the arbitrageur's immediate attention. These transactions typically have fast-moving developments, and the arbitrageur must be prepared to implement a trading strategy to take advantage of them. In contrast, mergers tend to be outstanding from 3 to 12 months. Because mergers and securities involved in mergers will be trading in the marketplace for these lengthy periods of time, it is less important for the arbitrageur to complete an analysis promptly. For contested takeovers, however, the arbitrageur must perform the analysis as soon as possible because the securities involved will trade shortly after any announcement. Numerous opportunities for profit open up for arbitrageurs who have made a proper analysis.

Professional arbitrageurs find it helpful, in their decision making, to monitor who is actually purchasing and selling the securities involved in arbitrage transactions. Through their relationships with numerous brokers who operate on the floors of the exchanges, the arbitrageurs are apprised of which firms are buying or selling any particular security. Some professional arbitrageurs find this information very useful. As they track who is buying and who is selling, they input that information into their decision framework and it guides their decisions on what to buy, hold, or sell.

Table 9.1   The Risk Arbitrage Deal Universe

		Target			Acq.	Deal
Deal Desc.	Type	Comp. Name	Symb	Price ($)	Co.	Value ($)
$14.25 Cash Tender	A-CT	Central Tractor	CIFC	$ 14.000	PRIV	$ 14.250
Unsolicited $17.00 Cash Tender	A-CT	Circon Corp	CCON	15.000	USS	17.000
$115 in Cash	A-CT	**Conrall-CXS**	C2	112.750	CSX	115.000
$13.00 Cash Tender	A-CT	Healthdyne Tech	HDTC	13.938	IVCR	13.000
$21.75 Cash Tender	A-CT	HealthSource	HS	20.625	CI	21.750
$13.75 Cash Tender	A-CT	Innotech	IIII	13.625	JNJ	13.750
$7 Cash Tender	A-CT	Maxserv	MAX	7.688	S	7.750
$30 Cash Tender	A-CT	Renaissance Hotel	RHG	29.875	MAR	30.000
$17.10 Cash Tender	A-CT	TheraTx Inc	THTX	16.625	VC	17.100
Dutch Tender (5m shs @ $12.50 to $15)	A-CT	Titan Wheel	TWI	14.250	OTHER	15.000
$17.50 Cash Merger	A-CT	Universal Hospital	UHOS	17.125	MFD	17.500
$31 Stock Tender Offer	A-ST	Kansas City Power & Light	KLT	28.375	WR	31.000
$5.00 Cash Merger	B-CM	AM International	AM	3.500	OTHER	5.000
$26 Cash Merger w/10% equity stub	B-CM	**Amphenal**	APH	25.375	OTHER	26.000
Unsolicited $12 cash offer	B-CM	Box Energy	BOXXB	7.250	FORCO	12.000
Speculative cash offer	B-CM	**Bre-X Minerals**	BXNMF	12.938	ABX	18.000
Unsolicited $20 Offer	B-CM	Carter-Wallace	CAR	14.500	PRIV	20.000
$21.65 Cash Merger	B-CM	Destec Energy	ENG	20.750	NGI	21.650
$36.00 Cash Merger	B-CM	Renaissance Comm	RRR	35.750	TRB	36.000
$59.00 Cash Merger	B-CM	Standard Federal	SFB	57.750	ARBI Y	59.000
$32 Cash Tender	B-CM	Syratech Corp.	SYR	31.750	OTHER	32.000
$15 Cash Merger	B-CM	UNC Inc.	UNC	14.250	GE	15.000
$22.50 Management Buyout Offer	B-CM	Xpedite	XPED	21.125	OTHER	22.500

To avoid being tracked by others, many arbitrageurs employ a protective strategy: They execute their orders through a firm (known as a "beard") so that other arbitrageurs will be unable to determine their origin. Effectively, these firms camouflage arbitrageurs' purchases and sales. Overall, this type of trading protection, although it can be useful at times, is not necessary to be a successful arbitrageur.

THE USE OF COMPUTERS TO AID TRADING TACTICS

Many arbitrageurs utilize computers to help them trade in arbitrage transactions. Most commonly, a personal computer is used to track the returns and risks in any given arbitrage situation. Many arbitrageurs, when a deal is initially announced, input their estimates of deal price,

Est. Close	Spreads Net ($)	Risk Adj N/Ann (%)	Dollar ($) Return (%)	Deal ($) Risk (Adj)	Even $ Size (M)	Risk Prob (%)	Reward
3/25/97	$0 250	59.253%	−20.74%	$ 1.596	$ 156	88.9%	6.4 : 1
6/16/97	2 000	51.773	−2.59	5.124	235	71 4	2.6 : 1
6/2/97	2.725	11.027	−5.35	32.707	9,100	93.3	12.1 : 1
3/24/97	(0.938)	−245.516	−559.78	4 512	157	123.4	−4.8 : 1
5/25/97	1 125	27 652	13.27	3.380	1,450	75.0	3 : 1
3/20/97	0.125	55.810	−50.23	4.591	125	97.4	36.7 : 1
3/15/97	0 063	296 748	−2480.81	3.185	95	98.1	51 : 1
3/29/97	0.125	10 181	−30 54	5 611	900	97.5	44.9 : 1
4/5/97	0 475	47.403	−54.89	3.605	350	88 4	7.6 : 1
3/24/97	0 750	192.105	115.26	1.344	75	62.5	1.8 : 1
4/5/97	0 375	36 330	−36 33	4 600	138	92.5	12.3 : 1
6/30/97	2 946	35.000	18 87	3 703	3,000	45.9	1.3 : 1
3/25/97	1.500	1422 078	681 41	1.385	35	52.0	0.9 : 1
4/15/97	0 625	28.094	19.10	2.792	1,500	84.4	4.5 · 1
6/30/97	4.750	221 424	165 49	(1.252)	200	−18.8	−0.3 : 1
5/30/97	5 063	185.488	137.40	(2 439)	3,850	−35.0	−0.5 : 1
6/15/97	5.540	149 952	73.78	1.464	611	31.1	0.3 . 1
9/30/97	0 900	7 916	6.77	0.158	1,270	−38.5	0.2 : 1
3/31/97	0.250	15 014	−75 07	(0 541)	1,130	95.8	−2.2 : 1
6/30/97	1.450	8.486	3.92	1 306	1,900	72.1	0.9 : 1
3/31/97	0 250	16.906	−91.29	5.583	280	96.9	22.3 : 1
7/15/97	0 750	15.618	7.29	1.487	345	62.5	2 · 1
5/31/97	1 375	30 458	11 08	1.049	200	45.0	0.8 : 1

(continued)

Table 9.1   (Continued)

Deal Desc.	Type	Target Comp. Name	Symb	Price ($)	Acq. Co.	Deal Value ($)
$36 Cash Offer	B-CM	Zurich Reinsurance	ZRC	$ 38.125	PRIV	$ 36.000
Mixed Merger ($7 in cash and $15 in stk)	B-MM	**ADT**	ADT	21.625	WR	22.500
Mixed Merger ($17.60 w/collar and 0.40 shs)	B-MM	Alimerican Prop & Caus	APY	31.500	AFC	32.150
Mixed Merger (0.75 shars and 125 ci A shs)	B-MM	Atlantic Energy	ATE	17.000	DEW	16.844
$30.00 Mixed Merger	B-MM	California Financial	CFHC	28.938	HN	30.000
Mixed Merger ($15.34 in cash and stock)	B-MM	CU Bancorp	CUBN	14.563	BOH	15.340
Mixed Merger ($43 in cash or stock)	B-MM	Dauphin Deposit	DAPN	42.125	AIB	43.000
Mixed $8 in TXU stk w/collar, 1 5 EEX	B-MM	**Enserch Corp**	ENS	21.625	TXU	22.813
Mixed Merger ($39 in cash and stock)	B-MM	Home Benefical	HBENB	38.250	ACC	39.000
Unsolicited 2 stop $55 offer	B-MM	**ITT Corp**	ITT	59.875	HIT	55.000
Mixed Merger ($6 and 0.54 shs)	B-MM	MCI Corp	MCIC	36.500	BTY	43.935
Stock Merger (0.7 shares)	B-MM	Morrison Petroleum	YYY	10.100	CANEN	10.150
Mixed Merger ($16.00 in cash and stk 50.50 prorate)	B-MM	NorAm Energy	NAE	15.000	HOU	16.000
Mixed Merger ($30, $15 and 0.5 shs or 1.0 shs)	B-MM	Panansal Corp	SPOT	28.875	CM	30.000
Mixed Merger (0.4211 shs, $22)	B-MM	Roosevelt Financial	RFED	22.500	MIL	24.161
$27 Offer	B-MM	Santa Anita Corp	SAR	28.625	PRIV	27.000
Mixed Merger (0.63 shs and eq stub)	B-MM	Valero Energy	VLO	32.750	PCG	32.648
$18.50 Cash (40%), 0.41 shs (60%)	B-MM	Wascana Energy	WE	19.450	HM	18.463
Mixed Merger (cash $5.90 lost in stk)	B-MM	Washington National	WNI	28.750	PLG	29.500
Mixed Merger ($2 stub and 0.625 shs w/collar)	B-MM	Wellsford Res. Prop	WRP	30.875	LQR	31.766
Stock Merger (0.611 shares)	B-SM	Allwaste Inc	ALW	8.375	PLV	9 318
Stock Merger (0.445 stock merger)	B-SM	American Federal	AMFB	29.625	CCB	30.761
Stock Merger (0.36 shares)	B-SM	Amisys Managed Care	AMCS	18.250	HBOC	18.944

Top Deal Picks: IN BOLD.

Est. Close	Spreads Net ($)	Risk Adj N/Ann (%)	Dollar ($) Return (%)	Deal ($) Risk (Adj)	Even $ Size (M)	Risk Prob (%)	Reward
4/10/97	($2.125)	–75 349%	–85.99%	$ 4.388	$332	170.8%	–2.1 : 1
5/30/97	0.771	16 894	2.56	2.863	3,500	76.4	3.7 : 1
9/10/97	1.049	6.751	1.06	4.898	800	82.2	4.7 : 1
12/31/97	0.706	5.193	2 18	1 664	951	65.5	2 4 : 1
5/15/97	1.172	23.854	5.21	3.481	150	80.8	3 : 1
7/15/97	0 848	17 270	9.90	1.687	190	64 8	2 : 1
8/30/97	1 475	7 562	–4.74	7 868	1,360	84.6	5.3 : 1
4/15/97	1 223	64.485	–21 38	5 677	1,700	85.0	4.6 : 1
3/31/97	0.818	45.923	–47.09	14.003	665	94.1	17.1 : 1
7/27/97	(4 875)	–22.013	–33.30	13.230	10,500	148.8	–2.7 : 1
12/31/97	8 067	27.628	18.94	3 340	24,000	36.4	0.4 : 1
3/25/97	0.065	21 451	385.62	(12.041)	650	100.6	–184.4 · 1
3/25/97	1 012	223.879	29 63	4 425	2,006	82.7	4 4 : 1
5/1/97	1 125	29.627	9.88	(0.107)	572	77.5	–0.1 : 1
6/30/97	2.007	30 146	17.38	3.808	1.072	64.6	1.9 : 1
4/15/97	(1 625)	64 752	–144.45	11 057	220	116.3	6.8 · 1
6/30/97	(0 134)	–1.381	–8.79	3.568	722	103.7	–26.7 · 1
4/25/97	(0 924)	–41.265	–63.43	4.369	1,700	127.9	–4.7 : 1
4/30/97	0.902	24.363	26 08	(0.994)	400	312.9	–1.1: 1
5/25/97	1 279	20.993	3.40	4.093	463	76.1	3 2 : 1
6/25/97	1.074	45.453	10.43	4.352	540	80.5	4.1 : 1
9/30/97	1 658	10.212	1.86	5.833	331	78.8	3.5 : 1
4/20/97	0 783	42.312	21.25	7 074	160	90.0	9 : 1

return, and estimated risk into a database. Depending on the computer's level of sophistication, these estimates may be revised automatically by overall market movements or may be individually adjusted by the arbitrageur over time. However, all current databases are designed to give the arbitrageur up-to-the-minute input as to each deal's estimated return and risk. This information allows the arbitrageur to monitor the spreads in the marketplace.

Table 9.1 on pages 144–147 shows a typical use of computers to monitor spreads and their risks. Each arbitrageur may customize the basic system to improve its decision-making assistance.

Given a comprehensive database, computer systems can generate potential trading opportunities. Some arbitrageurs maintain on their database as indication as to whether a deal has a signed definitive agreement. (See Table 9.2.) By having this information available and properly updated, the arbitrageur will be able to scroll through all the outstanding deals, or to print out a list of the deals that do not yet have definitive agreements. When an agreement in principle advances to become a signed definitive agreement, the spread in a transaction generally declines. By having a list of deals that are still only agreements in principle, the arbitrageur is able to focus his or her research on those transactions. If it can be predicted when the companies will reach a definitive agreement, the arbitrageur may be able to profit by setting up a position prior to the signing of the definitive agreement.

Computers can also be employed to monitor spreads. Arbitrageurs may be able to sort the outstanding transactions based on spread size or changes in spread. (See Table 9.3.) For many years, I have utilized systems that will print out a listing of deals in which the spread has narrowed or widened by a certain specified percentage. I stipulate the percentage that is to be used as a threshold, and the system gives me a listing of these securities. The dollar spread or percentage spread of transactions may change by, say, greater than $1 or 5 percent per day

Table 9.2 Deals Sorted by Definitive Agreements

Target Symbol	Acquiring Co Symbol	Target Co Price	Net Spread	$ Risk	Signed Definitive Agreement
PSY	GRAND	56.25	3.25	9.25	X
FEXC	ICH	14.625	−2.625	7.125	X
EEE	UTD	6.25	1.75	3.1	X
DMN	NOMAD	24.25	0.25	6.25	X
ARM	IV	45.625	0.375	8.375	X

Table 9.3 Deals Where Spread Has Changed by More Than $.25 During the Past Five Days

Target Symbol	Acquiring Co Symbol	Target Co Price	Net Spread Today	Net Spread Five Days Ago	Change in Spread
KDI	MAN	19.25	0.25	−0.125	0.375
POD	SHA	38.625	3.375	1.875	−1.5
WILF	DOSK	14.5	1.125	2	−0.875
HMA	IOA	14.75	0.75	0.25	0.5
DLCH	GAP	27	3	1.75	1.25

or over a three-to-five-day period. Most arbitrageurs may know, just from watching the prices of particular securities, that the spread has changed over that time period. But this method gives the arbitrageur a method to focus on these transactions and to print out their status if needed.

If spreads have widened, the arbitrageur may have an opportunity to establish or increase his or her position. If a spread has widened and the arbitrageur reevaluates the earlier analysis of the position (this should always be done), some new piece of information may surface. When the securities on this listing show a decline in spread, the arbitrageur may decide to rebalance the portfolio by selling the positions with the narrowed spreads and investing the money in deals that have a greater expected return.

If the arbitrageur has created a full database of transactions, along with their estimated risks and returns, the risk estimates can be used to generate a listing of attractive opportunities. As mentioned previously, the system I employ estimates the initial risk in any given transaction, and adjusts the risk for moves in the equity market. This process continually generates an adjusted risk on both the down side and the up side. If a transaction remains in the marketplace for many days, weeks, or months, the movement in the overall markets may have a significant or even a dramatic effect on the initial estimates of the down side and up side. The system can easily be instructed to generate a risk report that would show the original risk estimates as well as the adjusted estimates for an entire array of transactions. At times, an arbitrageur may be able to find a transaction that has a negative adjusted risk estimate. This can occur if the market has moved so significantly that, if this transaction now breaks up, given the level of the stock price in any particular transaction, the adjusted estimates would indicate that the target company's stock should rise. These estimates may not be extremely accurate, and they have to be continually reviewed by the

Table 9.4   Adjusted Risk Report

Target Company Symbol	Acquiring Company Symbol	Original Downside Estimate	Adjusted Downside Estimate	Target Company Price	Adjusted Downside Risk
DKT	CAR	37	41.37	45	3.63
DLA	GEN	4.75	5.62	5.5	−0.12
SDO	SCE	34.12	34.1	35.5	1.4
MFD	PAN	13.25	14.16	16.125	1.965
TSO	OWN	9.15	10.26	11.75	1.49

arbitrageur using some of the methods mentioned in prior chapters. Still, they give the arbitrageur a tool for improving his or her analysis of trading techniques. (See Table 9.4.)

Summary

Trading tactics can be an important aspect of doing risk arbitrage. The arbitrageur must be extremely disciplined and creative in utilizing his or her trading acumen. The actual methods of trading in arbitrage-related securities can dramatically influence the rate of return.

Chapter *10*

Portfolio Management

POSITION LIMITS AND PORTFOLIO DIVERSIFICATION

The first issue of portfolio management that the arbitrageur must deal with is position size. In general, an arbitrageur should set a maximum position size. A typical position size may be based on either the existing overall capital in the account or the overall buying power if the account is being managed with the use of leverage. Alternatively, the arbitrageur may use both measures to limit position size. The limit on position size that I have utilized over the years has been: No position should be more than 10 percent of the buying power in the portfolio. The percentage is calculated using the following formula:

$$\frac{\text{Dollars market value}}{\text{Buying power}} = \text{Maximum position size}$$

where Buying power (BP) = Capital $\times$ (1/MR)
        MR = Margin rate

Over the years, I have generally followed the discipline of having no more than 10 percent of my portfolio's total buying power in any given position. If an unusual reason has materialized, such as a contested takeover that has multiple bidders, I have, on occasion, set up a system that allowed the 10 percent of the portfolio to increase to an overall 15 percent limit. This increase has been employed only when there was very little dollar risk in the individual position *and* a very high probability of the transaction's closing.

By setting the 10 percent buying power limit, the portfolio is defined as having at least 10 different positions. At most times, however, the 10 percent limit, combined with the fact that not all positions are

151

maximum size, yields a portfolio that has between 20 and 30 risk arbitrage situations. This method of diversification can be a very effective way to limit risk.

The 10 percent limit alone, however, may not be adequate to limit the risk in an arbitrageur's portfolio. Why? Because 10 percent of the arbitrageur's buying power could be dedicated to a deal that has 20 points of downside risk. Or, another 10 percent position may be dedicated to a deal that has only 1 or 2 points of downside risk and is involved in a competitive bidding situation. If the current deal breaks up, the losing bidder may complete the transaction at a level $1 or $2 below the stock's trading price. These positions do not represent equal risk. The arbitrageur is much more vulnerable in the former position, which has 20 points of downside risk.

Wise arbitrageurs set a limit on position size that relates the risk in the position to the overall portfolio. This maximum risk can be calculated as follows:

$$\text{Maximum risk} = \frac{\text{Dollars of risk in one position}}{\text{Overall capital} \times 2}$$

The actual limits may be determined according to the arbitrageur's sensitivity to risk and loss. A conservative arbitrageur may set a relatively low limit of exposure. An arbitrageur who is willing to accept more aggressive risk profiles would set the percentage accordingly. Table 10.1 shows some typical limits that arbitrageurs might utilize, depending on their sensitivity to risk.

Most arbitrageurs use computers to track each position and its relative risk, to ensure that the prescribed position limits are holding firm. It is very important to maintain the position limits that are set. Because of the nature of the business, an arbitrageur can easily get caught up in the action in the marketplace and may be tempted to get overly aggressive.

Discipline is one of the most important traits of successful risk arbitrageurs. Risk arbitrage inevitably has dramatic turns. A downturn in the prices and securities held in a portfolio can be very damaging.

Table 10.1 Risk Arbitrage Position Limits

Arbitrageurs' Risk Profile	Individual Position Limit (In terms of buying power)
Conservative	2–3%
Moderate	3–4%
Aggressive	5–6%

Only by maintaining a disciplined approach to the position limits set for the portfolio will the arbitrageur be able to effectively contain risk.

Notes from the File ══

Lack of discipline has been the primary cause of arbitrageurs' exiting the business. I have seen a number of arbitrageurs "blow up" because they took outsized positions and outlandish risks. Arbitrageurs who have been able to operate continuously and generate favorable long-term performance records have almost always been the most disciplined arbitrageurs in the community.

ADDITIONAL METHODS TO LIMIT RISK

After an arbitrageur has determined his or her position limits, other disciplines can be applied to the portfolio to contain risk. One of the most obvious disciplines is to break down the portfolio according to deal type. Table 10.2 shows a typical example.

Each transaction has a particular risk profile. Hostile or contested takeover transactions, as we noted earlier, are historically volatile. They can be great opportunities, but they can also generate huge losses for arbitrageurs. Arbitrageurs who have a high percentage of hostile transactions in their portfolios must be prepared, financially and emotionally, to deal with an inordinate amount of risk.

FRIENDLY TRANSACTIONS

Compared to contested takeovers, friendly transactions, in general, should have less volatility, higher probabilities of completion, and relatively more certain rates of return. (The exceptions, of course, are transactions that involve antitrust questions or other regulatory issues.) However, some friendly transactions may have a larger risk in terms of absolute dollars.

Friendly cash transactions can usually be viewed as secure, as long as the financing is definitive in nature. Stock-for-stock transactions can contain an element of equity risk. If a stock-for-stock transaction contains a collar, the arbitrageur must monitor the collar and how it relates to the underlying security prices. Portfolios that contain a high percentage of stock-for-stock deals with collars may be subject to a higher risk level than those that contain a high degree of cash transactions.

Table 10.2   Risk Arbitrage Portfolio: Analysis by Deal Type

	No. of Deals	Long Mkt Value	Percent of Deals	Potential Gain	Potential Loss	Risk Reward
Tenders						
Cash Tenders	8	$ 4,162,375	33.0%	$ 115,056	$1,171,078	10.2 : 1
Stock Tenders	0	—	0.0	—	—	
Mixed Tenders	0	—	0.0	—	—	
All Tenders	8	$ 4,162,375	33.0%	$ 115,056	$1,171,078	10.2 : 1
Mergers						
Cash Mergers	0	$ —	0.0%	$ —	$ —	
Stock Mergers	10	3,244,052	25.7	779,584	1,250,726	1.6 : 1
Mixed Mergers	5	3,146,452	25.0	367,048	830,213	2.3 : 1
All Mergers	15	$ 6,390,504	50.7%	$1,146,632	$2,080,939	1.8 : 1
Miscellaneous						
Speculative	1	$ 230,000	1.8%	$ 50,000	$ 66,925	1.3 : 1
Spin-offs	0	—	0.0	—	—	
Other	0	—	0.0	—	—	
All Misc. Deals	1	$ 230,000	1.8%	$ 50,000	$ 66,925	1.3 : 1
Totals	24	$10,782,879	85.6%	$1,311,688	$3,318,942	2.53 : 1

Leveraged Buyouts

In general, leveraged transactions are highly sensitive to the overall economy, economic factors, interest rate changes, and earnings of the underlying companies.

Notes from the File ═══════

Actual experience has shown me that arbitrageurs should monitor their involvement in leveraged buyouts as it relates to the overall portfolio. Most leveraged buyouts are clearly friendly transactions, but there can be factors that affect all these types of transactions. A number of years ago, legislation was proposed that would have limited the loans that banks and institutions could make to finance what were described as highly leveraged transactions (HLTs). When this legislation was proposed, even though an arbitrageur may have been abiding by portfolio diversification limits, the entire portfolio and a group of leveraged buyouts held as security would have tended to constitute one entity because all these transactions were potentially going to be affected by the proposed legislation. This is why it is very important for an arbitrageur to examine how much of his or her portfolio is invested in any given type of transaction. With lever-aged buyouts in hand, an arbitrageur might have mistakenly thought that he or she had adequate diversification.

Arbitrageurs must be careful to avoid any overconcentration in any given area or group of deals that might react in a related fashion.

RECAPS AND SPIN-OFFS

Recapitalizations and spin-offs generally have an element of equity risk associated with them. The arbitrageur may choose to hedge or not to hedge this risk. If an arbitrageur breaks down his or her portfolio to determine the overall amount of capital committed to this equity-risk area, he or she may very well find it advantageous to set up a hedge against the equity risk. The arbitrageur may use futures, options, a combination of futures and options, or securities that are related to se-curities being issued in these transactions to help hedge the equity risk in this portion of the portfolio.

Arbitrageurs should generate a tabulation of their portfolio on a regular basis, to monitor the diversification achieved through the vari-ous types of deals. Table 10.2 can serve as a model.

GROUPING BY CASH FLOW

Another type of grouping that can prove helpful to the arbitrageur is based on an estimated investment time horizon. By going through the portfolio and grouping the individual positions according to their ex-pected closing dates, one can generate a compilation similar to Table 10.3.

This type of portfolio breakdown enables the arbitrageur to see (1) how much of the portfolio will be "turning over" as the deals close, and (2) how sensitive the portfolio may be to overall economic factors. If a relatively high percentage of the portfolio is dedicated to transac-tions that are due to close within the next one to three months, the portfolio and the individual positions will most likely *not* be heavily influenced by factors such as earnings and interest rates. If, however, only a small percentage of the portfolio is due to close over the next few months and a relatively high percentage is not expected to close for five or six (or more) months, the portfolio contains too much risk in re-lation to overall economic factors. The risk of having the economy or interest rates go against these positions is much greater in this type of

Table 10.3   Deal Completion Analysis

Time Until Close	Number of Deals	Potential Gain	Deal LMVs
Now–½ Month	2	$ 7,909.55	$ 959,150.00
½–1 Month	9	105,904.79	3,769,927.00
1–2 Months	5	795,595.86	1,926,975.00
2–3 Months	3	123,888.09	1,915,937.50
3–4 Months	3	16,604.95	454,125.00
4–5 Months	1	88,300.37	800,514.00
5–6 Months	0	—	—
6–9 Months	1	173,484.55	956,250.00
9–12 Months	0	—	—
1 Year On	0	—	—
Total potential profits	24	$1,311,688.00	$10,782,879.00

portfolio. Furthermore, the arbitrageur will have to be concentrating more on earnings estimates and fundamentals of the companies involved in these transactions. The arbitrageur must then become a fundamental securities analyst and economist in order to effectively monitor his or her portfolio.

Acquiring and using skills as a fundamental securities analyst may not be bad if the arbitrageur has been compensated for the additional risk and is aware of and comfortable with the possible outcomes. However, without generating a tabulation such as Table 10.3, it will be easy to lose sight of the overall exposure by concentrating on the individual transactions.

PORTFOLIO ANALYSIS BY SPREAD

Arbitrageurs use computers to monitor individual transactions and their estimated annual returns. Table 10.4 shows an example of how individual deals can be monitored by their spread. Using a computer-generated analysis such as this gives the arbitrageur the ability to analyze many potential investments quickly. This tool helps the arbitrageur deal with rapid changes occurring in the marketplace and aids in the monitoring of the arbitrageur's portfolio.

The next logical step for the arbitrageur is to utilize a computer to monitor the spread characteristics of the overall portfolio. By using the annualized spread to group the individual transactions held in the portfolio, the arbitrageur may get a valuable look at the portfolio's total sensitivity to risk. Table 10.5 shows a typical breakdown of a portfolio by annualized spread.

Table 10.4 Spread Monitor

Office Depot				Stock Merger (1.14 shares)				Retail-Spec Line			$3482 Million	
Target	**T**	**last**	**chg**	**%chg**	**bid**	**×**	**ask**	**size × size**	**vol**	**n**	**ex**	**amt**
ODP	–	17 7/8	+ 1/8	0.7%	17 7/8 ×		18	770 × 977	101,600		n/a	n/a
SPLS	+	23 3/8	+ 0	0.0%	23 5/16 ×		23 3/8	30 × 10	147,800		n/a	n/a

Terms:

		Collar:		
Cash:	$0.000	Up: none		
Stock	1.140	Dwn: none		
Deal val:	$26.648	Walk: none		
	Timing:	6/30/97	**18 days**	

Spreads:

Gross:	$8.773	995.2%		
Net:	$8.838	1002.6%	Div lg	$0.000
Lev:	$8.812	1999.2%	Div chg:	$0.000
Rsk/adj:	$0.299	33.9%	Rebate.	$0.066

Risk:

Downside:	$11.95	$5.923	Rsk/Rew.	0.7 : 1
Upside:	$23.96	$0.671	Ev $:	42%
	Total Risk	$6.59	Update:	9:51

Status: 1   Antitrust? But attractive.

Daily Spread

Spread values: $7.57, $7.57, $7.83, $8.19, $7.95, $8.49, $8.20, $8.75, $9.01, $8.98, $8.84

X-axis: 29-May, 30-May, 2-Jun, 3-Jun, 4-Jun, 5-Jun, 6-Jun, 9-Jun, 10-Jun, 11-Jun, now

Y-axis: $6.50 (750.0%), $7.00 (800.0%), $7.50 (850.0%), $8.00 (900.0%), $8.50 (950.0%), $9.00 (1000.0%), $9.50 (1050.0%)

Table 10.5   **Portfolio Breakdown by Annualized Spread**

Spread Range	Total $ Positions in Range	Percent of Total Portfolio
Premium (negative spread)	$ 271,290	3.05%
0 to 5%	567,291	6.38
6 to 10%	1,678,091	18.87
11 to 15%	3,690,085	41.50
16 to 20%	1,499,694	16.86
21 to 25%	883,547	9.94
26 to 30%	302,718	3.40
Over 30%	0	0
Total	$8,892,716	100%

Like the breakdown by type of deal, this portfolio breakdown gives the arbitrageur insight into the amount of risk contained in his or her portfolio. If the arbitrageur is attracted primarily to transactions with large spreads, the odds are that the portfolio will contain a high degree of risk. Deals have high rates of return for when they have:

1. A large dollar risk associated with the transaction;
2. A low estimate of the probability of the transaction's closing;
3. Both of the above.

Notes from the File

Early in my career, when I was trying to engage in risk arbitrage with relatively low amounts of capital, I found myself making good decisions for the portfolio I was running for the firm. Yet, my personal performance in my undercapitalized portfolio lagged the firm's portfolio significantly. By analyzing the types of transactions I was setting up in my personal portfolio, I realized I was concentrating on two types of transactions: (1) high relative expected returns and (2) contested takeovers. Both of these, while potentially rewarding, also generally contained either higher amounts of dollar risk or lower probability of success. By altering the types of transactions held in my portfolio, it was much easier to mirror the performance of an arbitrage portfolio that had strict disciplines.

Calculations on portfolios, such as those shown in Table 10.5, can be a valuable tool when an arbitrageur is assessing the overall risk in a portfolio.

HEDGING

The arbitrageur must be very careful to set up the proper hedges in transactions that involve stock-for-stock exchanges. As I have previously noted in several chapters of this book, it is important for arbitrageurs to maintain the discipline of setting up fully hedged positions. Any arbitrageur who does not fully hedge a position is taking a viewpoint on the market. Most likely, his or her profitability will be determined by the direction in which the market for that security moves. On the other hand, if a full hedge is set up for an individual transaction, the arbitrageur's profit will be determined by his or her ability to accurately predict the outcome.

Stock-for-stock transactions that involve collars must be analyzed carefully, and the short side of the position must take into account the individual collar for each particular deal. Over time, as the acquiring company's share price changes, the arbitrageur may have to make adjustments so as to maintain a fully hedged position.

MELDING A POSITION SHEET WITH A RISK ARBITRAGE ANALYSIS

Table 10.6 shows a typical position sheet for an arbitrageur's portfolio. A position sheet should be generated to show each individual position, and it should indicate the following items:

1. Cost basis per share;
2. Market price per share;
3. Total market value in dollars;
4. Percentage of the overall portfolio in terms of market value;
5. Percentage of buying power.

The arbitrageur can utilize this position sheet when decisions on the portfolio must be made. It may also help in determining which positions warrant additional purchases and which positions should be unwound.

A typical output sheet from a computer system maintained to monitor the database of outstanding deals was shown earlier (see Table 9.1). This output sheet generally indicates the estimated returns as well as the potential losses for each transaction. The system may also be set up to generate risk-adjusted returns and other important information that the arbitrageur may wish to monitor.

Table 10.6 Position Sheet for a Risk Arbitrage Account: Current Risk Analysis

Price as of close of the market·

Qty	Security Description	Symbol	Unit	Current Price	Purchase Cost	Current Mkt Value	Percent of Portfolio	Percent of Buying Power
25800	American Media Inc	ENQ	$17.037	$14.875	$ 439,548.511	$ 383,775.000	5.57	3.38
9000	American Medical Hol	AMI	24.131	24.125	217,181.628	217,125.000	2.75	1.67
-3700	National Medical Ent	NME	15.374	14.125	(64,572.837)	(52,262.500)		
15000	Associated Natural G	NGA	37.819	38.750	567,291.660	581,250.000	7.19	4.36
-8000	Panhandle Eastern CP	PEL	20.562	21.125	(172,719.238)	(169,000.000)		
26500	Borden Inc-W/RTS	BN	13.800	14.000	365,706.095	371,000.000	4.64	2.81
6500	Cardiovascular Imagi	CVIS	9.375	8.813	60,937.500	57,284.500	0.77	0.46
12800	Castle Energy Corp N	CECX	17.600	12.750	225,280.000	163,200.000	2.85	1.73
3500	Chiron Corp	CHIR	85.750	77.250	300,125.000	270,375.000	3.80	2.30
19500	Equicredit Corp	EQCC	29.523	29.875	575,704.740	582,562.500	7.30	4.42
17500	Great Lakes Bancorp	GLBC	25.750	24.750	450,625.000	433,125.000	5.71	3.46
5000	Healthtrust Inc	HTI	33.875	32.250	169,375.000	161,250.000	2.14	1.30
-4000	Columbia/HCA HealthC	COL	40.749	37.875	(85,572.140)	(151,500.000)		
4500	Hilton Hotels Corp	HLT	67.271	69.500	302,750.000	312,750.000	3.83	2.32
12000	Magma Power Co-New	MGMA	37.000	35.563	443,999.760	426,756.000	5.63	3.41
9500	Medstat Group Inc	MDST	26.500	26.703	251,750.000	253,678.500	3.19	1.93
7500	National Gypsum Co N	NGCO	44.200	42.875	331,497.195	321,562.500	4.20	2.54
12500	NBB Bancorp Inc	NBB	45.917	47.750	573,957.500	596,875.000	7.28	4.41
25000	Northeast Federal Co	NSB	9.924	8.250	248,100.750	206,250.000	3.15	1.91
6000	Powersoft Corp	PWRS	71.000	75.375	426,000.000	452,250.000	5.40	3.28
-9600	Sybase Inc	SYBS	47.250	48.500	(316,575.000)	(465,600.000)		
6500	Puritan Bennett Corp	PBEN	24.703	21.625	160,570.664	140,562.500	2.04	1.24
22500	Reliance Electric Co	REE	30.448	30.875	685,082.543	694,687.500	8.61	5.27
22000	Ropak Corporation	ROPK	10.303	10.250	226,663.448	225,500.000	2.87	1.74
19500	Santa Fe Pacific Cor	SFX	16.092	16.750	313,796.048	326,625.000	3.98	2.41
29600	Snapple Beverage Cor	SNPL	13.948	13.875	412,857.840	410,700.000	5.24	3.18
14500	Synergen Inc-W/RTS	SYGN	9.063	9.031	131,406.250	130,949.500	1.67	1.01
6500	USLICO Corp	USC	20.250	20.000	131,625.000	130,000.000	1.67	1.02
-4400	NWNL Companies Inc-W	NWN	30.380	27.750	(176,206.819)	(122,100.000)		
9500	Western Co of North	WSN	18.313	17.000	173,968.750	161,500.000	2.20	1.34
7500	Younkers Inc	YONK	18.622	17.250	139,665.435	129,375.000	1.77	1.07
					Cost	Market		
				Short:	($ 815,646.033)	($ 960,462.500)		
Grand Totals				Long:	$7,885,886.553	$7,757,193.500		

* The capital limit is currently: $13,000,000.00.

Table 10.7 on pages 162–163 shows a printout that melds the position sheet and the deal database. The arbitrageur can view not only each individual position and its potential return and risk, but also the portfolio as a whole. The printout is an important tool in monitoring the potential returns and risks in the portfolio. This type of report can generate data that show how much overall potential return is in the portfolio, and what the overall risk may be. These returns and risks can then be related so as to give the arbitrageur a relative upside–downside analysis. The report can also be utilized when the arbitrageur must estimate the risk-adjusted return on the overall portfolio (assuming all the estimates turn out to be correct).

This type of report must almost always be custom-generated by the arbitrageur. Whether the arbitrageur manages an arbitrage portfolio for a firm or maintains an account at a brokerage firm, the arbitrageur generally is only able to obtain a typical position report from offers. It is advisable for the arbitrageur to be able to massage this position report so as to include the factors shown in Table 10.7. Programs can then be written for and applied to the position sheet so as to generate a report like the one shown in Table 10.7.

The importance of this report cannot be overestimated. It gives the arbitrageur an important tool for monitoring the overall risk arbitrage portfolio.

OTHER RISK CONTAINMENT MEASURES

The arbitrageur may wish to utilize other types of hedges to contain the risk in his or her overall portfolio. For example, the arbitrageur may find that the portfolio contains a degree of equity risk originating from reorganizations, recapitalizations, or spin-offs in which the arbitrageur is to receive, upon completion of the transaction, a security that is not currently traded in the marketplace. Being unable to hedge the risk of this security's value at some future date, the arbitrageur may decide to set up a hedge that would simulate the performance of the security (or securities) expected to be received.

In setting up the hedge, either stock index futures or options could be utilized. If it is possible to find a security that trades in similar fashion to the security expected to be received, the arbitrageur could substitute a short sale of this security for the use of options or futures.

To develop this type of hedge, the arbitrageur will have to analyze the market movements of the tool being used to create the artificial hedge. The arbitrageur may run a correlation analysis to determine whether the security under study will properly hedge the risk

Table 10.7 Combined Position Sheet and Deal Database for a Risk Arbitrage Account: Current Risk Analysis

	Prices as of close of the market.	12/5/94		Current	Purchase	Current
Qty	Security Description	Symbol	Unit	Price	Cost	Mkt Value
25800	American Media Inc	ENQ	$17 037	$14.875	$ 439,548.511	$ 383,775.000
9000	American Medical Hol	AMI	24.131	24.125	217,181.628	217,125 000
−3700	National Medical Ent	NME	15.374	14.125	(64,572.837)	(52,262 500)
15000	Associated Natural G	NGA	37.819	38.750	567,291.660	581,250.000
−8000	Panhandle Eastern CP	PEL	20.562	21.125	(172,719 238)	(169,000.000)
26500	Borden Inc-W/RTS	BN	13.800	14.000	365,706.095	371,000.000
6500	Cardiovascular Imagi	CVIS	9.375	8.813	60,937.500	57,284.500
12800	Castle Energy Corp N	CECX	17.600	12.750	225,280.000	163,200.000
3500	Chiron Corp	CHIR	85.750	77 250	300,125.000	270,375 000
19500	Equicredit Corp	EQCC	29.523	29.875	575,704.740	582,562.500
17500	Great Lakes Bancorp	GLBC	25.750	24 750	450,625.000	433,125.000
5000	Healthtrust Inc-The	HTI	33.875	32.250	169,375.000	161,250.000
−4000	Columbia/HCA HealthC	COL	40.749	37.875	(85,572.140)	(151,500.000)
4500	Hilton Hotels Corp	HLT	67 271	69 500	302,750.000	312,750.000
12000	Magma Power Co-New	MGMA	37.000	35.563	443,999.760	426,756.000
9500	Medstat Group Inc	MDST	26.500	26.703	251,750.000	253,678 500
7500	National Gypsum Co N	NGCO	44.200	42.875	331,497.195	321,562.500
12500	NBB Bancorp Inc	NBB	45 917	47.750	573,957.500	596,875.000
25000	Northeast Federal Co	NSB	9.924	8.250	248,100.750	206,250.000
6000	Powersoft Corp	PWRS	71.000	75.375	426,000.000	452,250.000
−9600	Sybase Inc	SYBS	47.250	48 500	(316,575.000)	(465,600 000)
6500	Puritan Bennett Corp	PBEN	24.703	21.625	160,570 664	140,562.500
22500	Reliance Electric Co	REE	30.448	30.875	685,082.543	694,687.500
22000	Ropak Corporation	ROPK	10.303	10.250	226,663.448	225,500.000
19500	Santa Fe Pacific Cor	SFX	16.092	16.750	313,796.048	326,625.000
29600	Snapple Beverage Cor	SNPL	13.948	13.875	412,857 840	410,700.000
14500	Synergen Inc-W/RTS	SYGN	9 063	9.031	131,406.250	130,949.500
6500	USLICO Corp	USC	20.250	20 000	131,625.000	130,000.000
−4400	NWNL Companies Inc-W	NWN	30.380	27.750	(176,206.819)	(122,100.000)
9500	Western Co of North	WSN	18.313	17 000	173,968.750	161,500.000
7500	Younkers Inc	YONK	18.622	17 250	139,665.435	129,375.000

		Cost	Market
	Short:	($ 815,646.033)	($ 960,462.500)
Grand Totals	Long·	$7,885,886.553	$7,757,193.500

* The capital limit is currently: $13,000,000.00.

in this position. Such an analysis can be very helpful in setting up the hedge.

FUTURES

After the arbitrageur analyzes the portfolio and identifies where the elements of risk are, he or she may decide to utilize futures to hedge

Percent of Portfolio	Percent of Buying Power	Net Sprd Unlev	Current P&L	Potential Dollars In: Profit	Loss	Percentage Of Equity	Limit*
5.57	3.38	$1.175	($ 55,773.511)	$ 30,315.000	$ 541 322	5.34%	2.00%
2 75	1 67	0 964	12,263.709	8,674.363	48,086.999	3.02	1.00
7 19	4 36	0 322	17,677.578	4,831 849	166,102.183	8 09	4.00
4.64	2 81	0.285	5,293.905	7,556 130	218,625.000	5.17	2 00
0 77	0 46	1 688	(3,653.000)	10,968.750	13,346.479	0.80	0.40
2.85	1.73	6 750	(62,080 000)	86,400 000	15,658.914	2 27	1.20
3.80	2 30	3.000	(29,750 000)	10,500.000	66,084 988	3.77	2.00
7 30	4.42	2.125	6,857.760	41,437.500	101,697.460	8.11	4.40
5.71	3 46	3 467	(17,500 000)	60,666 428	69,228.584	6.03	3.30
2.14	1.30	1.427	(74,052.860)	7,132.970	42,459 042	2.25	1.20
3 83	2 32	6 100	10,031 252	27,450.000	63,381 368	4.36	2.40
5.63	3 41	2.941	(17,243.760)	35,294.384	100,206.732	5.94	3.20
3 19	1 93	0 297	1,928 500	2,820 313	102,231 084	3 53	1.90
4 20	2 54	0 625	(9,934 695)	4,687.500	73,096.047	4.48	2 40
7.28	4.41	1 250	22,917 500	15,625 000	32,171 527	8.31	4.59
3 15	1 91	0 766	(41,850 750)	19,147.311	70,476.945	2.87	1.59
5.40	3.28	3.230	(122,775 000)	19,377.288	126,388 568	6.30	3.48
2 04	1.24	2.875	(20,008 164)	18,687.500	23,170.345	1.96	1.08
8.61	5 27	0.125	9,604 958	2,812.500	176,403 933	9.67	5.34
2 87	1 74	0.250	(1,163 448)	5,500 000	23,064.399	3 14	1 73
3 98	2 41	0 559	12,828.953	10,897.606	94,463.706	4.55	2 51
5.24	3.18	0 125	(2,157.840)	3,700.000	155,106 654	5.72	3.16
1 67	1.01	0.219	(456.750)	3,171.875	61,265 356	1.82	1.01
1 67	1 02	(0.340)	52,481 819	(2,210 320)	15,720 366	1.81	1.00
2.20	1.34	4.427	(12,468 750)	42,056.292	67,787 286	2.25	1.24
1.77	1 07	(0 250)	(10,290 435)	(1,875 000)	840.593	1.80	1.00

			Current Unrealized P&L	Total Potential Dollars In Profit	Loss	Percentage Of Equity	Limit*
			($329,283.03)	$475,625.24	$1,927,605 88	100.00%	55.23%

individual or overall risks. If the portfolio contains a degree of equity risk, the arbitrageur may look to the S&P 500 futures contracts for help in hedging this equity risk.

The most difficult aspect of this hedge is determining the proper amount of futures to be sold. As we discussed in previous chapters, the arbitrageur will use correlation analysis to aid in determining which—and how many—futures contracts should be used. Computer models and simulations will be enlisted to determine how much of the contracts should be sold as a hedge.

If the arbitrageur also finds interest rate risk in the portfolio, interest rate futures may offer a method of reducing that risk. Interest rate futures may come into play when the arbitrageur expects to receive securities upon completion of transactions whose value is directly related to interest rates. By performing a sensitivity and correlation analysis of the expected security, and comparing it to securities that are available to hedge these types of transactions, the arbitrageur tries to decide which instrument should be utilized for the hedge.

Some arbitrageurs may become quite creative in setting up these types of hedges. I once took a large position in a closed-end fund that was converting to open-end status. The transaction was very similar to a cash merger. After the shareholders approved the transaction and all regulatory approvals were received, the closed-end fund, which tended to trade at a discount to its net asset value, was to be converted to an open-end fund. When the fund became open-ended, the position could be liquidated by redeeming the shares at the open-end fund. The redemption process would allow the arbitrageur to receive proceeds and therefore to profit from the difference between the net asset value and the open-end value. The fund that I was trading held Japanese securities, so the transaction had various risks associated with it. In a typical closed-end fund, the net asset value of the portfolio is related to the securities held in that portfolio. These securities were related to the equity market in Japan. By analyzing the relationship between the movement in the Japan Fund's net asset value and the movement in the Nikkei futures, I was able to establish a hedge position: I shorted a certain amount of Nikkei futures against my long position in the Japan Fund. This hedge offset a very high percentage of my equity risk in the Japan Fund holding.

The arbitrageur must be continually looking for and analyzing these types of creative hedges. However, the arbitrageur should be very careful to compare the cost of any given hedge versus the potential return in the individual position. It may be wise not to enter into any complex transactions that do not yield an adequate net return on the arbitrageur's capital. A cost is always associated with setting a hedge. The arbitrageur must realize that if the cost of setting up the hedge, when matched against the estimate of expected return, does not yield an adequate return, it is best to look for an entirely different opportunity.

OPTION HEDGING

The arbitrageur has at his or her disposal the ability to hedge individual or overall portfolio positions by utilizing: (1) options on various indexes such as the OEX contract or (2) options on individual securities. If the portfolio has a degree of equity risk imbedded in it because of holding positions such as spin-offs or recapitalizations, the arbitrageur may find that OEX options are an effective way to hedge this equity risk. The analysis of this hedge would be similar to the analysis described above.

The arbitrageur may also be able to utilize puts and calls on the securities held in his or her portfolio, if they are traded in the marketplace. The use of puts and calls in conjunction with setting up an arbitrage transaction may allow the arbitrageur a risk–reward profile in any given transaction.

By using a "buy-write"—a technique of selling calls against a long stock position—the arbitrageur may establish a hedge that he or she can profit from if the underlying stock price rises. The remainder of this chapter details how, as an alternative to shorting a security involved in a transaction, an arbitrageur could alter a risk–reward profile by utilizing the buy-write or put purchase strategies.

A Buy-Write Example

Date: May 1, 1999
Deal: Company A is buying Company T through a merger. Company T's shareholders are to receive .5 shares of Company A stock for each share of Company T stock. The relevant stock prices are:

Company T:	$23.50
Company A:	$50.00
Company T (June 20 calls):	$ 4.25

The merger is expected to take 90 days. If the deal breaks up, Company T stock is expected to trade at $17 per share.

As an alternative to buying 100 shares of Company T stock and shorting 50 shares of Company A stock to hedge the transaction, the arbitrageur could execute a buy-write: Buy 100 shares of Company T stock and sell one June 20 call contract. The sale of the call would be in lieu of selling 50 shares of Company A stock.

Strategy 1

- Buy: 100 shares of Company T stock @ $23.50 per share.
- Sell short: 50 shares of Company A stock @ $50.00 per share.

$$\text{Gross spread} = (\$50.00 \times .5) - \$23.50$$
$$= \$25.00 - \$23.50$$
$$= \$1.50$$

$$ER_{UL} = \frac{\$1.50}{\$23.50} \times \frac{365}{90}$$
$$= 25.8 \text{ percent}$$

$$\text{Downside risk} = \$23.50 - \$17.00$$
$$= \$6.50 \text{ per share}$$

$$\text{Upside risk} = (\$55 - 50) \times .5$$
$$= \$2.50 \text{ per share}$$

$$\text{Total risk} = \text{Downside risk} + \text{Upside risk}$$
$$= \$2.50 + \$6.50$$
$$= \$9.00$$

(Company A's stock is expected to trade at $55 if the deal is cancelled.)

Strategy 2

- Buy: 100 shares of Company T stock @ $23.50 per share.
- Sell: One June 20 call on Company T stock @ $4.25.

If, at the end of June, the shares of Company T are trading in excess of $20.00, the call will be exercised and the arbitrageur will have the following position:

Exercise (Sales) price	=	$20.00
Plus: Premium received		+4.24
Sales proceeds	=	$24.25
Less: Cost		−23.50
Gross profit	=	$ .75

$$ER_{UL} = \frac{\$.75}{(\$23.50 - \$4.25)^*} \times \frac{365}{50^{2\dagger}}$$
$$= 28.4 \text{ percent}$$

---

[*] The arbitrageur receives the $4.25 premium at the same time he or she purchases Company T shares, so the net outlay is only $19.25.
[†] We are assuming that, at the expiration of the call, it is exercised, and this occurs only 50 days after the call was sold.

$$\text{Downside risk} = (\$23.50 - \$17.00) - \$4.25$$
$$= \$2.25$$
$$\text{Total risk} = \text{Downside risk} + \text{Upside risk}$$
$$= \$2.25 + 0$$
$$= \$2.25$$

The arbitrageur has only a one-sided risk with the buy-write approach. Had he or she used Strategy 1, the risk would have been greater due to the short position.

The arbitrageur may also utilize puts to help limit the risk for any given position in the overall portfolio. Some portfolio transactions contain a high degree of absolute risk. By purchasing a put against the stock held in the position, the arbitrageur is able to limit the downside risk if the transaction fails to close. The next example utilizes puts to limit the risk in a proposed transaction.

A Sale or Put Example

Date: May 1, 1999
Deal: Company A is buying Company T through a merger. Company T's shareholders are to receive .5 shares of Company A stock for each share of Company T stock.

Company T June 20 put price: $1.00

Strategy 3

- Buy: 100 shares of Company T stock @ $23.50
- Sell: 50 shares of Company A stock @ $50.00
- Buy: One Company T June 20 put @ $1.00

If the merger closes as expected, the arbitrageur's gross return is as follows:

$$ER_{UL} = \frac{[(\$50.00 \times .5) - \$23.50] - \$1.00}{\$23.50 + \$1.00} \times \frac{365}{90}$$

$$= \frac{\$.50}{\$24.50} \times 4.555$$

$$= 8.3 \text{ percent}$$

The arbitrageur's return was dropped from 25.8 percent to 8.3 percent, and the risk profile is significantly altered.

$$\text{Downside risk} = (\$23.50 + \$1.00) - \$20.00$$
$$= \$4.50$$

$$\text{Total risk} = \text{Downside risk} + \text{Upside risk}$$
$$= \$4.50 + 0$$
$$= \$4.50$$

Instead of risking $6.50 per short (Strategy 1), the arbitrageur's maximum risk is reduced to $4.50. By giving up a portion of the return, the arbitrageur has been able to reduce the risk.

Arbitrageurs should utilize any tool available to help contain risk in the portfolio. They must also continually review and try to improve all the tools utilized to carry out this objective. Active containment of risk can be an important aspect of arbitrageurs' long-term and short-term performance records.

Chapter **11**

The Exciting World of Risk Arbitrage

Over the course of the previous ten chapters, we have examined in depth the various elements of risk arbitrage, as well as methods for trading and monitoring the risk arbitrage portfolio.

The three elements of risk arbitrage—return, risk, and probability—have been demonstrated. The estimates are highly subjective and they are based on the arbitrageur's ability to forecast many variables. The arbitrageur's analysis of these variables and of the transactions cannot be summarized via a computer model or a mathematical algorithm.

In pulling together these three elements, it will be helpful to examine a recent deal that incorporated many of the various elements. The MCI/British Telecom (BTY)/GTE/WorldCom transaction was a deal that "had it all": friendly agreements, a hostile bid, bidding wars, and regulatory problems. Almost anything that could possibly have happened in a transaction occurred in the MCI deal.

It started as a friendly merger transaction with British Telecom. When that deal developed problems, uncertainty caused a traumatic swing in profits for the arbitrage community. Ultimately, after the deal was recut with British Telecom at a lower price, causing losses for most arbitrageurs, the unforeseen occurred: WorldCom initiated a hostile takeover bid. This bid ultimately ended up prevailing in a friendly merger transaction.

The prices of MCI, British Telecom, GTE, and WorldCom are shown in Figure 11.1. The individual events are marked on these charts as well as on the charts of the spreads involved in the transactions (Figure 11.2). The spreads of the individual deals are shown later in the chapter.

169

Figure 11.1   Prices of MCIC, British Telecom, GTE, and WorldCom

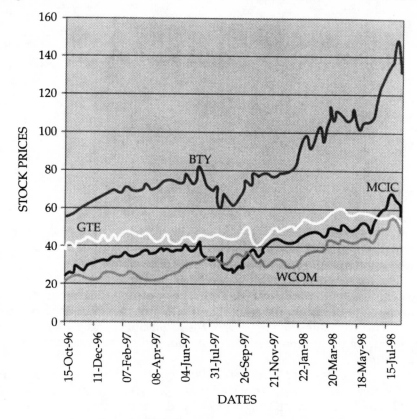

THE EVENT TIMELINE: THE MCI/BTY/GTE/WORLDCOM DEAL

Event 1   November 3, 1996
British Telecom announces a friendly merger pact with MCI for $21 billion. MCI shareholders are to receive $6 in cash plus .54 BTY share for each of their MCI shares. BTY shareholders are to receive a 35-pence special dividend.

December 2, 1997
MCI shareholders approve the BTY transaction.

Event 2   July 10, 1997
MCI discloses that its losses in its local phone businesses could total $800 million in 1997. This $800 million is more than double its previous estimate.

Figure 11.2   Deal Spreads for British Telecom, GTE, and WorldCom

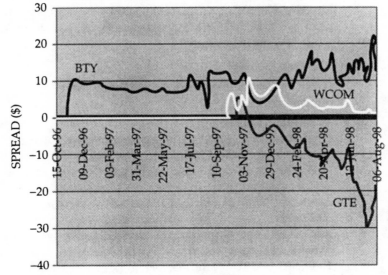

July 11, 1997
BTY announces it will study and review MCI's books
and records regarding the write-off.

July 16, 1997
At BTY's annual meeting, BTY's chairman, Ian Vallance,
states that the United States market and the relationship
with MCI continue to be strategically important for BTY.

Event 3   August 20, 1997
MCI discloses that changes in the terms of the merger
agreement are being discussed with BTY.

August 21, 1997
BTY receives FCC approval for the merger with MCI.

Event 4   August 21, 1997
MCI and BTY agree to revise their earlier terms. MCI
shareholders are to receive $7.75 in cash plus .375 share
of BTY per MCI share, under the revised merger
agreement.

Event 5   October 1, 1997
WorldCom makes an unsolicited $30 billion stock offer for MCI Communications. Shareholders of MCI are to receive WorldCom stock valued at $41.50 per share for each MCI share owned.

Event 6   October 15, 1997
GTE announces an unsolicited $40-per-share cash merger offer.

Event 7   November 9, 1997
MCI announces a definitive agreement with WorldCom to merge MCI into WorldCom. The terms are as follows. If WorldCom shares were worth less than $29 during the pricing period, MCI shareholders would receive a maximum of 1.7586 WorldCom shares. If WorldCom, during the pricing period, was trading between $29 and $41 a share, MCI shareholders were to receive $51 worth of WorldCom stock. Finally, if WorldCom stock was trading in excess of $41 during the pricing period, MCI shareholders would receive 1.2439 shares of WorldCom common stock.

Had an arbitrageur set up a position on the initial announcement date with BTY, November 3, 1996, he or she would have had the following position:

Date: November 3, 1996

Long position: Bought 100 shares of MCI @ $30.1875

Short position: Short 54 shares of BTY @ $55.50

Gross spread = [$6 + .54 ($55.50)] – $30.1875
              = $5.78

By purchasing 100 shares of MCI at $30.1875 and selling short 54 shares of BTY at $55.50, the arbitrageur created a spread of $5.78. If the deal were to take a year to close, the arbitrageur would have been expecting an annualized unleveraged gross return of 19 percent.

That would have been a very attractive return. However, the arbitrageur had no preparation for the unusual twists and turns that the deal would endure.

The charts in Figure 11.2 show that the spread versus the BTY deal had widened out to $10.59 on November 15, 1997. The arbitrageur at that point would have had a loss of $481.25 on a mark-to-market basis on his or her position in MCI. Here are its origins:

Date: November 15, 1996	Cost Basis	11/15/96 Market Value per Share	Total Market Value	Profit or Loss
Long position: Bought 100 shares of MCI	$3,018.75	$28.75	$2,875	($143.75)
Short position: Short 54 shares of BTY	$2,997.00	$61.75	$3,334	($337.50)
		Net mark-to-market loss		($481.25)

Figure 11.2 shows that the spread, while varying, usually traded between $7 and $9.50 over a great number of months during 1996 and 1997, as the companies waited for shareholders and regulators to approve the transaction. The spread reached a low of $6.87 on May 5, 1997. At this point, the arbitrageur would still have shown a loss had he or she set up the position (not including dividends and short interest credit) on the initial announcement date.

The spread widened to a high of $12.20 on July 11, 1997, as MCI disclosed that it had unforeseen substantial losses in its local phone business, and BTY was reconsidering the price that it would pay to MCI.

On August 21, 1997, MCI and BTY announced that they had reached an agreement on revised terms. MCI shareholders would receive .375 share of BTY plus $7.75 in cash. One would have thought that this deal was now secure.

Notes from the File

One of the safest deals to get involved with is a deal that has had its terms revised. This means it has been evaluated at least twice by the involved parties. Historically, these types of transactions have had a very high probability of closing.

WorldCom surprised MCI, the arbitrageurs, and investors by announcing a hostile bid of $41.50 on October 1, 1997. Arbitrageurs who got in on the initial announcement date were still losing money because of the recutting of the original BTY deal. MCI stock on October 1 jumped $5.875 to $35.25, but that still left a $6.25 spread versus the WorldCom $41.50 bid. The spread versus the BTY transaction was $9.62.

GTE's entrance into the transaction, on October 15, 1997, caused MCI's price to rise and the spreads to decline as arbitrageurs attempted to determine who would be the final winner and what the ultimate terms of the transaction might be. Not many transactions have three bidders for a target company.

The big news for arbitrageurs and shareholders came on November 9, 1997, when WorldCom announced a definitive agreement to acquire MCI. The terms of this transaction were complicated, but they were quite favorable overall to MCI shareholders, who were to receive one of the following:

1. If WorldCom was less than $29, MCI shareholders would receive 1.7586 shares of WorldCom.

2. If WorldCom was between $29 and $41, shareholders would receive $51 in WorldCom stock.

3. If WorldCom shares were trading in excess of $41, MCI shareholders would receive 1.2439 shares of WorldCom stock.

The MCI/WorldCom deal initially started trading at a spread of approximately $9 to the new bid. Arbitrageurs who had established their position on the initial announcement date, however, were STILL underwater! Their loss was reduced to $389.50, but that gave small comfort:

Date: November 9, 1997	Cost Basis	11/9/97 Market Value per Share	Total Market Value	Profit or Loss
Long position: Bought 100 shares of MCI	$3,018.75	$35.125	$3,513.50	$494.75
Short position: Short 54 shares of BTY	$2,997.00	$71.875	$3,881.25	($884.25)
		Net mark-to-market loss		($389.50)

It is difficult to determine when an arbitrageur actually would have reversed out of the short position in BTY, but, by November 9, 1997, most arbitrageurs would have been looking to get out of their short BTY position and to set up a proper hedge for the WorldCom transaction. The arbitrageur's logic at this time would have been: There are now three bidders and no reliable estimate of which bidder will win MCI. The arbitrageur could not know which company's shares to short versus his or her MCI position. In all probability, he or she would not have had a short position at this point in time.

WorldCom was, at this point, in the "collar." Arbitrageurs would receive $51 a share in stock with a floating ratio, so they would have a one-sided risk in MCI on the long side. If the price of WorldCom rose to the top end of the collar ($41) and WorldCom then issued the maximum number of shares, the arbitrageur would look to short WorldCom to lock in his or her spread.

This actually occurred on March 16, 1998, when the price of World-Com rose above $41 a share. The spread at that point (see Figure 11.2) had been trading between $2 and $9 a share but had recently been in the $5-a-share range.

If the price of WorldCom exceeded $41 a share, arbitrageurs looked to short the proper ratio to lock-in the spread. If the price of WorldCom continued to rise and the transaction closed, the arbitrageurs would re-alize the $3.83 to $4.48 spread, regardless of the price of WorldCom. However, if WorldCom's stock price dropped below the $41 collar level before the transaction closed, arbitrageurs would have an additional benefit. They would receive $51 in stock plus an additional gain on the shares of WorldCom they had shorted at higher prices.

At this point, the arbitrageurs did not have to worry about additional headaches sparked by a decline in the WorldCom stock price. However, they did have to worry about regulatory issues. Figure 11.2 shows how the spread in the MCI/WorldCom deal continued to oscillate as regulators in Europe and in Washington (DC) evaluated the transaction. At one point, the spread exceeded $4 per MCI share. When regulators in Europe and the United States signed off on the regulatory aspects of the transaction, the spread finally began to react in a normal fashion.

By July 29, 1998, the gross spread had declined to $1.15, and the arbitrageurs who had entered the transaction on the initial merger announcement had the following position:

Date: July 29, 1998	Cost Basis	7/29/98 Market Value per Share	Total Market Value	Profit or Loss
Long position: Bought 100 shares of MCI	$3,018.75	$65.	$6,500.	$3,481.25
Short position #1: Short 54 shares of BTY	$2,997.00	$72.	($3,889.)	($891.00)
Short position #2: Short 124 shares of WorldCom on 3/16/98 at $41.875 per share	$5,192.00	$53.1875	$6,595.25	($1,402.75)
		Net mark-to-market gain		$1,187.50

Arbitrageurs who had established positions upon the entrance of WorldCom into the transaction had a much more attractive return. If an arbitrageur had established a position in MCI on March 16, 1998, and hedged it off after WorldCom's price lowered through the collar ($4c1), he or she would have shown the following position:

Date: July 29, 1998	Cost Basis	7/29/98 Market Value per Share	Total Market Value	Profit or Loss
Long position: Bought 100 shares of MCI on 10/1/97 at $35.25	$3,525.00	$65.	$6,500.	$2,975.00
Short position: Short 124 shares of WorldCom on 3/16/98 at $41.875	$5,192.50	$53.1875	$6,595.25	($1,402.75)
			Profit	$1,572.25

$$\text{Annual gross return} = \frac{\$1,572.25}{(\$3,525 + .50 \text{ of } \$5,192.50)} \times \frac{365}{302}$$

$$= \$1,572.25 / \$6,121.25$$

$$= 31 \text{ percent}^*$$

The return for the arbitrageur was 31 percent on an annualized gross basis.

The twists and turns exhibited in the MCI/BTY/GTE/WorldCom deal illustrates how there can be many possible outcomes to a proposed transaction. The arbitrageur requires special skills to predict the likelihood of any outcome. Over the course of this book, I hope I have clarified that the practice of risk arbitrage, while being extremely exciting, is an art rather than a science.

---

*Assumes that the arbitrageur had to put up 50 percent of short value as margin.

Appendix **1**

Tender Offer Document

ALUMAX INC.

Filing Type: SC 14D1
Description: N/A
Filing Date: 03/13/98

Ticker: AMX
Cusip: 022197
State: GA
Country: US
Primary SIC: 3334
Primary Exchange: NYS
Billing Cross Reference:
Date Printed: 04/13/98

OFFER TO PURCHASE FOR CASH
UP TO
27,000,000 SHARES OF COMMON STOCK
OF
ALUMAX INC.
AT
$50.00 NET PER SHARE
BY
AMX ACQUISITION CORP.
A WHOLLY OWNED SUBSIDIARY OF
ALUMINUM COMPANY OF AMERICA

THE OFFER, PRORATION PERIOD AND WITHDRAWAL RIGHTS WILL
EXPIRE AT 12:00 MIDNIGHT, NEW YORK CITY TIME, ON APRIL 9,
1998, UNLESS THE OFFER IS EXTENDED.

THE OFFER IS CONDITIONED UPON, AMONG OTHER THINGS, THE WAIT-
ING PERIOD UNDER THE HART-SCOTT-RODINO ANTITRUST IMPROVE-
MENTS ACT OF 1976, AS AMENDED, APPLICABLE TO THE PURCHASE OF
THE SHARES PURSUANT TO THE OFFER HAVING EXPIRED OR BEEN TERMI-
NATED. SEE "SECTION 14. CONDITIONS TO THE OFFER," WHICH SETS
FORTH IN FULL THE CONDITIONS TO THE OFFER.

THE BOARD OF DIRECTORS OF ALUMAX INC. (THE "COMPANY") HAS
UNANIMOUSLY (WITH ONE DIRECTOR ABSENT) APPROVED THE MERGER
AGREEMENT AND THE TRANSACTIONS CONTEMPLATED THEREBY, DETER-
MINED THAT THE TERMS OF THE OFFER AND THE MERGER (EACH AS HERE-
INAFTER DEFINED) ARE FAIR TO, AND IN THE BEST INTERESTS OF, THE
COMPANY AND ITS STOCKHOLDERS AND RECOMMENDS THAT STOCK-
HOLDERS ACCEPT THE OFFER, TENDER THEIR SHARES PURSUANT TO THE
OFFER AND ADOPT THE MERGER AGREEMENT. SEE "SECTION 10. BACK-
GROUND OF THE OFFER; CONTACTS WITH THE COMPANY; THE MERGER
AGREEMENT."

IMPORTANT

<u>POINT 1</u>: *The most important thing to note in tender offers is the proper ten-*
der offer deadlines. Page one of all tender offers discloses the time and date on
which the offer expires. The arbitrageur must tender the shares by this date.
Otherwise, he or she risks receiving a drastically reduced price on the invest-
ment. Also, on this cover page, there is usually a summary of the major contin-
gencies and conditions of the deal. This section tells the price being paid per
share as well as how many shares will be purchased at that price. If the offer is
for all the shares, one need not worry about proration. However, if it is only a
partial cash tender offer, the numbers are the basis for calculating the mini-
mum proration ratio.

Any stockholder desiring to tender all or any portion of such stockholder's shares of common stock, par value $.01 per share (the "Shares"), of the Company, should either (1) complete and sign the Letter of Transmittal (or a facsimile thereof) in accordance with the instructions in the Letter of Transmittal and mail or deliver it together with the certificate(s) evidencing tendered Shares, and any other required documents, to the Depositary or tender such Shares pursuant to the procedure for book-entry transfer set forth in "Section 3. Procedures for Accepting the Offer and Tendering Shares," or (2) request such stockholder's broker, dealer, commercial bank, trust company or other nominee to effect the transaction for such stockholder. Any stockholder whose Shares are registered in the name of a broker, dealer, commercial bank, trust company or other nominee must contact such broker, dealer, commercial bank, trust company or other nominee if such stockholder desires to tender such Shares.

A stockholder who desires to tender Shares and whose certificates evidencing such Shares are not immediately available or who cannot comply with the procedure for book-entry transfer on a timely basis may tender such Shares by following the procedure for guaranteed delivery set forth in "Section 3. Procedures for Accepting the Offer and Tendering Shares."

Questions or requests for assistance may be directed to the Information Agent or to the Dealer Manager at their respective addresses and telephone numbers set forth on the back cover of this Offer to Purchase. Additional copies of this Offer to Purchase, the Letter of Transmittal and other tender offer materials may also be obtained from the Information Agent or the Dealer Manager.

The Dealer Manager for the Offer is:

CREDIT   FIRST

SUISSE   BOSTON

March 13, 1998

TABLE OF CONTENTS

To the Holders of Common Stock of Alumax Inc.:

INTRODUCTION

AMX Acquisition Corp., a Delaware corporation (the "Purchaser") and a wholly owned subsidiary of Aluminum Company of America, a Pennsylvania corporation (the "Parent"), hereby offers to purchase up to 27,000,000 shares of common stock, par value $.01 per share (the "Shares"), of Alumax Inc., a Delaware corporation (the "Company"), at a price of $50.00 per Share, net to the seller in cash, upon the terms and subject to the conditions set forth in this Offer to Purchase and in the related Letter of Transmittal (which together constitute the "Offer").

Tendering stockholders who have Shares registered in their own name and who tender such Shares directly to the Depositary will not be obligated to pay brokerage fees or commissions or, except as otherwise provided in Instruction 6 of the Letter of Transmittal, stock transfer taxes with respect to the purchase of Shares by the Purchaser pursuant to the Offer. Stockholders who hold their Shares through a bank or broker should check with such institution as to whether there are any fees applicable to a tender of Shares. The Purchaser will pay all charges and expenses of Credit Suisse First Boston Corporation ("Credit Suisse First Boston"), which is acting as Dealer Manager for the Offer (the "Dealer Manager"), First Chicago Trust Company of New York (the "Depositary") and D.F. King & Co., Inc. (the "Information Agent") incurred in connection with the Offer. See "Section 16. Fees and Expenses."

THE BOARD OF DIRECTORS OF THE COMPANY (THE "BOARD") HAS UNANIMOUSLY (WITH ONE DIRECTOR ABSENT) APPROVED THE MERGER AGREEMENT AND THE TRANSACTIONS CONTEMPLATED THEREBY, DETERMINED THAT THE TERMS OF THE OFFER AND THE MERGER ARE FAIR TO, AND IN THE BEST INTERESTS OF, THE COMPANY AND ITS STOCKHOLDERS AND RECOMMENDS THAT STOCKHOLDERS ACCEPT THE OFFER, TENDER THEIR SHARES PURSUANT TO THE OFFER AND ADOPT THE MERGER AGREEMENT.

<u>**POINT 2**</u>: *The document discloses that this transaction is friendly and has been approved by the Board of Alumax, Inc. This is important. Having the deal identified as friendly may minimize other potential problems.*

For a discussion of the Board's recommendation, see "Item 4. The Solicitation or Recommendation" set forth in the Company's Solicitation/Recommendation Statement on Schedule 14D-9 (the "Schedule 14D-9"), which is being mailed to stockholders with this Offer to Purchase.

BT Wolfensohn ("BT Wolfensohn") has delivered to the Board its written opinion that, as of March 8, 1998, and based upon and subject to the matters set forth therein the consideration to be received pursuant to the Merger Agreement by the stockholders of the Company in the Offer and the Merger, taken together, is fair from a financial point of view to such stockholders. A copy of the opinion of BT Wolfensohn is contained in the Schedule 14D-9.

POINT 3: Always try to find the investment bankers' opinions relating to the fairness of the offer. In this case, B.T. Wolfensohn has delivered to Alumax's board an opinion that the $50 price to be received is fair from a financial point of view. These opinions can become quite important if the underlying stock prices change. On occasion, these fairness opinions have been revoked. They can become an important aspect of a successful or a broken transaction.

THE OFFER IS CONDITIONED UPON, AMONG OTHER THINGS, THE WAITING PERIOD UNDER THE HART-SCOTT-RODINO ANTITRUST IMPROVEMENTS ACT OF 1976, AS AMENDED, APPLICABLE TO THE PURCHASE OF THE SHARES PURSUANT TO THE OFFER HAVING EXPIRED OR BEEN TERMINATED. THE OFFER IS ALSO SUBJECT TO CERTAIN OTHER CONDITIONS SET FORTH IN THIS OFFER TO PURCHASE. SEE "SECTION 14. CONDITIONS TO THE OFFER."

The Offer is being made pursuant to the Agreement and Plan of Merger, dated as of March 8, 1998 (the "Merger Agreement"), among the Parent, the Purchaser and the Company. The Merger Agreement provides, among other things, that, upon the terms and subject to the conditions set forth in the Merger Agreement, following the purchase of Shares pursuant to the Offer, the Company will be merged with and into the Purchaser (the "Merger"), which will be the surviving corporation in the Merger (the "Surviving Corporation"). At the effective time of the Merger (the "Effective Time"), each issued and outstanding Share (other than Shares owned by the Parent, the Purchaser, the Company or any of their respective subsidiaries and Dissenting Shares (as defined in the Merger Agreement)) will be converted into, and become exchangeable for, the right to receive: (i) 0.6975 (the "Exchange Ratio") of a share of common stock, par value $1.00 per share, of the Parent ("Parent Common Stock"), if the Purchaser purchases at least 27,000,000 Shares or such other number of Shares which equals the 50% Share Number (as hereinafter defined); or (ii) a combination of cash and a fraction of a share of Parent Common Stock, if the Purchaser purchases fewer Shares than the 50% Share Number. The "50% Share Number" equals that number of Shares which represents an absolute majority of the excess of (x) the number of issued and outstanding Shares on a fully diluted basis on the Expiration Date (as hereinafter defined), minus (y) the total number of Shares issuable upon the exercise of all outstanding employee/director stock options. The per Share consideration determined pursuant to clause (i) or clause (ii) above is referred to herein as the "Merger Consideration."

On the Expiration Date, if the Purchaser purchases all Shares validly tendered and such number of Shares is less than 27,000,000, then in the Merger each Share will be converted into the right to receive a prorated amount of the cash remaining available from the Offer (the "Merger Cash Prorate Amount") and a fraction of a share of Parent Common Stock (the "Adjusted Exchange Ratio"), each determined as follows. The Merger Cash Prorate Amount will equal the U.S. dollar amount (rounded up to the nearest cent) determined by dividing (1) the product of the per Share amount paid by the Purchaser pursuant to the Offer times the excess of the 50% Share Number over the number of Shares purchased by the Purchaser in the Offer by (2) the total number of Shares outstanding immediately prior to the Effective Time of the Merger minus the number of Shares owned by the Parent and its subsidiaries immediately prior to the Effective Time (the "Final Outstanding Number"). The Adjusted Exchange Ratio will be determined by dividing (3) the product of the 50% Share Number times .6975 by (4) the Final Outstanding Number. For example, if 26,000,000 Shares were purchased by the Purchaser in the Offer and at the Effective Time the 50% Share Number were 27,000,000 and the Final Outstanding Number were 28,000,000, then in the Merger each Share (other than those owned by the Parent or its subsidiaries and Dissenting Shares) would be converted into the right to receive $1.79 in cash and .6726 of a share of Parent Common Stock.

POINT 4: *In addition to the terms of the tender offer, this document will describe the exact terms, if any, of the proposed follow-up merger. The arbitrageur must be careful to understand all these terms so that they can be included in the proration calculations.*

Pursuant to the Merger Agreement, the Company has advised the Parent that as of March 8, 1998, 53,458,062 Shares were issued and outstanding, 4,436,350 Shares were issuable upon the exercise of stock options (2,275,355 of which are currently exercisable), 441,111 Shares were subject to other stock-based awards and deferred awards, and 190,564 Shares may be issued upon the occurrence of certain future events, including a change of control. The 27,000,000 Shares to which the Offer relates represent approximately 50% of the issued and outstanding Shares of the Company.

POINT 5: *This document gives the arbitrageur the most up-to-date estimate of how many shares of the target company are outstanding, as well as the number of shares that are issuable upon exercise of stock options. These numbers must be used in any of the arbitrageur's calculations of proration.*

Because the market price of the shares of Parent Common Stock will fluctuate and the Exchange Ratio will not be adjusted as a result of such price fluctuation, the value of the Merger Consideration at the Effective Time may be greater or less than the $50.00 per Share in cash payable pursuant to the Offer. Based on the closing price of the Parent Common Stock on the New York Stock Exchange, Inc. ("NYSE") on March 12, 1998, the value of the fraction of a share of Parent Common Stock which would have been received in the Merger had it occurred on such date for each Share pursuant to the Exchange Ratio would have been $49.78 (assuming 27,000,000 Shares were purchased in the Offer).

POINT 6: Any description of the future exchange ratio must be studied by the arbitrageur. The ratio is the key to accurate calculation of spreads.

The Merger Agreement provides that, promptly upon the purchase of Shares by the Purchaser pursuant to the Offer, the Parent will be entitled to designate that number of directors, rounded up to the next whole number, which equals the product obtained by multiplying the total number of directors on the Company's Board (giving effect to the directors designated pursuant to such provision of the Merger Agreement) by the percentage that the number of Shares accepted for payment pursuant to the Offer bears to the total number of Shares then outstanding. In the Merger Agreement, the Company has agreed to increase the size of the Board or exercise its best efforts to secure the resignations of incumbent directors or both as is necessary to enable the Parent's designees to be so elected.

The consummation of the Merger is subject to the satisfaction of certain conditions, including the approval and adoption of the Merger Agreement and the transactions contemplated thereby by the affirmative vote of a majority of the outstanding Shares (the "Company Stockholder Approval"). The Company has agreed to convene a special meeting of its stockholders (the "Company Special Meeting") as promptly as practicable for such purpose. If the Company Special Meeting is held subsequent to the consummation of the Offer and if the Purchaser has acquired (pursuant to the Offer or otherwise) a majority of the outstanding Shares, the Purchaser will have sufficient voting power to approve and adopt the Merger Agreement and the Merger without the vote of any other stockholder. If the Company Special Meeting is held prior to the Expiration Date and the stockholders of the Company fail to approve and adopt the Merger and the Merger Agreement as required under the applicable provisions of the Delaware General Corporation Law (the "DGCL"), either the Parent or the Company may terminate the Merger Agreement, in which event the Offer will be terminated.

Pursuant to the Merger Agreement, the Company has redeemed the preferred stock purchase rights outstanding pursuant to the Rights Agreement, dated February 22, 1996 (the "Rights Agreement"), between the Company and Chemical Mellon Shareholder Services, L.L.C., as rights agent. Payment of the $.01 per right redemption price will be made to stockholders of record as of March 18, 1998.

The Merger Agreement is more fully described in "Section 10. Background of the Offer; Contacts with the Company; the Merger Agreement."

THIS OFFER TO PURCHASE AND THE RELATED LETTER OF TRANSMITTAL CONTAIN IMPORTANT INFORMATION WHICH SHOULD BE READ BEFORE ANY DECISION IS MADE WITH RESPECT TO THE OFFER.

1. Terms of the Offer; Expiration Date. Upon the terms and subject to the conditions of the Offer (including, if the Offer is extended or amended, the terms

and conditions of such extension or amendment), the Purchaser will accept for payment and pay for up to 27,000,000 Shares validly tendered pursuant to the Offer prior to the Expiration Date and not withdrawn as permitted by "Section 4. Withdrawal Rights." The term "Expiration Date" means 12:00 midnight, New York City time, on April 9, 1998, unless and until the Purchaser, in its sole discretion (but subject to the limitations set forth below), shall have extended the period during which the Offer is open, in which event the term "Expiration Date" shall mean the latest time and date at which the Offer, as so extended by the Purchaser, shall expire. If more than 27,000,000 Shares are validly tendered prior to the Expiration Date and not withdrawn, the Purchaser will accept for payment (and thereby purchase) 27,000,000 Shares, on a pro rata basis, with adjustments to avoid purchases of fractional Shares, based upon the number of Shares validly tendered on or prior to the Expiration Date and not withdrawn by each tendering stockholder. In the event that proration of tendered Shares is required, because of the difficulty of determining the precise number of Shares properly tendered and not withdrawn (due in part to the guaranteed delivery procedure described under "Section 3. Procedures for Accepting the Offer and Tendering Shares"), the Purchaser does not expect that it will be able to announce the final results of such proration or pay for any Shares until at least five NYSE trading days after the Expiration Date. Preliminary results of proration will be announced by press release as promptly as practicable after the Expiration Date. Stockholders may obtain such preliminary information from the Information Agent and may be able to obtain such information from their brokers. Tendering stockholders will not receive payment for Shares accepted for payment pursuant to the Offer until the final proration factor is known.

POINT 7: *Again, the arbitrageur must be extremely careful to have the precise date and time when the offer is due to expire.*

Pursuant to the Merger Agreement, the Purchaser is obligated to purchase up to 27,000,000 Shares validly tendered and not withdrawn pursuant to the Offer (or such other number of Shares as equals the 50% Share Number). In the event that on the Expiration Date 27,000,000 Shares is less than the 50% Share Number by more than 2% of the then outstanding Shares and the Offer is scheduled to expire at any time earlier than the tenth business day following the date the Purchaser's notice of acceptance for payment of Shares pursuant to the Offer is first published, sent or given, the Offer will be extended until the expiration of such ten business day period.

Pursuant to the Merger Agreement, the Purchaser may, without the consent of the Company, (i) extend the Offer if, at the Expiration Date, any of the conditions to the Purchaser's obligation to accept for payment and to pay for the Shares are not satisfied or waived, or (ii) extend the Offer for any period required by any rule, regulation or interpretation of the Securities and Exchange Commission (the "Commission") or the staff thereof applicable to the Offer. So long as the Merger Agreement is in effect and the applicable waiting period under the Hart-Scott-Rodino Antitrust Improvements Act of 1976, as amended (the "HSR Act"), has not expired or been terminated, the Purchaser has agreed to extend the Offer from time to time for a period or successive periods, each not to exceed ten business days after the previously scheduled Expiration Date. See "Section 15. Certain Legal Matters and Regulatory Approvals—Antitrust." During any such extension, Shares previously tendered and not withdrawn will remain subject to the terms of the Offer, including the right of a tendering stockholder to withdraw such Shares.

Subject to the applicable regulations of the Commission, the Purchaser also expressly reserves the right, in its sole discretion (but subject to the terms and conditions of the Merger Agreement), at any time and from time to time, (i) to terminate the Offer and not accept for payment any Shares upon the occurrence of any of the conditions specified in "Section 14. Conditions to the Offer" immediately prior to the Expiration Date, and (ii) to waive any condition or otherwise amend the Offer in any respect, by giving oral or written notice of such termination, waiver or amendment to the Depositary and by making a public announcement thereof. Subject to the terms of the Merger Agreement, the Purchaser expressly reserves the right to increase the price per Share payable in the Offer and to make any other changes in the terms and conditions of the Offer, except that without the consent of the Company, the Purchaser will not (i) decrease the price per Share payable pursuant to the Offer, (ii) reduce the number of Shares to be purchased in the Offer, (iii) change the form of consideration to be paid in the Offer, (iv) modify any of the conditions to the Offer set forth in "Section 14. Conditions to the Offer" in a manner adverse to the holders of Shares, or (v) extend the Offer except as described above.

Any such extension, delay, termination, waiver or amendment will be followed as promptly as practicable by public announcement thereof, such announcement in the case of an extension to be made no later than 9:00 A.M., New York City time, on the next business day after the previously scheduled Expiration Date. Subject to applicable law (including Rules 14d-4(c) and 14d-6(d) under the Securities Exchange Act of 1934, as amended (the "Exchange Act"), which require that material changes be promptly disseminated to stockholders in a manner reasonably designed to inform them of such changes) and without limiting the manner in which the Purchaser may choose to make any public announcement, the Purchaser shall have no obligation to publish, advertise or otherwise communicate any such public announcement other than by issuing a press release to the Dow Jones News Service.

If the Purchaser makes a material change in the terms of the Offer or the information concerning the Offer, or if it waives a material condition of the Offer, the Purchaser will extend the Offer to the extent required by Rules 14d-4(c) and 14d-6(d) under the Exchange Act.

The Company has provided the Purchaser with the Company's stockholder list and security position listings for the purpose of disseminating the Offer to holders of Shares. This Offer to Purchase, the related Letter of Transmittal and other relevant materials will be mailed to record holders of Shares whose names appear on the Company's stockholder list and will be furnished, for subsequent transmittal to beneficial owners of Shares, to brokers, dealers, commercial banks, trust companies and similar persons whose names, or the names of whose nominees, appear on the stockholder list or, if applicable, who are listed as participants in a clearing agency's security position listing.

2. Acceptance for Payment and Payment for Shares. Upon the terms and subject to the conditions of the Offer (including, if the Offer is extended or amended, the terms and conditions of any such extension or amendment), the Purchaser will accept for payment, and will pay for, up to 27,000,000 Shares validly tendered prior to the Expiration Date (subject to any pro rata adjustment in accordance with the terms of the Offer in the event more than 27,000,000 Shares are validly tendered in the Offer) and not properly withdrawn. The Purchaser expressly reserves the right, in its sole discretion, to delay acceptance for payment of, or payment for, Shares in order to comply in whole or in part with any applicable law. Any such delays will be effected in compliance with Rule 14e-1(c) under the Exchange Act, relating to a bidder's obligation to pay the consideration offered or return the securities deposited by or on behalf of holders of securities promptly after the termination or withdrawal of such bidder's offer.

In all cases, payment for Shares tendered and accepted for payment pursuant to the Offer will be made only after timely receipt by the Depositary of (i) the certificates evidencing such Shares (the "Share Certificates") or timely confirmation (a "Book-Entry Confirmation") of a book-entry transfer of such Shares into the Depositary's account at The Depository Trust Company (the "Book-Entry Transfer Facility") pursuant to the procedures set forth in "Section 3. Procedures for Accepting the Offer and Tendering Shares," (ii) the Letter of Transmittal (or a facsimile thereof), properly completed and duly executed, with any required signature guarantees, or an Agent's Message (as hereinafter defined) in connection with a book-entry transfer, and (iii) any other documents required under the Letter of Transmittal. The per Share consideration paid to any holder of Shares pursuant to the Offer will be the highest per Share consideration paid to any other holder of such Shares pursuant to the Offer.

For purposes of the Offer, the Purchaser will be deemed to have accepted for payment (and thereby purchased) Shares validly tendered to the Purchaser (subject to any pro rata adjustment in accordance with the terms of the Offer in the event more than 27,000,000 Shares are validly tendered in the Offer) and not properly withdrawn as, if and when the Purchaser gives oral or written notice to the Depositary of the Purchaser's acceptance for payment of such Shares pursuant to the Offer. Upon the terms and subject to the conditions of the Offer, payment for Shares accepted for payment pursuant to the Offer will be made by deposit of the purchase price therefor with the Depositary, which will act as agent for tendering stockholders for the purpose of receiving payments from the Purchaser and transmitting such payments to tendering stockholders whose Shares have been accepted for payment. Under no circumstances will interest on the purchase price for Shares be paid, regardless of any delay in making such payment.

POINT 8: *Shares are accepted for payment only after all conditions are met. The arbitrageur may have to wait a period of time for this precise date.*

If any tendered Shares are not accepted for payment for any reason pursuant to the terms and conditions of the Offer, or if Share Certificates are submitted evidencing more Shares than are tendered, Share Certificates evidencing unpurchased Shares will be returned, without expense to the tendering stockholder (or, in the case of Shares tendered by book-entry transfer into the Depositary's account at the Book-Entry Transfer Facility pursuant to the procedure set forth in "Section 3. Procedures for Accepting and Tendering Shares," such Shares will be credited to an account maintained at the Book-Entry Transfer Facility), as promptly as practicable following the expiration or termination of the Offer.

The Purchaser reserves the right to transfer or assign, in whole or from time to time in part, to one or more of its affiliates, the right to purchase all or any portion of the Shares tendered pursuant to the Offer, but any such transfer or assignment will not relieve the Purchaser of its obligations under the Offer and will in no way prejudice the rights of tendering stockholders to receive payment for Shares validly tendered and accepted for payment pursuant to the Offer.

3. Procedures for Accepting the Offer and Tendering Shares. In order for a holder of Shares validly to tender Shares pursuant to the Offer either (a) the Letter of Transmittal (or a facsimile thereof), properly completed and duly executed, together with any required signature guarantees or, in the case of a book-entry transfer, an Agent's Message, and any other documents required by the Letter of Transmittal, must be received by the Depositary at one of its addresses set forth on the back cover of this Offer to Purchase and either the Share Certificates evidencing tendered Shares must be received by the Depositary at such address or such Shares must be tendered pursuant to the procedure for book-entry transfer described below and a Book-Entry Confirmation must be received by the Depositary, in each case prior to the Expiration Date, or (b) the tendering stockholder must comply with the guaranteed delivery procedures described below.

THE METHOD OF DELIVERY OF SHARE CERTIFICATES AND ALL OTHER REQUIRED DOCUMENTS, INCLUDING DELIVERY THROUGH THE BOOK-ENTRY TRANSFER FACILITY, IS AT THE OPTION AND RISK OF THE TENDERING STOCKHOLDER, AND THE DELIVERY WILL BE DEEMED MADE ONLY WHEN ACTUALLY RECEIVED BY THE DEPOSITARY. IF DELIVERY IS BY MAIL, REGISTERED MAIL WITH RETURN RECEIPT REQUESTED, PROPERLY INSURED, IS RECOMMENDED. IN ALL CASES, SUFFICIENT TIME SHOULD BE ALLOWED TO ENSURE TIMELY DELIVERY.

Book-Entry Transfer. The Depositary will establish an account with respect to the Shares at the Book-Entry Transfer Facility for purposes of the Offer within two business days after the date of this Offer to Purchase. Any financial institution that is a participant in the Book-Entry Transfer Facility may make a book-entry delivery of Shares by causing the Book-Entry Transfer Facility to transfer such Shares into the Depositary's account at the Book-Entry Transfer Facility in accordance with the Book-Entry Transfer Facility's procedures for such transfer. Although delivery of Shares may be effected through book-entry transfer at the Book-Entry Transfer Facility, the Letter of Transmittal (or a facsimile thereof), properly completed and duly executed, together with any required signature guarantees, or an Agent's Message, and any other required documents, must, in any case, be received by the Depositary at one of its addresses set forth on the back cover of this Offer to Purchase prior to the Expiration Date, or the tendering stockholder must comply with the guaranteed delivery procedure described below. DELIVERY OF DOCUMENTS TO THE BOOK-ENTRY TRANSFER FACILITY DOES NOT CONSTITUTE DELIVERY TO THE DEPOSITARY.

The term "Agent's Message" means a message transmitted by the Book-Entry Transfer Facility to, and received by, the Depositary and forming a part of a Book-Entry Confirmation, which states that the Book-Entry Transfer Facility has received an express acknowledgment from the participant in the Book-Entry Transfer Facility tendering the Shares that such participant has received and agrees to be bound by the terms of the Letter of Transmittal and that the Purchaser may enforce such agreement against such participant.

Signature Guarantees. Signatures on all Letters of Transmittal must be guaranteed by a firm which is a financial institution (including most commercial banks, savings and loan associations and brokerage houses) that is a participant in the Securities Transfer Agents Medallion Program, the New York Stock Exchange Medallion Signature Guarantee Program or the Stock Exchange Medallion Program (each, an "Eligible Institution"), except in cases where Shares are tendered (i) by a registered holder of Shares who has not completed either the box entitled "Special Payment Instructions" or the box entitled "Special Delivery Instructions" on the Letter of Transmittal or (ii) for the account of an Eligible Institution. If a Share Certificate is registered in the name of a person other than the signer of the Letter of Transmittal, or if payment is to be made, or a Share Certificate not accepted for payment or not tendered is to be returned, to a person other than the registered holder(s), then the tendered Share Certificate must be endorsed or accompanied by appropriate stock powers, in either case signed exactly as the name(s) of the registered holder(s) appear on the Share Certificate, with the signature(s) on such Share Certificate or stock powers guaranteed by an Eligible Institution. See Instructions 1 and 5 of the Letter of Transmittal.

Guaranteed Delivery. If a stockholder desires to tender Shares pursuant to the Offer and such stockholder's Share Certificates evidencing such Shares are not immediately available or such stockholder cannot deliver the Share Certificates and all other required documents to the Depositary prior to the Expiration Date, or such stockholder cannot complete the procedure for delivery by book-entry transfer on a timely basis, such Shares may nevertheless be tendered, provided that all the following conditions are satisfied:

(i)   such tender is made by or through an Eligible Institution;

(ii)   a properly completed and duly executed Notice of Guaranteed Delivery, substantially in the form made available by the Purchaser, is received prior to the Expiration Date by the Depositary as provided below; and

(iii) the Share Certificates (or a Book-Entry Confirmation) evidencing all tendered Shares, in proper form for transfer, in each case together with the Letter of Transmittal (or a facsimile thereof), properly completed and duly executed, with any required signature guarantees, or, in the case of a book-entry transfer, an Agent's Message, and any other documents required by the Letter of Transmittal are received by the Depositary within three NYSE trading days after the date of execution of such Notice of Guaranteed Delivery. A "NYSE trading day" is any day on which securities are traded on the NYSE.

POINT 9: *Regarding the procedure of tendering shares, the arbitrageur must always note the length of the guarantee period. If the arbitrageur is not physically tendering the shares and, instead, has a broker guarantee delivery, this guarantee must be made on time or the arbitrageur risks not receiving a consideration under the tender offer.*

The Notice of Guaranteed Delivery may be delivered by hand or mail or transmitted by telegram or facsimile transmission to the Depositary and must include a guarantee by an Eligible Institution in the form set forth in the form of Notice of Guaranteed Delivery made available by the Purchaser.

In all cases, payment for Shares tendered and accepted for payment pursuant to the Offer will be made only after timely receipt by the Depositary of the Share Certificates evidencing such Shares, or a Book-Entry Confirmation of the delivery of such Shares, and the Letter of Transmittal (or a facsimile thereof), properly completed and duly executed or, in the case of a book-entry transfer, an Agent's Message, with any required signature guarantees, and any other documents required by the Letter of Transmittal. Accordingly, tendering stockholders may be paid at different times depending upon when Share Certificates, Book-Entry Confirmations and such other documents are actually received by the Depositary. Under no circumstances will interest be paid by the Purchaser on the purchase price of the Shares to any tendering stockholders, regardless of any extension of the Offer or any delay in making such payment.

Determination of Validity. All questions as to the validity, form, eligibility (including time of receipt) and acceptance for payment of any tender of Shares will be determined by the Purchaser in its sole discretion, which determination shall be final and binding on all parties. The Purchaser reserves the absolute right to reject any and all tenders determined by it not to be in proper form or the acceptance for payment of which may, in the opinion of its counsel, be unlawful. The Purchaser also reserves the absolute right, subject to the terms of the Merger Agreement, to waive any condition of the Offer or any defect or irregularity in the tender of any Shares of any particular stockholder, whether or not similar defects or irregularities are waived in the case of other stockholders. No tender of Shares will be deemed to have been validly made until all defects and irregularities have been cured or waived. None of the Purchaser, the Parent, the Dealer Manager, the Depositary, the Information Agent or any other person will be under any duty to give notification of any defects or irregularities in tenders or incur any liability for failure to give any such notification. The Purchaser's interpretation of the terms and conditions of the Offer (including the Letter of Transmittal and the instructions thereto) will be final and binding.

Other Requirements. By executing the Letter of Transmittal as set forth above (including through delivery of an Agent's Message), a tendering stockholder irrevocably appoints designees of the Purchaser as such stockholder's proxies, each with full power of substitution, in the manner set forth in the Letter of Transmittal, to the full extent of such stockholder's rights with respect to the Shares tendered by such stockholder and accepted for payment by the Purchaser (and with respect to any and all other Shares or other securities issued or issuable in respect of such Shares on or after the Expiration Date). All such proxies shall be considered coupled with an interest in the tendered Shares. Such appointment will be effective when, and only to the extent that, the Purchaser accepts such Shares for payment. Upon such acceptance for payment, all prior proxies given by such stockholder with respect to such Shares (and such other Shares and securities) will be revoked without further action, and no subsequent proxies may be given nor any subsequent written consent executed by such stockholder (and, if given or executed, will not be deemed to be effective) with respect thereto. The designees of the Purchaser will, with respect to the Shares for which the appointment is effective, be empowered to exercise all voting and other rights of such stockholder as they in their sole discretion may deem proper at any annual or special meeting of the Company's stockholders or any adjournment or postponement thereof, by written consent in lieu of any such meeting or otherwise. The Purchaser reserves the right to require that, in order for Shares to be deemed validly tendered, immediately upon the Purchaser's payment for such Shares, the Purchaser must be able to exercise full voting rights with respect to such Shares.

The acceptance for payment by the Purchaser of Shares pursuant to any of the procedures described above will constitute a binding agreement between the tendering stockholder and the Purchaser upon the terms and subject to the conditions of the Offer.

UNDER THE "BACKUP WITHHOLDING" PROVISIONS OF U.S. FEDERAL INCOME TAX LAW, THE DEPOSITARY MAY BE REQUIRED TO WITHHOLD 31% OF THE AMOUNT OF ANY PAYMENTS OF CASH PURSUANT TO THE OFFER. IN ORDER TO PREVENT BACKUP FEDERAL INCOME TAX WITHHOLDING WITH RESPECT TO PAYMENT TO CERTAIN STOCKHOLDERS OF THE PURCHASE PRICE OF SHARES PURCHASED PURSUANT TO THE OFFER, EACH SUCH STOCKHOLDER MUST PROVIDE THE DEPOSITARY WITH SUCH STOCKHOLDER'S CORRECT TAXPAYER IDENTIFICATION NUMBER AND CERTIFY THAT SUCH STOCKHOLDER IS NOT SUBJECT TO BACKUP WITHHOLDING BY COMPLETING THE SUBSTITUTE FORM W-9 IN THE LETTER OF TRANSMITTAL. CERTAIN STOCKHOLDERS (INCLUDING, AMONG OTHERS, ALL CORPORATIONS AND CERTAIN FOREIGN INDIVIDUALS AND ENTITIES) ARE NOT SUBJECT TO BACKUP WITHHOLDING. IF A STOCKHOLDER DOES NOT PROVIDE ITS CORRECT TIN OR FAILS TO PROVIDE THE CERTIFICATIONS DESCRIBED ABOVE, THE INTERNAL REVENUE SERVICE MAY IMPOSE A PENALTY ON THE STOCKHOLDER AND PAYMENT OF CASH TO THE STOCKHOLDER PURSUANT TO THE OFFER MAY BE SUBJECT TO BACKUP WITHHOLDING. ALL STOCKHOLDERS SURRENDERING SHARES PURSUANT TO THE OFFER SHOULD COMPLETE AND SIGN THE SUBSTITUTE FORM W-9 INCLUDED IN THE LETTER OF TRANSMITTAL TO PROVIDE THE INFORMATION NECESSARY TO AVOID BACKUP WITHHOLDING (UNLESS AN APPLICABLE EXEMPTION EXISTS AND IS PROVED IN A MANNER SATISFACTORY TO THE

DEPOSITARY). NON-CORPORATE FOREIGN STOCKHOLDERS SHOULD COM-
PLETE AND SIGN A FORM W-8, CERTIFICATE OF FOREIGN STATUS (A COPY
OF WHICH MAY BE OBTAINED FROM THE DEPOSITARY), IN ORDER TO
AVOID BACKUP WITHHOLDING. SEE INSTRUCTION 10 OF THE LETTER OF
TRANSMITTAL.

4. Withdrawal Rights. Tenders of Shares made pursuant to the Offer are ir-
revocable except that such Shares may be withdrawn at any time prior to the Expiration Date and, unless theretofore accepted for payment by the Purchaser
pursuant to the Offer, may also be withdrawn at any time after May 11, 1998. If
the Purchaser extends the Offer, is delayed in its acceptance for payment of
Shares or is unable to accept Shares for payment pursuant to the Offer for any
reason, then, without prejudice to the Purchaser's rights under the Offer, the
Depositary may, nevertheless, on behalf of the Purchaser, retain tendered Shares,
and such Shares may not be withdrawn except to the extent that tendering stockholders are entitled to withdrawal rights as described in this "Section 4. Withdrawal Rights."

For a withdrawal to be effective, a written, telegraphic or facsimile transmission notice of withdrawal must be timely received by the Depositary at one of its
addresses set forth on the back cover page of this Offer to Purchase. Any such notice of withdrawal must specify the name of the person who tendered the Shares
to be withdrawn, the number of Shares to be withdrawn and the name of the registered holder of such Shares, if different from that of the person who tendered
such Shares. If Share Certificates evidencing Shares to be withdrawn have been
delivered or otherwise identified to the Depositary, then, prior to the physical release of such Share Certificates, the serial numbers shown on such Share Certificates must be submitted to the Depositary and the signature(s) on the notice of
withdrawal must be guaranteed by an Eligible Institution, unless such Shares have
been tendered for the account of an Eligible Institution. If Shares have been tendered pursuant to the procedure for book-entry transfer as set forth in "Section 3.
Procedures for Accepting the Offer and Tendering Shares," the notice of withdrawal must specify the name and number of the account at the Book-Entry
Transfer Facility to be credited with the withdrawn Shares.

*POINT 10: Withdrawal rights can sometimes be very important. The arbi-
trageur should always note when withdrawal rights have been granted. Developments at later stages of any transaction may cause the arbitrageur to want
to withdraw securities already tendered.*

All questions as to the form and validity (including time of receipt) of any
notice of withdrawal will be determined by the Purchaser, in its sole discretion,
whose determination will be final and binding. None of the Purchaser, the Parent, the Dealer Manager, the Depositary, the Information Agent or any other
person will be under any duty to give notification of any defects or irregularities in any notice of withdrawal or incur any liability for failure to give any such
notification.

Any Shares properly withdrawn will thereafter be deemed not to have been validly tendered for purposes of the Offer. However, withdrawn Shares may be re-tendered at any time prior to the Expiration Date by following one of the procedures described in "Section 3. Procedures for Accepting the Offer and Tendering Shares."

5. Certain Federal Income Tax Consequences. The summary of U.S. federal income tax consequences set forth below is for general information only and is based on the Purchaser's understanding of the law as currently in effect. It is assumed for purposes of this discussion that the Shares are held and will continue to be held as "capital assets" within the meaning of Section 1221 of the Internal Revenue Code of 1986, as amended (the "Code"). The tax consequences to each stockholder will depend in part upon such stockholder's particular situation. Special tax consequences not described herein may be applicable to particular classes of taxpayers, such as financial institutions, insurance companies, tax-exempt organizations, broker-dealers, persons who are not citizens or residents of the United States and stockholders who acquired their Shares through the exercise of an employee stock option or otherwise as compensation. ALL STOCKHOLDERS SHOULD CONSULT WITH THEIR OWN TAX ADVISORS AS TO THE PARTICULAR TAX CONSEQUENCES OF THE OFFER AND THE MERGER, INCLUDING THE APPLICABILITY AND EFFECT OF THE ALTERNATIVE MINIMUM TAX AND ANY STATE, LOCAL OR FOREIGN INCOME AND OTHER TAX LAWS AND OF CHANGES IN SUCH TAX LAWS.

Tax Consequences of the Offer and the Merger Generally. The Offer and the Merger are intended to qualify as a reorganization within the meaning of Section 368(a) of the Code. If they are so treated, for U.S. federal income tax purposes (i) no gain or loss will be recognized by the Parent, the Purchaser or the Company pursuant to the Offer or the Merger, (ii) a stockholder of the Company who exchanges all of such stockholder's Shares solely for cash in the Offer (or upon the exercise of appraisal rights in connection with the Merger) will recognize gain or loss in an amount equal to the difference between the cash received and such stockholder's adjusted tax basis in the Shares surrendered, (iii) a stockholder of the Company who does not exchange any Shares pursuant to the Offer and who receives solely Parent Common Stock in exchange for Shares in the Merger will not recognize any gain or loss, and (iv) a stockholder of the Company who receives a combination of cash and Parent Common Stock in the Offer and the Merger or in the Merger only will not recognize loss but will recognize gain, if any, on the Shares so exchanged to the extent of any cash received. It is a condition to the respective obligations of each of the Company and the Purchaser that such party receive an opinion from its tax counsel to the effect that the Merger qualifies as a reorganization.

Exchange of Shares Solely for Cash. In general, a stockholder of the Company who exchanges all of such stockholder's Shares for cash in the Offer (or upon the exercise of appraisal rights in connection with the Merger) will recognize capital gain or loss equal to the difference between the amount of cash received and such stockholder's adjusted tax basis in the Shares surrendered. The gain or loss will be long-term capital gain or loss if, as of the date of the exchange, the stockholder has held such Shares for more than one year.

Exchange of Shares Solely for Parent Common Stock. A stockholder of the Company who does not exchange any Shares pursuant to the Offer and who receives solely Parent Common Stock in exchange for Shares in the Merger will not recognize any gain or loss upon such exchange. Such stockholder may recognize gain or loss, however, to the extent cash is received in lieu of a fractional share of Parent Common Stock, as discussed below. The aggregate adjusted tax basis of the Shares of Parent Common Stock received in such exchange will be equal to the aggregate adjusted tax basis of the Shares surrendered therefor, and the holding period of Parent Common Stock will include the holding period of the Shares surrendered therefor.

Exchange of Shares for Parent Common Stock and Cash. A stockholder of the Company who receives a combination of cash and shares of Parent Common Stock in the Offer and the Merger or in the Merger only will not recognize loss but will recognize gain, if any, on the Shares so exchanged to the extent of any cash received. Any such recognized gain will be treated as capital gain unless the receipt of the cash has the effect of the distribution of a dividend for U.S. federal income tax purposes, in which case such gain will be treated as ordinary dividend income to the extent of such stockholder's ratable share of the Company's accumulated earnings and profits. Any capital gain will be long- term capital gain if, as of the date of the exchange, the stockholder has held such Shares for more than one year.

The aggregate adjusted tax basis of the shares of Parent Common Stock received in such exchanges will be equal to the aggregate tax basis of the Shares surrendered therefor, decreased by the cash received and increased by the amount of gain recognized, if any. The holding period of Parent Common Stock will include the holding period of the Shares surrendered therefor.

Cash Received in Lieu of a Fractional Interest of Parent Common Stock. Cash received in lieu of a fractional share of Parent Common Stock will be treated as received in redemption of such fractional interest and gain or loss will be recognized, measured by the difference between the amount of cash received and the portion of the basis of the Shares allocable to such fractional interest. Such gain or loss will be long-term capital gain or loss if, as of the date of the exchange, the holding period for such Shares was greater than one year.

The Taxpayer Relief Act of 1997 (the "1997 Act") created several new categories of capital gains applicable to noncorporate taxpayers. Under prior law, noncorporate taxpayers were generally taxed at a maximum rate of 28% on net capital gain (generally, the excess of net long-term capital gain over net short-term capital loss). Noncorporate taxpayers are now generally taxed at a maximum rate of 20% on net capital gain attributable to the sale of property held for more than eighteen months, and a maximum rate of 28% on net capital gain attributable to the sale of property held for more than one year but not more than eighteen months. The 1997 Act did not affect the treatment of short- term capital gain or loss (generally, gain or loss attributable to capital assets held for one year or less) and did not affect the taxation of capital gains in the hands of corporate taxpayers.

A stockholder whose Shares are purchased in the Offer may be subject to 31% backup withholding unless certain information is provided to the Parent and the Purchaser or an exemption applies. "Section 3. Procedures for Accepting the Offer and Tendering Shares."

6. Price Range of Shares; Dividends. The Shares are listed and principally traded on the NYSE under the symbol AMX. The following table sets forth, for the quarters indicated, the high and low sales prices per Share on the NYSE. The Company has not paid cash dividends on Shares in the past and has publicly disclosed that it does not anticipate doing so in the foreseeable future. In addition, the Merger Agreement prohibits the payment of dividends by the Company. See "Section 12. Dividends and Distributions."

***POINT 11*: The arbitrageur should always consult these tender offer documents to help determine whether any dividends that are paid during the pendency of the offer accrue to the holder. In some deals, if the target company were to pay a dividend during the pendency of the tender offer, the consideration being offered by the acquiring company may be reduced by the amount of that dividend. In this case, the merger agreement specifically allowed for the payment of dividends by Alumax, Inc.**

	HIGH	LOW
1996:		
First Quarter	$40	$26 5/8
Second Quarter	36 1/2	29 1/8
Third Quarter	34	29
Fourth Quarter	34 1/8	30 5/8
1997:		
First Quarter	$40 3/8	$33 7/8
Second Quarter	39 1/8	34 1/4
Third Quarter	45 1/4	37 3/8
Fourth Quarter	42 1/4	30 1/2
1998:		
First Quarter (through March 12, 1998)	$47 3/4	$31 3/16

On March 6, 1998, the last full trading day prior to the announcement of the execution of the Merger Agreement and the Purchaser's intention to commence the Offer, the closing price per Share as reported on the NYSE was $36 11/16. On March 12, 1998, the last full trading day prior to the commencement of the Offer, the closing price per Share as reported on the NYSE was $45 9/16.

STOCKHOLDERS ARE URGED TO OBTAIN A CURRENT MARKET QUOTATION FOR THE SHARES.

7. Certain Information Concerning the Company. Except as otherwise set forth herein, the information concerning the Company contained in this Offer to Purchase, including financial information, has been furnished by the Company or has been taken from or based upon publicly available documents and records on file with the Commission and other public sources. Neither the Purchaser nor the Parent assumes any responsibility for the accuracy or completeness of the information concerning the Company furnished by the Company or contained in such documents and records or for any failure by the Company to disclose events which may have occurred or may affect the significance or accuracy of any such information but which are unknown to the Purchaser or the Parent.

General. The Company is a Delaware corporation with its principal executive offices located at 3424 Peachtree Road, N.E., Suite 2100, Atlanta, Georgia 30326. The Company is an integrated producer of aluminum products, operating in a single segment: aluminum processing. Using alumina purchased primarily from an affiliate of the Parent, the Company produces primary aluminum employing an electrolytic process at five reduction plants in the United States and Canada. Primary products are sold externally or further processed by the Company into a broad range of semi-fabricated and fabricated products. The Company's products are sold to a wide variety of markets, including transportation, distributors, building and construction, consumer durables, and packaging. The Company operates over 70 plants and other manufacturing and distribution facilities in 22 states, Canada, Western Europe, Mexico, Australia, the People's Republic of China and Poland.

Relationship with the Company. The Company does not mine bauxite or refine alumina. Alcoa of Australia Limited, a subsidiary of the Parent, has been the Company's principal supplier of alumina for over 20 years and currently provides substantially all of the alumina for the Company's reduction operations under a long-term contract which, with renewal options, expires in increments between 2007 and 2018. Pricing under the contract is determined in part on a cost basis and in part on a market basis, providing the Company with protection against spot market price extremes during periods of tight supply. In fiscal years 1997, 1996 and 1995, the Company made aggregate payments under such contract of $257.7 million, $255.4 million and $182.1 million, respectively.

Selected Consolidated Financial Information. Set forth below is certain selected financial information relating to the Company which has been excerpted or derived from the audited financial statements contained in the Company's Annual Report on Form 10-K for the fiscal year ended December 31, 1997 (the "Company Form 10-K"). More comprehensive financial information is included in the Company Form 10-K and other documents filed by the Company with the Commission. The financial information that follows is qualified in its entirety by reference to such reports and other documents, including the financial statements and related notes contained therein. Such reports and other documents may be examined and copies may be obtained from the offices of the Commission in the manner set forth under "Company Available Information" on page 196.

ALUMAX INC.

SELECTED CONSOLIDATED FINANCIAL INFORMATION
(DOLLARS IN MILLIONS, EXCEPT PER SHARE AMOUNTS)

	Year Ended December 31,		
	1997	1996	1995
OPERATING RESULTS			
Net sales	$2,930.9	$3,159.3	$2,926.1
Earnings (loss) from operations	$ 293.0	$ 231.9	$ 305.8
Gain on sales of assets		242.9	128.8
Interest expense, net	(57.8)	(62.8)	(65.4)
Other income, net	2.0	10.6	7.3
Income tax (provision) benefit	(203.5)	(172.6)	(139.1)
Cumulative effect of accounting changes			
Net earnings (loss)	$ 33.7	$ 250.0	$ 237.4
Earnings (loss) applicable to common shares	$ 33.7	$ 240.7	$ 228.1
EARNINGS (LOSS) PER COMMON SHARE			
Basic	$ 0.62	$ 5.26	$ 5.11
Diluted	$ 0.60	$ 4.53	$ 4.34
FINANCIAL POSITION			
Working capital	$ 754.3	$ 660.6	$ 767.9
Property, plant and equipment, net	2,026.9	2,027.4	1,611.9
Total assets	3,453.0	3,298.7	3,135.0
Long-term debt	955.6	672.0	708.9
Total debt	1,002.0	710.4	845.9
Stockholders' equity	$1,621.7	$1,640.8	$1,399.3
OTHER DATA			
Total debt to invested capital	38.2%	30.2%	37.7%
Return on sales	1.1%	7.9%	8.1%
Return on average stockholders' equity	2.1%	16.4%	18.5%
Return on average invested capital	3.0%	13.5%	14.1%
Book value per Share	$ 30.37	$ 30.00	$ 25.73

Company Available Information. The Company is subject to the informational filing requirements of the Exchange Act and, in accordance therewith, is required to file periodic reports, proxy statements and other information with the Commission relating to its business, financial condition and other matters.

Information as of particular dates concerning the Company's directors and officers, their remuneration, stock options granted to them, the principal holders of the Company's securities and any material interest of such persons in transactions with the Company is required to be disclosed in proxy statements distributed to the Company's stockholders and filed with the Commission. Such reports, proxy statements and other information should be available for inspection at the public reference facilities maintained by the Commission at Judiciary Plaza, 450 Fifth Street, N.W., Washington, D.C. 20549, and also should be available for inspection at the Commission's regional offices located at Seven World Trade Center, Suite 1300, New York, New York 10048 and the Citicorp Center, 500 West Madison Street, Suite 1400, Chicago, Illinois 60661. Copies of such materials may also be obtained by mail, upon payment of the Commission's customary fees, by writing to its principal office at Judiciary Plaza, 450 Fifth Street, N.W., Washington, D.C. 20549. The Commission also maintains a World Wide Web site on the Internet at http://www.sec.gov that contains reports, proxy statements and other information regarding registrants that file electronically with the Commission.

POINT 12: This document gives basic information on both the target company and the acquiring company. The arbitrageur, of course, would normally have utilized all other available sources of information to supplement what is disclosed in this document.

    8. Certain Information Concerning the Parent and the Purchaser.

    General. The Parent is a corporation organized under the laws of Pennsylvania. The principal offices of the Parent and the Purchaser are located at 425 Sixth Avenue, Pittsburgh, Pennsylvania 15219. The Parent is the world's largest aluminum company and the world's largest alumina producer, with over 180 operating locations in 28 countries.

    The Purchaser is a newly incorporated Delaware corporation organized in connection with the Offer and the Merger and has not carried on any activities other than in connection with the Offer and the Merger. The Purchaser is a wholly owned subsidiary of the Parent. Until immediately prior to the time that the Purchaser purchases Shares pursuant to the Offer, it is not anticipated that the Purchaser will have any significant assets or liabilities or engage in activities other than those incident to its formation and capitalization and the transactions contemplated by the Offer and the Merger. Because the Purchaser is newly formed and has minimal assets and capitalization, no meaningful financial information regarding the Purchaser is available.

    Directors and Officers. The name, citizenship, business address, principal occupation or employment, and five-year employment history for each of the directors and executive officers of the Parent and the Purchaser and certain other information are set forth in Schedule I hereto.

    Except as described in this Offer to Purchase, (i) none of the Purchaser, the Parent nor, to the best knowledge of the Purchaser and the Parent, any of the persons listed in Schedule I to this Offer to Purchase or any associate or majority-owned subsidiary of the Purchaser, the Parent or any of the persons so listed beneficially owns or has any right to acquire, directly or indirectly, any Shares, and (ii) none of the Purchaser, the Parent nor, to the best knowledge of the Purchaser and the Parent, any of the persons or entities referred to above nor any director, executive officer or subsidiary of any of the foregoing has effected any transaction in the Shares during the past 60 days.

Except as provided in the Merger Agreement and as otherwise described in this Offer to Purchase, none of the Purchaser, the Parent nor, to the best knowledge of the Purchaser and the Parent, any of the persons listed in Schedule I to this Offer to Purchase, has any contract, arrangement, understanding or relationship with any other person with respect to any securities of the Company, including, but not limited to, any contract, arrangement, understanding or relationship concerning the transfer or voting of such securities, joint ventures, loan or option arrangements, puts or calls, guaranties of loans, guaranties against loss or the giving or withholding of proxies. Except as set forth in this Offer to Purchase, since January 1, 1995, neither the Purchaser nor the Parent nor, to the best knowledge of the Purchaser and the Parent, any of the persons listed on Schedule I hereto, has had any business relationship or transaction with the Company or any of its executive officers, directors or affiliates that is required to be reported under the rules and regulations of the Commission applicable to the Offer. Except as set forth in this Offer to Purchase, since January 1, 1995, there have been no contracts, negotiations or transactions between any of the Purchaser, the Parent, or any of their respective subsidiaries or, to the best knowledge of the Purchaser and the Parent, any of the persons listed in Schedule I to this Offer to Purchase, on the one hand, and the Company or its affiliates, on the other hand, concerning a merger, consolidation or acquisition, tender offer or other acquisition of securities, an election of directors or a sale or other transfer of a material amount of assets.

POINT 13: *Arbitrageurs should always try to determine the amount of stock held by all officers and directors of the respective companies. This document also requires officers and directors to indicate whether they plan on tendering their shares.*

Financial Information. Set forth below are certain selected financial data relating to the Parent and its subsidiaries for the Parent's last three fiscal years, which have been excerpted or derived from the audited financial statements contained in the Parent's Annual Report on Form 10-K for the fiscal year ended December 31, 1997 (the "Parent Form 10-K"). More comprehensive financial information is included in the Parent Form 10-K and other documents filed by the Parent with the Commission, and the following financial information is qualified in its entirety by reference to such reports and other documents, including the financial information and related notes contained therein. Such reports and other documents may be inspected and copies may be obtained from the offices of the Commission in the manner set forth under "Parent Available Information" on page 199.

ALUMINUM COMPANY OF AMERICA

SELECTED CONSOLIDATED FINANCIAL DATA
(DOLLARS IN MILLIONS, EXCEPT PER SHARE AMOUNTS)

	Fiscal Year Ended		
	December 31, 1997	December 31, 1996	December 31, 1995
INCOME STATEMENT DATA			
Sales and operating revenues	$13,319.2	$13,061.0	$12,499.7
Net income[a]	805.1	514.9	790.5
Basic earnings per common share	4.66	2.94	4.43
Diluted earnings per common share	4.62	2.91	4.39
Cash dividends per common share	.975	1.33	.90
	As of December 31, 1997	As of December 31, 1996	As of December 31, 1995
BALANCE SHEET DATA			
Total assets	$13,070.6	$13,499.9	$13,643.4
Long-term debt	1,457.2	1,689.8	1,215.5
Stockholders' equity	4,419.4	4,462.4	4,444.7

[a] Includes a net after-tax gain of $43.9 or $0.25 per basic share in 1997; and net charges of $122.3 or $0.70 per basic share in 1996; and $10.1 or $0.06 per basic share in 1995.

Parent Available Information. The Parent is subject to the informational filing requirements of the Exchange Act and, in accordance therewith, is required to file periodic reports, proxy statements and other information with the Commission relating to its business, financial condition and other matters. Information as of particular dates concerning the Parent's directors and officers, their remuneration, stock options granted to them, the principal holders of the Parent's securities and any material interest of such persons in transactions with the Parent is required to be disclosed in proxy statements distributed to the Parent's stockholders and filed with the Commission. Such reports, proxy statements and other information should be available for inspection at the public reference facilities maintained by the Commission at Judiciary Plaza, 450 Fifth Street, N.W., Washington, D.C. 20549, and also should be available for inspection at the Commission's regional offices located at Seven World Trade Center, Suite 1300, New York, New York 10048 and the Citicorp Center, 500 West Madison Street, Suite 1400, Chicago, Illinois 60661. Copies of such materials may also be obtained by mail, upon payment of the Commission's customary fees, by writing to its principal office at Judiciary Plaza, 450 Fifth Street, N.W., Washington, D.C. 20549. The Commission also maintains a World Wide Web site on the Internet at http://www.sec.gov that contains reports, proxy statements and other information regarding registrants that file electronically with the Commission.

9. Financing of the Offer and the Merger. The total amount of funds required by the Purchaser to consummate the Offer and the Merger and to pay related fees and expenses is estimated to be approximately $1.4 billion. The Purchaser will obtain all of such funds from the Parent. The Parent presently intends to utilize available cash and the proceeds from the public sale of debt securities pursuant to its effective shelf registration statement and the private placement of hybrid equity securities. The Parent expects the debt securities to bear interest at prevailing market rates for such instruments at the time of issuance and to have maturities of up to 30 years.

POINT 14: The financing of any offer is of extreme importance. In this case, the total cost of the offer is $1.4 billion in cash. The acquiring company intends to utilize available cash on hand as well as proceeds from a sale of debt securities under a shelf-offering. This is a very secure type of financing. Normally, an acquiring company goes to banks to borrow money. The arbitrageur must then be very careful and should try to determine what stage the financing agreements have reached. In an ideal situation, the documents have been signed and the company has ready access to the cash that will be needed to pay for the target company's stock.

10. Background of the Offer; Contacts with the Company; the Merger Agreement.

POINT 15: The sections describing the background of the offer and the financing of the offer are the most important sections of the document. In this section, we learn details that are generally not disclosed prior to a document's release. One may learn all types of information relating to how the transaction was negotiated and any potential problems that may have occurred along the way. In hostile takeover transactions, we may find information that sheds a whole new light on the history and analysis of the deal. In this particular case, we can see the specific steps that the two companies took in trying to arrive at the definitive agreement. Both sides negotiated back and forth, ultimately arriving at an agreement that resulted in Aluminum Company's making the offer.

By reading about the background of an offer, one can gain tremendous insight into the likelihood of the transaction's completion, as well as the potential for any increase in the price received by the target company's shareholders. If, as in this case, a merger agreement has been reached, many of the specific terms will be detailed, including all conditions that could result in termination of the merger agreement. The arbitrageur should analyze all the potential conditions that would allow the companies to terminate the agreement.

In February 1996, Mr. Paul H. O'Neill, Chairman and Chief Executive Officer of the Parent, called Mr. Allen Born, Chairman and Chief Executive Officer of the Company, to offer the Parent's support and assistance in light of the publicly announced unsolicited acquisition proposal made by Kaiser Aluminum Corporation. Mr. Born told Mr. O'Neill that he appreciated the Parent's support and would let the Parent know if assistance was necessary or appropriate.

During September 1996, Mr. O'Neill and Mr. Born had discussions concerning the acquisition of the Company by the Parent. On October 6, 1996, Mr. O'Neill proposed a merger transaction in which the Company's stockholders would receive .66 of a share of Parent Common Stock which at that time represented a per Share value of $39.88. Mr. Born informed Mr. O'Neill that the Company would not consider the Parent's proposal.

On December 9, 1996, Mr. O'Neill sent the following letter to Mr. Born:

December 9, 1996

Mr. Allen Born
Chairman and C.E.O.
Alumax Inc.
5655 Peachtree Parkway
Norcross, GA 30092-2812

Dear Al:

I am writing to you in an effort to rekindle our discussions of a possible combination of Alumax and Alcoa. As you know, I believe that this combination is so attractive that we should exhaust every possibility to see whether it can be accomplished. As I have reflected on our prior discussions, I believe market movements over the last thirty days make a share-for-share combination even more compelling today than it was last month. For these reasons, I would like once again to outline our proposed transaction and its rationale for what I hope will be favorable consideration by you and your Board of Directors.

As we have discussed and, I believe agreed upon, the market has established a trading range for the shares of our two companies at about .53 Alumax share to 1 Alcoa share. We believe this ratio furnishes a logical basis upon which to develop an appropriate exchange ratio for the combination of the two companies. In light of this historical ratio, our Board of Directors authorized me to pursue a combination through a share exchange in which each Alumax share would be exchanged for .66 of an Alcoa share. Based on the closing prices of Alumax and Alcoa shares last Friday, this represented $41.50 of market value for each Alumax share, or a premium of 32%. In addition, the exchange ratio of .66 represents a 26% premium to the historical ratio of .53.

I would like to point out two special features of the proposed combination. First, your shareholders will receive Alcoa shares tax free and will be able to defer recognizing gain on their Alumax investment until they wish to sell the Alcoa shares they receive. Second, since they will receive Alcoa common stock, your shareholders will have the opportunity to participate in the upside potential of our combined companies. Given the substantial overlap of our very large institutional shareholders, I am confident that they will enthusiastically support our combination on the basis we are proposing.

I also want to emphasize the importance of maintaining stability among employees during a transitional period. It would be our desire to have your employees harmoniously integrated into the Alcoa family. We have significant experience and have achieved excellent success integrating acquired companies into our group, and we have done so on a basis which new employees have found to be an attractive and secure opportunity. We would expect to do the same for Alumax employees.

We hope that you and your Board of Directors will view this proposal as the Alcoa Board of Directors and I do—a unique opportunity for Alumax shareholders to realize full value for their shares while maintaining an enhanced investment in a stronger combined company with superior growth potential. Please let me know if there is anything I can do to help you with your deliberations.

Sincerely,

/s/

Paul H. O'Neill

cc: Members of the Board of Directors

Following receipt of the letter, the Board of Directors of the Company met and determined that the proposal outlined in Mr. O'Neill's December 9, 1996 letter was inadequate. Thereafter, Mr. Born sent the following letter to the Parent:

PERSONAL AND CONFIDENTIAL
December 16, 1996

Mr. Paul H. O'Neill
Chairman of the Board and Chief Executive Officer
Aluminum Company of America
425 Sixth Avenue
Alcoa Building
Pittsburgh, Pennsylvania 15219-1850

Dear Paul:

The Alumax Board of Directors has unanimously determined that it is not in the best interests of Alumax or our shareholders to pursue a business combination at this time and that the financial terms suggested by your proposal are wholly inadequate. None of the Alumax directors is willing to permit Alumax to be sold for an inadequate price at an inopportune time. The Board has full confidence that our strategic plan will result in significant value to our shareholders and believes that the current aluminum price has resulted in an undervaluation of Alumax relative to other aluminum companies.

I trust that with this communication we can continue as before to be friends and vigorous competitors.

Very truly yours,

/s/

Allen Born

cc: Members of the Alumax Board of Directors

In early January 1998, in a telephone conversation with Mr. Born, Mr. O'Neill briefly mentioned their prior discussions, reaffirmed the Parent's interest in a business combination with the Company and suggested they meet to discuss the Parent's interest. Mr. Born told Mr. O'Neill that the Company's position with respect to those discussions had not changed since December 1996. Nonetheless, on January 14, 1998, Mr. Born and Mr. O'Neill met, and Mr. O'Neill discussed with Mr. Born the possibility of merging their two companies in a transaction in which the Company's stockholders would receive .66 of a share of Parent Common Stock. At that time, .66 of a share of Parent Common Stock represented a per Share value of $43.68. Mr. Born and Mr. O'Neill could not reach agreement at that value.

On Thursday, January 29, 1998, Mr. O'Neill telephoned Mr. Born and proposed an acquisition transaction in which the Company's stockholders would receive .66 of a share of Parent Common Stock for each outstanding Share. Mr. O'Neill suggested that the two companies and their advisors proceed with the mechanical steps required to complete a transaction. Mr. Born requested that Mr. O'Neill memorialize the Parent's proposal in a letter which he could share with his Board of Directors. Later that day, Mr. Born called Mr. O'Neill and requested that the Parent's .66 share exchange proposal include collar protection for the Company's stockholders. The following day, Mr. O'Neill called Mr. Born to discuss Mr. Born's request and suggested that the simplest method for dealing with Mr. Born's concern was to offer the Company's stockholders $50 per Share in cash. Mr. Born arranged to receive the letter containing the $50 cash proposal by facsimile transmission at his home early Sunday morning.

On February 1, 1998, the following letter was faxed to Mr. Born:

February 1, 1998

Mr. Allen Born
Chairman and CEO
Alumax Inc.
3424 Peachtree, NE
Suite 2100
Atlanta, GA 30326
Via Fax: x-xxx/xxx-xxxx

Dear Al:

As you requested, I am writing to summarize the economic terms of our proposal for a business combination of Alcoa and Alumax, which we have discussed recently. I understand this will afford you a definitive basis for seeking authorization from your Board of Directors to proceed. In the meantime, let me thank you very much for taking the time and trouble to meet with me on this subject two weeks ago and again to return my telephone call Thursday afternoon in the midst of your travels.

As I told you Thursday, I believe the conditions you outlined in our meeting on January 14 for pursuing a transaction have now been satisfied and we should proceed to sign and announce an agreement as quickly as is possible. Accordingly, Alcoa is prepared to begin documenting and implementing an acquisition of Alumax by Alcoa in which the stockholders of Alumax would receive $50 in cash for each of their shares. This purchase price represents a premium of more than 43% over Friday's closing price for Alumax common shares. Promptly following signature and announcement of the agreement Alcoa would commence a tender offer for all outstanding common shares of Alumax. The tender offer would be subject to customary conditions, including applicable regulatory approvals and receipt of tenders of at least a majority of the outstanding shares on a fully diluted basis.

As I mentioned in our conversation Friday morning, we are prepared to dispatch our transaction team (including outside advisors) to New York promptly in order to accommodate Board meetings as early as Tuesday and an announcement before the opening of the market on Wednesday. We expect that the acquisition agreement would be customary for a transaction of this type and magnitude. We would expect that the agreement would contain appropriate and customary fiduciary termination and transaction "break-up" arrangements. Overall, we see no obstacle to reaching agreement on the form of the agreement promptly, which is, of course, a prerequisite for moving ahead with the proposed transaction.

Maintaining stability among Alumax employees during the transitional period is a very high priority for us. To that end, we would in general expect to provide programs, plans and benefits which in the aggregate should be comparable to what Alumax employees enjoy as a group. We would hope to engender a spirit of enthusiastic anticipation among your employees for an attractive and secure opportunity with Alcoa.

I am confident your Board of Directors will view this proposal as Alcoa's Board of Directors and I do—a unique opportunity for Alumax stockholders to realize a substantial premium for their shares. As I indicated to you on Friday, I would be happy to discuss or clarify any aspect of this letter over the weekend, and I will plan to call you at 10 AM (EST) on Sunday morning February 1. I understand you can be reached at x-xxx/xxx-xxxx. I look forward to talking to you.

Sincerely,

/s/
Paul H. O'Neill

At a meeting attended by each of the Company's directors on February 4, 1998 prior to the regularly scheduled Board meeting to be held the following day, Mr. Born reviewed the proposal set forth in Mr. O'Neill's letter of February 1, 1998. After presentations from the Company's legal and financial advisors, the directors discussed various financial, commercial and regulatory aspects of the proposal among themselves and concluded that Mr. Born should advise Mr. O'Neill that the Company was not interested in entertaining the Parent's proposal at the specified price but would be willing to consider a higher offer. This conclusion was affirmed at the meeting of the Board held on February 5, 1998, following further discussion and consultation with representatives of the Company's financial advisor. Later that day, Mr. Born telephoned Mr. O'Neill and informed him that the Company's Board of Directors declined to pursue the Parent's proposal but would be prepared to discuss a business combination at a higher price. In addition, Mr. Born offered to provide the Parent with non-public evaluation material concerning the Company if the Parent would sign a confidentiality agreement.

The following week Mr. Born telephoned Mr. O'Neill to determine whether the Parent would be willing to enter into the confidentiality agreement and commence an evaluation of the Company. In the meantime, Mr. O'Neill spoke by telephone with two directors of the Company and expressed the Parent's very strong interest in pursuing a transaction with the Company and indicated that, if it would assist the Company's Board with consideration of the Parent's proposal, the Parent was prepared to permit the Company to shop the Parent's proposal and to enter into a transaction with another acquiror at a price higher than the price being offered by the Parent. Mr. O'Neill was informed by one of the directors that offering Parent Common Stock as consideration might be viewed as a more attractive alternative by the Company's Board of Directors than the Parent's cash proposal.

On Thursday, February 19, 1998, Mr. O'Neill and Mr. Richard B. Kelson, Executive Vice President and Chief Financial Officer of the Parent, met with Messrs. Born, Harold Brown and Paul W. MacAvoy, two of the Company's directors, and Thomas G. Johnston, President and Chief Operating Officer of the Company, to discuss generally the Parent's proposal. They discussed the merits of a business combination, the value of such a combination to the Parent and the appropriate level of consideration for such a transaction. The Parent's representatives emphasized their view that at $50 per Share the transaction was fully priced and that the Parent remained prepared to permit the Company to shop the Company and to seek a transaction at a price higher than $50 per Share. The Parent's representatives also indicated that the Parent was prepared to offer half cash and half Parent Common Stock as the consideration for the transaction. The Company's representatives informed the Parent's representatives that they would reply to the proposal after consulting with all of the Company's directors the next week.

On Wednesday, February 25, 1998, Mr. Born telephoned Mr. O'Neill to inform him that the Board had rejected the Parent's proposal. That same day he also sent the following letter to Mr. O'Neill:

February 25, 1998

Mr. Paul O'Neill
Chairman and CEO
Aluminum Company of America
Alcoa Building
425 Sixth Avenue
Pittsburgh, PA 15219-1850

Dear Paul:

As I have previously advised you, I have again reviewed with our Board your unsolicited offer of $50 a share in cash or ALCOA stock for each share of Alumax stock. We believe this offer is inadequate and unacceptable.

Having said that, I reiterate to you our willingness to discuss a transaction between our companies at a price significantly higher than you proposed.

Sincerely,

/s/
Allen Born
Chairman and Chief Executive Officer

On Monday, March 2, 1998, Mr. O'Neill spoke by telephone in separate conversations with two members of the Company's Board and discussed the Company's rejection of the Parent's proposal. Mr. O'Neill reiterated his strong belief in the timeliness of a combination, the desirability of the proposed transaction from the Company's stockholders' point of view and, in particular, the desirability of offering those stockholders the chance to exchange a part of their investment into Parent Common Stock. The directors indicated that they believed the Parent's proposal should be discussed at the meeting of the directors on Wednesday evening and the regularly scheduled Board meeting on Thursday of that week and that a brief explanation of the desirability of the transaction and the opportunity to invest in the Parent Common Stock might be helpful.

In response to the directors' comments described above, on Wednesday, March 4, 1998, the Parent provided the following list of "talking points" to one of the directors for use at the Board meeting:

- Merger of Alumax with Alcoa
  - Approximately ½ the outstanding Alumax shares exchanged for $50 worth of Alcoa stock
  - Remaining shares exchanged for $50 in cash
- Merger Agreement provides floor against which to seek superior economics elsewhere

- No limit on post-signature shopping of Alumax
- The Agreement may be terminated with "fiduciary out"
- No requirement for breakup fee if company sold elsewhere for more money
- Attractive premium
  - $50—35.6% over yesterday's closing price
  - Share portion—Exchange at 39.9% premium to historical trading ratio for last 12 months
- Historical trading ratios—Alumax/Alcoa
  - 3 years—.55
  - 2 years—.51
  - 1 year—.49
  - 6 months—.48
- Alcoa's higher, more consistent margins (EBIT/Revenues)

	Alcoa	Alumax
1997	12.2%	10.0%
1996	10.8%	7.3%
1995	12.7%	10.5%

- Annual dividend
  - Alcoa current dividend $1.00 plus 30% of net income over $3 per share—$1.50 per share in 1998
  - Alumax currently pays no dividend
- Alcoa's premium price-to-earnings trading multiple
  - 13.1 times vs. 11.7 times estimated 1998 net income
  - 9.8 times vs. 8.3 times estimated 1999 net income
- Alcoa's greater trading liquidity
  - Approximately 6.6 times the average daily dollar volume of Alumax
- Alcoa's superior balance sheet strength
  - Alumax—NR/BBB
  - Alcoa—A1/A+

During the meeting of directors on the evening of March 4, the Company's directors concluded that Mr. Born and certain other representatives of the Company should meet with Mr. O'Neill to discuss and obtain clarification of the Parent's proposal. Mr. O'Neill was called that evening and a meeting was scheduled for the following afternoon. Mr. O'Neill was asked to be prepared to present the Parent's proposal in writing at the meeting. At its regularly scheduled Board meeting on March 5, the Company's Board again considered the factors discussed the prior evening. After lengthy discussion, the Board formally authorized management to pursue the proposal. That afternoon Messrs. O'Neill, Alain J.P. Belda, President and Chief Operating Officer of the Parent, and Kelson met with Messrs. Born, Johnston and Brown and presented the following letter to them:

March 5, 1998

The Board of Directors
Alumax Inc.
3424 Peachtree Road, NE
Atlanta, GA 30326

Lady and Gentlemen:

    This letter is to formalize the discussions we have been having concerning a transaction between Alumax and Alcoa as requested. Alcoa is prepared to proceed immediately with a merger transaction in which approximately one-half the total number of outstanding Alumax shares would be exchanged for $50 worth of Alcoa stock and the remaining shares would be exchanged for $50 in cash. The merger agreement would contain no limitation on your ability to shop the company and would permit termination on fiduciary grounds with no requirement to pay a break-up fee if you were able to sell the company to someone else for more money. We would expect to structure the transaction in two steps, commencing with a cash tender offer and finishing with a merger in which the remaining shares are converted into Alcoa stock. We assume you would like to negotiate a reasonable collar and market test period for the stock portion of the consideration, and we are prepared to do that with you. The agreement would provide for a cash out of all options. The transaction will be subject only to usual and customary conditions.

    In our discussions with your Chairman and certain other of your members we have discussed a variety of considerations for Alumax stockholders which would lead them to conclude that our proposal is one they should accept, and, in particular, that the opportunity to convert a portion of their investment in Alumax into an investment in a combined Alcoa and Alumax is especially attractive. We hope you will give special weight and attention to the following factors which strongly favor an investment in Alcoa compared with an investment in Alumax alone:

- Attractive premium
    - $50—37.2% over yesterday's closing price
    - Share portion—Exchange at 42.4% premium to one-year historical trading ratio
- Historical trading ratios—Alumax/Alcoa
    - 3 years—.55
    - 2 years—.51
    - 1 year—.49
    - 6 months—.48
- Alcoa's higher, more consistent margins (EBIT/Revenues)

	Alcoa	Alumax
1997	12.2%	10.0%
1996	10.8%	7.3%
1995	12.7%	10.5%

- Annual dividend
  - Alcoa current dividend $1.00 plus 30% of net income over $3 per share—$1.50 per share in 1998
  - Alumax currently pays no dividend
- Alcoa's premium price-to-earnings trading multiple
  - 12.8 times vs. 11.6 times estimated 1998 net income
  - 9.6 times vs. 8.2 times estimated 1999 net income
- Alcoa's greater trading liquidity
  - Approximately 6.6 times the average daily dollar volume of Alumax
- Alcoa's superior balance sheet strength
  - Alumax—NR/BBB
  - Alcoa—A1/A+

Our transaction team is present and available in New York to take steps necessary to permit a press release on Sunday and an announcement before the opening on Monday.

Sincerely,

/s/
Paul H. O'Neill

BY HAND DELIVERY

In the course of the discussions of the proposal set forth in the March 5 letter, the Company's representatives requested that there be a fixed exchange ratio for the stock portion of the consideration based on the prior day's closing market price of the Parent Common Stock so that the value of this portion of the consideration payable in the transaction would fluctuate with future changes in the market price of the Parent Common Stock. In the course of the negotiations the Parent representatives agreed to a fixed exchange ratio at .6975. The parties also agreed in principle that subject to Board approvals and to negotiation and execution of a satisfactory form of merger agreement they were prepared to proceed with a transaction. Thursday evening, the Parent's representatives delivered a draft merger agreement to the Company's representatives. On Friday, March 6, the Company requested a new letter revising certain provisions in the letter delivered on Thursday, including changes to reflect the Exchange Ratio and to provide that all Company stock options would be "rolled over" into options to acquire Parent Common Stock—which the Parent delivered that afternoon.

On Friday, March 6, the Parent's Board of Directors met and authorized management to negotiate the final documentation for the transactions contemplated by the Merger Agreement. That same day the Company's Board convened for an informational meeting and the directors agreed that the Company should proceed to negotiate a definitive agreement incorporating the proposal set forth in the Parent's March 6th letter. Negotiation of the definitive acquisition agreement continued throughout Friday, Saturday and Sunday.

On Saturday, March 7, the Company's Board met and approved in principle the transaction outlined in the revised letter delivered by the Parent on March 6, subject to the completion of the negotiation of an acceptable definitive acquisition agreement.

On Sunday, March 8, the Company's Board of Directors met and approved the transactions contemplated by the Merger Agreement. The Merger Agreement was thereafter executed and delivered on March 8, 1998.

THE MERGER AGREEMENT

The following is a summary of the Merger Agreement, a copy of which is filed as an Exhibit to the Tender Offer Statement on Schedule 14D-1 (the "Schedule 14D-1") filed by the Purchaser and the Parent with the Commission in connection with the Offer. Such summary is qualified in its entirety by reference to the Merger Agreement.

The Offer. The Merger Agreement provides for the making of the Offer as provided in this Offer to Purchase.

The Merger. The Merger Agreement provides that, upon the terms and subject to the conditions thereof and in accordance with the DGCL, the Company shall merge with and into the Purchaser and the separate corporate existence of the Company will thereupon cease, and the Purchaser will be the Surviving Corporation in the Merger. Upon consummation of the Merger, each Share that is owned by the Parent, the Purchaser, any of their respective subsidiaries, the Company or any subsidiary of the Company shall automatically be cancelled and retired and shall cease to exist, and no consideration shall be delivered in exchange therefor. Each issued and outstanding Share, other than Excluded Shares (as hereinafter defined) and Dissenting Shares, shall be converted into, and become exchangeable for the right to receive: (A) 0.6975 of a share of Parent Common Stock if the Purchaser purchased no fewer than the 50% Share Number of Shares in the Offer; or (B) that fraction of a share of Parent Common Stock equal to the Adjusted Exchange Ratio plus an amount in cash equal to the Merger Cash Prorate Amount, if the Purchaser purchased fewer than the 50% Number of Shares in the Offer. The term "Excluded Shares" means that number of Shares owned by the Parent and its subsidiaries immediately prior to the Effective Time (excluding Shares held by the Company and its subsidiaries). The Merger Agreement provides that if, prior to the Effective Time, the Parent effects a change in the number of shares of Parent Common Stock or securities convertible or exchangeable into or exercisable therefor, the Merger Consideration will be equitably adjusted.

Charter Documents; Initial Directors and Officers. The Merger Agreement provides that, at the Effective Time, the Certificate of Incorporation of the Purchaser, as in effect immediately prior to the Effective Time, will be the Certificate of Incorporation of the Surviving Corporation; provided, however, that Article FIRST of the Certificate of Incorporation of the Surviving Corporation will be amended in its entirety to read as follows: "FIRST: The name of the corporation is Alumax Inc." The Merger Agreement also provides that, at the Effective Time the By-laws of the Purchaser, as in effect immediately prior to the Effective Time, will be the By-laws of the Surviving Corporation. Pursuant to the Merger Agreement, the directors of the Purchaser at the Effective Time will be the directors of the Surviving Corporation, and the officers of the Purchaser at the Effective Time will be the officers of the Surviving Corporation, in each case, until their respective successors are duly elected and qualified or their earlier death, resignation or removal in accordance with the Certificate of Incorporation and By-laws of the Surviving Corporation.

Stockholders' Meeting. The Merger Agreement provides that as promptly as practicable following the date of the Merger Agreement, the Company, acting through its Board of Directors, will, in accordance with applicable law duly call, give notice of, convene and hold the Company Special Meeting for the purposes of considering and taking action upon the approval of the Merger and the approval and adoption of the Merger Agreement.

Filings. The Merger Agreement provides that the Company will, as promptly as practicable following the date of the Merger Agreement, prepare and file with the Commission a preliminary proxy or information statement relating to the Merger and the Merger Agreement and will cause a definitive proxy or information statement, including any amendment or supplement thereto (the "Proxy Statement") to be mailed to its stockholders at the earliest practicable date after the Registration Statement (as hereinafter defined) is declared effective by the Commission. In addition, the Merger Agreement obligates the Company to use its reasonable best efforts to obtain the necessary approvals of the Merger and the Merger Agreement by its stockholders. The Company has agreed that unless the Merger Agreement has been terminated in accordance with its terms it will include in the Proxy Statement the recommendation of the Board that stockholders of the Company vote in favor of the approval of the Merger and the approval and adoption of the Merger Agreement; provided, however, that if the Board of Directors of the Company, based on the advice of outside legal counsel, determines in good faith that there is an Acquisition Proposal (as hereinafter defined) which is a Superior Proposal (as hereinafter defined) and it is necessary for the Board of Directors of the Company in order to avoid breaching its fiduciary duties to the Company's stockholders under applicable law, the Board may amend or withdraw its recommendation.

The Merger Agreement provides that the Parent shall as promptly as practicable following the date of the Merger Agreement prepare and file with the Commission a registration statement (the "Registration Statement"), in which the Proxy Statement shall be included as a prospectus, and shall use its reasonable best efforts to have the Registration Statement declared effective by the Commission as promptly as practicable.

Conduct of Business Pending the Merger. Pursuant to the Merger Agreement, the Company has agreed that, from and after the date of the Merger Agreement and prior to the Effective Time or the date, if any, on which the Merger Agreement is earlier terminated pursuant to the terms and conditions thereof, and except as may be agreed in writing by the other parties to the Merger Agreement or as may be expressly permitted pursuant to the Merger Agreement, the Company:

(i) will, and will cause each of its subsidiaries to, conduct its operations according to their ordinary and usual course of business in substantially the same manner as conducted prior to the date of the Merger Agreement;

(ii) will use its reasonable best efforts, and cause each of its subsidiaries to use its reasonable best efforts, to preserve intact its business organization and goodwill, keep available the services of its current officers and other key employees and preserve its relationships with those persons having business dealings with the Company and its subsidiaries;

(iii) will confer at such times as the Parent may reasonably request with one or more representatives of the Parent to report material operational matters and the general status of ongoing operations;

(iv) will notify the Parent of any emergency or other change in the normal course of its or its subsidiaries' respective businesses or in the operation of its or its subsidiaries' respective properties and of any complaints or hearings (or communications indicating that the same may be contemplated) of any governmental entity, if such emergency, change, complaint, investigation or hearing would have a Material Adverse Effect (as defined in the Merger Agreement) on the Company;

(v) will not, and will not permit any of its subsidiaries that is not wholly owned to, authorize or pay any dividends on or make any distribution with respect to its outstanding shares of stock;

(vi) will not, and will not permit any of its subsidiaries to, except as otherwise provided in the Merger Agreement, establish, enter into or amend any employee benefit plan or increase the compensation payable or to become payable or the benefits provided to its officers or employees, subject to certain exceptions;

(vii) subject to certain exceptions will not, and will not permit any of its subsidiaries to, authorize, propose or announce an intention to authorize or propose, or enter into an agreement with respect to, any merger, consolidation or business combination (other than the Merger), any acquisition or disposition of an amount of assets or securities, in each case in excess of $1 million, except (x) for the sale of goods and products manufactured by the Company and held for sale in the ordinary course and (y) certain expenditures not in excess of $150 million in the aggregate;

(viii) will not, and will not permit any of its subsidiaries to, propose or adopt any amendments to its certificate of incorporation or by-laws (or other similar organizational documents);

(ix) will not, and will not permit any of its subsidiaries to, issue or authorize the issuance of, or agree to issue or sell any shares of capital stock of any class (whether through the issuance or granting of options, warrants, commitments, subscriptions, rights to purchase or otherwise) other than certain issuances expressly permitted by the Merger Agreement;

(x) will not, and will not permit any of its subsidiaries to, reclassify, combine, split, purchase or redeem any shares of its capital stock or purchase or redeem any rights, warrants or options to acquire any such shares;

(xi) other than in the ordinary course of business consistent with past practice, will not, and will not permit any of its subsidiaries to, (a) incur, assume or prepay any indebtedness or any other material liabilities or issue any debt securities, or (b) assume, guarantee, endorse or otherwise become liable or responsible (whether directly, contingently or otherwise) for the obligations of any other person, other than guarantees of obligations of wholly owned subsidiaries of the Company in the ordinary course of business;

(xii) will not, and will not permit any of its subsidiaries to, (a) sell, lease, license, mortgage or otherwise encumber or subject to any lien or otherwise dispose of any of its properties or assets (including securitizations), other than in the ordinary course of business consistent with past practice; (b) modify, amend or terminate any of its material contracts or waive, release or assign any material rights (contract or other); or (c) permit any insurance policy naming it as a beneficiary or a loss payable payee to lapse, be cancelled for reasons within the Company's control or expire unless a new policy with substantially identical coverage is in effect as of the date of lapse, cancellation or expiration;

(xiii) will not, and will not permit any of its subsidiaries to, (a) make any material tax election or settle or compromise any material tax liability or (b) change any of the accounting methods used by it unless required by GAAP; and

(xiv) will not, and will not permit any of its subsidiaries to, agree, in writing or otherwise, to take any of the foregoing actions or knowingly take any action which would (y) make any representation or warranty in the Merger Agreement untrue or incorrect in any material respect or (z) result in any of the conditions to the Offer set forth in "Section 14. Conditions to the Offer" or any of the conditions to the Merger set forth in the Merger Agreement not being satisfied.

Directors. The Merger Agreement provides that, promptly upon the purchase of and payment for any Shares by the Purchaser or any of its affiliates pursuant to the Offer, the Parent will be entitled to designate such number of directors, rounded up to the next whole number, on the Board of Directors of the Company as is equal to the product obtained by multiplying the total number of directors on such Board (giving effect to the directors designated by the Parent pursuant to this sentence) by the percentage that the number of Shares so accepted for payment bears to the total number of Shares then outstanding. In furtherance thereof, the Merger Agreement provides that the Company is obligated, upon request of the Purchaser, to increase promptly the size of its Board of Directors or exercise its best efforts to secure the resignations of such number of directors, or both, as is necessary to enable the Parent's designees to be so elected to the Company's Board and will cause the Parent's designees to be so elected. The Company has agreed that, at such time, the Company will, if requested by the Parent, cause directors designated by the Parent to constitute at least the same percentage (rounded up to the next whole number) as is on the Company's Board of Directors of (i) each committee of the Company's Board of Directors, (ii) each board of directors (or similar body) of each Significant Subsidiary (as defined in the Merger Agreement) of the Company, and (iii) each committee (or similar body) of each such board. Notwithstanding the foregoing, if Shares are purchased pursuant to the Offer, the Merger Agreement requires there be at least one member of the Company's Board of Directors who was a director on the date of the Merger Agreement and is not an employee of the Company until the Effective Time.

Solicitation by the Company. The Merger Agreement provides that nothing contained in the Merger Agreement prohibits the Board of Directors of the Company from furnishing information to, or entering into discussions with, any Person that makes a bona fide Acquisition Proposal. The term "Acquisition Proposal" as defined in the Merger Agreement means any tender or exchange offer involving the capital stock of the Company or any of its subsidiaries, any proposal or offer to acquire in any manner a substantial equity interest in, or a substantial portion of the business or assets of, the Company or any of its subsidiaries, any proposal or offer with respect to any merger, consolidation, business combination, recapitalization, liquidation, dissolution or restructuring of or involving the Company or any of its subsidiaries, or any proposal or offer with respect to any other transaction similar to any of the foregoing with respect to the Company or any of its subsidiaries, other than the transactions contemplated by the Merger Agreement. Additionally, the Merger Agreement provides that nothing contained in the Merger Agreement prohibits the Company from taking and disclosing to its stockholders a position contemplated by Rule 14e-2(a) promulgated under the Exchange Act or from making any disclosure to the Company's stockholders if the Board of Directors of the Company determines in good faith, after consultation with outside legal counsel, that it is necessary to do so in order to avoid breaching its fiduciary duties under applicable law; provided, however, that neither the Company nor its Board of Directors nor any committee thereof may withdraw or modify, or propose publicly to withdraw or modify, its position with respect to the Merger Agreement, the Offer or the Merger, or approve or recommend, or propose publicly to approve or recommend, an Acquisition Proposal, except if, and only to the extent that, the Board of Directors of the Company, based on the advice of outside legal counsel, determines in good faith that such Acquisition Proposal is a bona fide Acquisition Proposal made by a third party to acquire, directly or indirectly, 20% or more of the outstanding Shares on a fully diluted basis or all or substantially all the assets of the Company and its subsidiaries and otherwise on terms and conditions which the Board of Directors of the Company determines in good faith, after consultation with and based upon the written opinion of its financial advisor, to be a superior financial alternative to the stockholders of the Company than the Offer and the Merger (a "Superior Proposal") and that such action is necessary for the Board of Directors of the Company to avoid breaching its fiduciary duties to the Company's stockholders under applicable law; and provided, further, that the Board is not required to violate applicable laws.

Directors' and Officers' Indemnification. The Merger Agreement provides that from and after the Effective Time, the Parent will indemnify and hold harmless each present and former director and officer of the Company and its subsidiaries (the "Indemnified Parties"), against any costs or expenses (including attorneys' fees), judgments, fines, losses, claims, damages or liabilities incurred in connection with any claim, action, suit, proceeding or investigation, whether civil, criminal, administrative or investigative, arising out of or pertaining to matters existing or occurring at or prior to the Effective Time, to the fullest extent that the Company or such subsidiary would have been permitted under applicable law and the Certificate of Incorporation or By-laws of the Company or such subsidiary in effect on the date of the Merger Agreement to indemnify such person (and the Parent shall also advance expenses as incurred to the fullest extent permitted under applicable law provided the Person to whom expenses are advanced provides an undertaking to repay such advances if it is ultimately determined that such Person is not entitled to indemnification).

Employee Stock Options. The Merger Agreement provides that simultaneously with the Merger, (i) each outstanding option (the "Company Stock Options") to purchase or acquire a Share under employee incentive or benefit plans, programs or arrangements and non-employee director plans presently maintained by the Company (the "Company Option Plans") will be converted into an option to purchase the number of shares of Parent Common Stock equal to the product of (x) the Exchange Ratio multiplied by (y) the number of Shares which could have been issued prior to the Effective Time upon the exercise of such option, at an exercise price per share (rounded upward to the nearest cent) equal to the exercise price for each Share subject to such option divided by the Exchange Ratio, and all references in each such option to the Company will be deemed to refer to the Parent, where appropriate, provided, however, that with respect to any option which is an "incentive stock option," within the meaning of Section 422 of the Code, such adjustments shall, if applicable, be modified in a manner so that the adjustments are consistent with requirements of Section 424(a) of the Code, and (ii) the Parent will assume the obligations of the Company under the Company Option Plans. The Merger Agreement also provides that the other terms of each such option, and the plans under which they were issued, will continue to apply in accordance with their terms, including any provisions providing for acceleration and that at or prior to the Effective Time, the Parent has agreed to take all corporate action necessary to reserve for issuance a sufficient number of shares of Parent Common Stock for delivery upon exercise of Company Stock Options assumed by it in accordance with the Merger Agreement. The Parent has agreed that, as soon as practicable after the Effective Time, if necessary, it will file a registration statement on Form S-8 (or any successor or other appropriate forms), or another appropriate form with respect to the shares of Parent Common Stock subject to such Company Stock Options, and will use its best efforts to maintain the effectiveness of such registration statement (and maintain the current status of the prospectus or prospectuses contained therein) for so long as the former Company Stock Options remain outstanding.

Representations and Warranties. The Merger Agreement contains various customary representations and warranties of the parties thereto including representations by the Company as to the Company's corporate organization and qualification, capital stock, corporate authority, filings with the Commission and other governmental authorities, financial statements, litigation, employee matters, employment benefit matters, intellectual property, tax matters, environmental matters, compliance with law, the absence of certain changes or events, opinion of financial advisor and undisclosed liabilities.

Conditions to Consummation of the Merger. The Merger Agreement provides that the respective obligations of each party to effect the Merger are subject to the following conditions: (a) the Merger Agreement and the transactions contemplated thereby will have been approved and adopted by the affirmative vote of the holders of a majority of the outstanding Shares; (b) no statute, rule, regulation, executive order, decree, ruling or injunction will have been enacted, entered, promulgated or enforced by any Governmental Entity (as defined in the Merger Agreement) which prohibits the consummation of the Merger substantially on the terms contemplated in the Merger Agreement or has the effect of making the acquisition of Shares by the Parent or the Purchaser or any affiliate of either of them illegal; (c) the Parent or the Purchaser or any affiliate of either of them have purchased Shares pursuant to the Offer, except that this condition will not apply if the Parent, the Purchaser or such affiliate has failed to purchase Shares pursuant to the Offer in breach of their obligations under the Merger Agreement; (d) the applicable waiting period under the HSR Act shall have expired or been terminated; (e) the shares of Parent Common Stock to be issued in the Merger will have been approved for listing on the NYSE, subject to official notice of issuance and (f) the Registration Statement shall have become effective in accordance with the provisions of the Securities Act of 1933, as amended. In addition, the Merger Agreement provides (i) that the obligation of the Parent and the Purchaser to effect the Merger shall be subject to the receipt by the Parent of an opinion of Skadden, Arps, Slate, Meagher & Flom LLP, tax counsel to the Parent, dated as of the Effective Time, to the effect that the Merger will qualify as a reorganization within the meaning of Section 368(a) of the Code and that (ii) that the obligation of the Company to effect the Merger shall be subject to the receipt by the Company of an opinion of Sullivan & Cromwell, tax counsel to the Company, dated as of the Effective Time, to the effect that the Merger will qualify as a reorganization within the meaning of Section 368(a) of the Code.

The Merger Agreement also provides that, in the event that the Purchaser purchases a number of Shares in the Offer which is less than the 50% Share Number, the respective obligations of the Parent and the Purchaser and the Company to effect the Merger shall be subject to the fulfillment at or prior to the Effective Time of the following conditions, unless waived in writing by the party to which the condition applies or unless the Company Stockholder Approval is obtained prior thereto, in which event such conditions will thereupon be deemed fulfilled: (i) that the representations and warranties of the other party or parties, as the case may be, set forth in the Merger Agreement will be true and correct, ignoring for this purpose any qualification as to materiality or Material Adverse Effect, as if such representations or warranties were made as of the Effective Time, except for such inaccuracies as, individually or in the aggregate, would not have a Material Adverse Effect on such party or parties, (ii) that the other party will have performed and complied in all material respects with all agreements, obligations and conditions required by the Merger Agreement to be performed and complied with by it on or prior to the closing date and (iii) that such party or parties will have furnished a certificate of an officer to evidence compliance with the conditions set forth in clauses (i) and (ii) of this sentence.

Termination. The Merger Agreement may be terminated and the Merger and the other transactions contemplated thereby may be abandoned at any time prior to the Effective Time, notwithstanding any requisite approval by the stockholders of the Company: (a) by mutual written consent of the Parent, the Purchaser and the Company; (b) by either the Parent or the Company if (i) (1) the Offer has expired without any Shares being purchased pursuant thereto, or (2) the Offer has not been consummated on or before September 30, 1998 (the "Termination Date"); provided, however, that such right to terminate the Merger Agreement is not available to any party whose failure to fulfill any obligation under the Merger Agreement has been the cause of, or resulted in, the failure of the Shares to have been purchased pursuant to the Offer; (ii) a statute, rule, regulation or executive order has been enacted, entered or promulgated prohibiting the consummation of the Offer or the Merger substantially on the terms contemplated by the Merger Agreement; or (iii) an order, decree, ruling or injunction has been entered permanently restraining, enjoining or otherwise prohibiting the consummation of the Offer or the Merger substantially on the terms contemplated by the Merger Agreement and such order, decree, ruling or injunction has become final and nonappealable; provided further that the Termination Date will be extended by one business day for each business day which elapses from March 16, 1998, until the date upon which the applicable filings under the HSR Act are made by the Company with the appropriate governmental entity; (c) by the Parent, (i) if due to an occurrence or circumstance, other than as a result of a breach by the Parent or the Purchaser of its obligations hereunder, resulting in a failure to satisfy any condition set forth in "Section 14. Conditions to the Merger," hereto, the Purchaser has (1) failed to commence the Offer within 30 days following the date of the Merger Agreement, or (2) terminated the Offer without having accepted any Shares for payment thereunder; or (ii) if either the Parent or the Purchaser is entitled to terminate the Offer as a result of the occurrence of any event set forth in paragraph (e) of "Section 14. Conditions to the Merger" hereto; (d) by the Company, upon approval of its Board of Directors, if due to an occurrence or circumstance, other than as a result of a breach by the Company of its obligations under the Merger Agreement, that would result in a failure to satisfy any of the conditions set forth in "Section 14. Conditions to the Merger," hereto, the Purchaser terminates the Offer without having accepted any Shares for payment thereunder; (e) by the Company, if the Company receives a Superior Proposal and the Board of Directors of the Company, based on the advice of outside legal counsel, determines in good faith that such action is necessary for the Board of Directors to avoid breaching its fiduciary duties to the Company's stockholders under applicable law; or (f) by the Parent or the Company, if after the Company convenes and holds the Company Special Meeting and certifies the vote with respect to the Merger, the Company's stockholders have voted against granting the Company Stockholder Approval.

POINT 16: *The arbitrageur must pay close attention to all the terms that allow the parties to terminate the transaction.*

Fees and Expenses. The Merger Agreement provides that except as expressly contemplated by the Merger Agreement, all costs and expenses incurred in connection therewith and the transactions contemplated thereby shall be paid by the party incurring such costs and expenses.

Amendment. At any time prior to the Effective Time, the Merger Agreement may be amended or supplemented in any and all respects, whether before or after Company Stockholder Approval, by written agreement of the parties thereto, by action taken by their respective Boards of Directors (which, following the election of the Parent's designees upon consummation of the Offer, in the case of the Company, will require the concurrence of a majority of the directors of the Company then in office who were neither designated by the Parent nor are employees of the Company), with respect to any of the terms contained in the Merger

Agreement; provided, however that following the Company Stockholder Approval there shall be no amendment or change to the provisions thereof which would reduce the amount or change the type of consideration into which each Share shall be converted upon consummation of the Merger without further approval by the stockholders of the Company.

11. Purpose of the Offer; Plans for the Company after the Offer and the Merger.

Purpose of the Offer. The purpose of the Offer is for the Purchaser to acquire a majority of the outstanding Shares as a first step in acquiring the entire equity interest in the Company. The purpose of the Merger is for the Purchaser to acquire all Shares not acquired pursuant to the Offer. Assuming that all the conditions to the Merger are satisfied, pursuant to the Merger, the Company will be merged with and into the Purchaser, with the Purchaser surviving the Merger as a direct, wholly owned subsidiary of the Parent. The Offer is being made pursuant to the Merger Agreement.

Under the DGCL, the approval of the Company's Board and the affirmative vote of the holders of a majority of the outstanding Shares are required to approve and adopt the Merger Agreement and the transactions contemplated thereby, including the Merger. The Board of Directors of the Company has unanimously (with one director absent) approved the Merger Agreement and the transactions contemplated thereby and determined that the terms of the Offer and the Merger are fair to, and in the best interests of, the Company and its stockholders. The only remaining required corporate action of the Company is the approval and adoption of the Merger Agreement and the transactions contemplated thereby by the affirmative vote of the holders of a majority of the Shares. In the Merger Agreement, the Company has agreed to duly call, give notice of, convene and hold a special meeting of its stockholders as promptly as practicable after the date of the Merger Agreement for the purpose of considering and taking action on the Merger Agreement and the transactions contemplated thereby.

The Purchaser has agreed that all Shares owned by it and any of its affiliates will be voted in favor of the Merger Agreement and the transactions contemplated thereby.

If the Purchaser purchases Shares pursuant to the Offer, the Merger Agreement provides that the Parent will be entitled to designate representatives to serve on the Board of the Company substantially in proportion to the Purchaser's ownership of Shares following such purchase. See "Section 10. Background of the Offer; Contacts with the Company; the Merger Agreement." If the Purchaser purchases a number of Shares greater than or equal to the 50% Share Number, the Purchaser expects that such representation would permit the Parent effectively to control the Company's conduct of its business and operations.

Appraisal Rights. No appraisal rights are available in connection with the Offer. If a number of Shares less than the 50% Share Number is purchased pursuant to the Offer, a portion of the Merger Consideration will be paid in cash as described in "Introduction." In such event, stockholders of the Company will have certain rights under the DGCL to dissent and demand appraisal of, and to receive payment in cash of the fair value of, their Shares. Such rights, if the statutory procedures are complied with, could lead to a judicial determination of the fair value (excluding any element of value arising from the accomplishment or expectation of the Merger) required to be paid in cash to such dissenting holders for their Shares. Any such judicial determination of the fair value of Shares could be based upon considerations other than or in addition to the price paid in the Offer and the market value of the Shares, including asset values and the investment value of the Shares. The value so determined could be more or less than the purchase price per Share pursuant to the Offer or the consideration per Share to be paid in the Merger.

In addition, several decisions by Delaware courts have held that, in certain instances, a controlling stockholder of a corporation involved in a merger has a fiduciary duty to the other stockholders that requires the merger to be fair to such other stockholders. In determining whether a merger is fair to minority stockholders, the Delaware courts have considered, among other things, the type and amount of consideration to be received by the stockholders and whether there were fair dealings among the parties. The Delaware Supreme Court has indicated in recent decisions that in most cases the remedy available in a merger that is found not to be "fair" to minority stockholders is the right to appraisal described above or a damages remedy based on essentially the same principles.

The foregoing summary of the rights of dissenting stockholders does not purport to be a complete statement of the procedures to be followed by stockholders desiring to exercise their appraisal rights. The preservation and exercise of appraisal rights are conditioned on strict adherence to the applicable provisions of the DGCL.

Plans for the Company. It is expected that, initially following the Merger, the business and operations of the Company will, except as set forth in this Offer to Purchase, be continued substantially as they are currently being conducted. The Parent will continue to evaluate the business and operations of the Company during the pendency of the Offer and after the consummation of the Offer and the Merger and will take such actions as it deems appropriate under the circumstances then existing. The Parent intends to seek additional information about the Company during this period. Thereafter, the Parent intends to review such information as part of a comprehensive review of the Company's business, operations, capitalization and management with a view to optimizing development of the Company's potential in conjunction with the Parent's businesses.

Except as indicated in this Offer to Purchase, the Parent does not have any present plans or proposals which relate to or would result in an extraordinary corporate transaction, such as a merger, reorganization or liquidation, involving the Company or any Company subsidiary, a sale or transfer of a material amount of assets of the Company or any Company subsidiary or any material change in the Company's capitalization or dividend policy or any other material changes in the Company's corporate structure or business.

12. Dividends and Distributions. The Company has not paid cash dividends to date and has advised the Parent that it intends to retain future earnings for use in the business.

The Merger Agreement provides that between the date of the Merger Agreement and the Effective Time, without the prior written consent of the Parent, the Company, (a) will not, and will not permit any of its subsidiaries that is not wholly owned to, authorize or pay any dividends on or make any distribution with respect to its outstanding shares of stock; (b) will not, and will not permit any of its subsidiaries to, issue or authorize the issuance of, or agree to issue or sell any shares of capital stock of any class (whether through the issuance or granting of options, warrants, commitments, subscriptions, rights to purchase or otherwise) except for certain issuances expressly provided for in the Merger Agreement; or (c) will not, and will not permit any of its subsidiaries to, reclassify, combine, split, purchase or redeem any shares of its capital stock or purchase or redeem any rights, warrants or options to acquire any such shares.

13. Effect of the Offer on the Market for the Shares, Exchange Listing; Exchange Act Registration. The purchase of Shares by the Purchaser pursuant to the Offer will reduce the number of Shares that might otherwise trade publicly and will reduce the number of holders of Shares, which could adversely affect the liquidity and market value of the remaining Shares held by the public. The Parent believes, however, that, following the consummation of the Offer, the Shares will continue to meet the standards for continued listing on the NYSE.

The Shares are currently "margin securities," as such term is defined under the rules of the Board of Governors of the Federal Reserve System, which has the effect, among other things, of allowing brokers to extend credit on the collateral of such securities. It is likely that the Shares will continue to be "margin securities" following consummation of the Offer.

The Shares are currently registered under the Exchange Act. Such registration may be terminated upon application by the Company to the Commission if the Shares are not listed on a national securities exchange and there are fewer than 300 record holders. The termination of the registration of the Shares under the Exchange Act would substantially reduce the information required to be furnished by the Company to holders of Shares and to the Commission and would make certain provisions of the Exchange Act, such as the short-swing profit recovery provisions of Section 16(b), the requirement of furnishing a proxy statement in connection with stockholders' meetings and the requirements of Rule 13e-3 under the Exchange Act with respect to "going private" transactions, no longer applicable to the Shares. In addition, "affiliates" of the Company and persons holding "restricted securities" of the Company may be deprived of the ability to dispose of such securities pursuant to Rule 144 promulgated under the Securities Act of 1933, as amended. If registration of the Shares under the Exchange Act were terminated, the Shares would no longer be "margin securities" or be eligible for NYSE listing. The Purchaser currently intends to seek to cause the Company to terminate the registration of the Shares under the Exchange Act as soon after consummation of the Offer as the requirements for termination of registration are met. However, the Parent does not believe that the Company will meet such requirements as a consequence of the Offer.

14. Conditions to the Offer. Notwithstanding any other provision of the Offer and subject to the terms of the Merger Agreement, the Purchaser will not be required to accept for payment any Shares tendered pursuant to the Offer, and may terminate the Offer and may postpone the acceptance for payment of and payment for Shares tendered, if (i) any applicable waiting period under the HSR Act shall not have expired or been terminated prior to the expiration of the Offer,

or (ii) immediately prior to the acceptance for payment of Shares, any of the following conditions shall be reasonably determined by the Parent to be existing:

(a) there shall have been entered, enforced, promulgated or issued by any court or governmental, administrative or regulatory authority or agency of competent jurisdiction, domestic or foreign, any judgment, order, injunction or decree, (i) which makes illegal or prohibits or makes materially more costly the making of the Offer, the acceptance for payment of, or payment for, any Shares by the Parent, the Purchaser or any other affiliate of the Parent, or the consummation of any other transaction contemplated by the Merger Agreement, or imposes material damages in connection with any transaction contemplated by the Merger Agreement; (ii) which prohibits the ownership or operation by the Company or any of its subsidiaries or, as a result of the transactions contemplated by the Merger Agreement, the Parent and its subsidiaries, of all or any material portion of the business or assets of the Company, the Parent or any of their subsidiaries as a whole, or compels the Company, the Parent or any of their subsidiaries to dispose of or hold separate all or any material portion of the business or assets of the Company, the Parent or any of their subsidiaries as a whole; (iii) which imposes or confirms limitations on the ability of the Parent, the Purchaser or any other affiliate of the Parent to exercise effectively full rights of ownership of any Shares, including, without limitation, the right to vote any Shares acquired by the Purchaser pursuant to the Offer or otherwise on all matters properly presented to the Company's stockholders, including, without limitation, the approval and adoption of the Merger Agreement and the transactions contemplated by the Merger Agreement; (iv) requires divestiture by the Parent, the Purchaser or any other affiliate of the Parent of any Shares; or (v) which otherwise would have a Material Adverse Effect on the Company or, as a result of the transactions contemplated by the Merger Agreement, the Parent and its subsidiaries;

(b) there shall have been any action taken, or any statute, rule, regulation, legislation or interpretation enacted, entered, enforced, promulgated, amended, issued or deemed applicable to (i) the Company or any subsidiary of the Company or, as a result of the transactions contemplated by the Merger Agreement, the Parent or any subsidiary or affiliate of the Parent, or (ii) any transaction contemplated by the Merger Agreement, by any legislative body, court, government or governmental, administrative or regulatory authority or agency, domestic or foreign, other than the routine application of the waiting period provisions of the HSR Act to the Offer or the Merger, which is reasonably likely to result, directly or indirectly, in any of the consequences referred to in clauses (i) through (v) of paragraph (a) above;

(c) there shall have occurred and be continuing, (i) any general suspension of, or limitation on prices for, trading in securities on the NYSE other than a shortening of trading hours or any coordinated trading halt triggered solely as a result of a specified increase or decrease in a market index, (ii) a declaration of a banking moratorium or any suspension of payments in respect of banks in the United States, (iii) the commencement of a war, material armed hostilities or any other material international or national calamity involving the United States, or (iv) in the case of any of the foregoing existing at the time of the commencement of the Offer, a material acceleration or worsening thereof;

(d) the representations or warranties of the Company set forth in the Merger Agreement shall not be true and correct, ignoring for this purpose any qualification as to materiality or Material Adverse Effect, as if such representations or warranties were made as of such time on or after the date of the Merger Agreement, except where the failure to be so true and correct, individually and in the aggregate would not have a Material Adverse Effect;

(e) the Company shall have failed to perform in any material respect any obligation or to comply in any material respect with any agreement or covenant of the Company to be performed or complied with by it under the Merger Agreement;

(f) the Merger Agreement shall have been terminated in accordance with its terms; or

(g) the Purchaser and the Company shall have agreed that the Purchaser shall terminate the Offer or postpone the acceptance for payment of or payment for Shares thereunder;

which, in the reasonable good faith judgment of the Purchaser in any such case, and regardless of the circumstances (including any action or inaction by the Parent or any of its affiliates) giving rise to any such condition, makes it inadvisable to proceed with such acceptance for payment or payment.

The foregoing conditions are for the sole benefit of the Purchaser and the Parent and may be asserted by the Purchaser or the Parent regardless of the circumstances giving rise to any such condition or may be waived by the Purchaser or the Parent in whole or in part at any time and from time to time in their sole discretion. The failure by the Parent or the Purchaser at any time to exercise any of the foregoing rights shall not be deemed a waiver of any such right; the waiver of any such right with respect to particular facts and other circumstances shall not be deemed a waiver with respect to any other facts and circumstances; and each such right shall be deemed an ongoing right that may be asserted at any time and from time to time.

Point 17: *This is one of the most important sections of the tender offer document. The arbitrageur must read and understand all the potential conditions that would allow the bidder to terminate the offer. This section will reveal potential problems—such as whether the bidder has allowed itself an out if the equity market declines by a certain amount.*

15. Certain Legal Matters and Regulatory Approvals.

General. Based upon an examination of publicly available information with respect to the Company and the representations and warranties of the Company contained in the Merger Agreement, neither the Purchaser nor the Parent is aware of any license or other regulatory permit that appears to be material to the business of the Company and its subsidiaries, taken as a whole, which might be adversely affected by the acquisition of Shares by the Purchaser pursuant to the Offer, or, except as set forth below, of any approval or other action by any domestic (federal or state) or foreign governmental, administrative or regulatory authority or agency which would be required prior to the acquisition of Shares by the Purchaser pursuant to the Offer. Should any such approval or other action be required, it is the Purchaser's present intention to seek such approval or action.

The Purchaser does not currently intend, however, to delay the purchase of Shares tendered pursuant to the Offer pending the outcome of any such action or the receipt of any such approval. There can be no assurance that any such approval or other action, if needed, would be obtained without substantial conditions or that adverse consequences might not result to the business of the Company, the Purchaser or the Parent or that certain parts of the businesses of the Company, the Purchaser or the Parent might not have to be disposed of or held separate or other substantial conditions complied with in order to obtain such approval or other action or in the event that such approval was not obtained or such other action was not taken. The Purchaser's obligation under the Offer to accept for payment and pay for Shares is subject to certain conditions, including conditions relating to the legal matters discussed in this "Section 15. Certain Legal Matters and Regulatory Approvals." See "Section 14. Conditions to the Offer."

Litigation. Following the March 9, 1998 announcement of the proposed acquisition of the Company by the Parent and the Purchaser, five putative class actions on behalf of stockholders of the Company were filed in the Delaware Court of Chancery against the Company, the Company's directors and the Parent. The plaintiffs in those actions allege, among other things, that the director defendants have agreed to a buyout of the Company at an inadequate price, that they have failed to provide the Company's stockholders with all necessary information about the value of the Company, that they failed to make an informed decision as no market check of the Company's value was obtained, and that the acquisition is structured to ensure that stockholders will tender their shares and is coercive. Plaintiffs seek to enjoin the acquisition or to rescind it in the event that it is consummated and to cause the Company to implement a "full and fair" auction for the Company. Plaintiffs also seek compensatory damages in an unspecified amount, costs and disbursements, including attorneys' fees, and such other relief as the Court deems appropriate.

State Takeover Laws. A number of states throughout the United States have enacted takeover statutes that purport, in varying degrees, to be applicable to attempts to acquire securities of corporations that are incorporated or have assets, stockholders, executive offices or places of business in those states. In 1982, in Edgar v. MITE Corp., the Supreme Court of the United States held that the Illinois Business Takeover Act, which involved state securities laws that made the takeover of certain corporations more difficult, imposed a substantial burden on interstate commerce and was therefore unconstitutional. However, in 1987, in CTS Corp. v. Dynamics Corp. of America, the Supreme Court of the United States held that a state may, as a matter of corporate law and, in particular, those laws concerning corporate governance, constitutionally disqualify a potential acquirer from voting on the affairs of a target corporation without prior approval of the remaining stockholders; provided that the laws were applicable only under certain conditions. Section 203 of the DGCL limits the ability of a Delaware corporation to engage in business combinations with "interested stockholders" (defined generally as any person that directly or indirectly beneficially owns 15% or more of the outstanding voting stock of the subject corporation) for three years following the date such person became an "interested stockholder," unless, among other things, the board of directors of the subject corporation has given its prior approval of either the transaction in which such person became an interested stockholder or the business combination. The Company has represented in the Merger Agreement that it approved the Merger Agreement and the transactions contemplated thereby, including the Offer and the Merger, and has taken all appropriate action so that neither the Parent nor the Purchaser will be an "interested stockholder" within the meaning of Section 203 of the DGCL by virtue of the Parent, the Purchaser and the Company entering into the Merger Agreement and consummating the transactions contemplated thereby.

The Company, directly or through subsidiaries, conducts business in a number of states throughout the United States, some of which have enacted takeover laws. The Purchaser does not know whether any of these laws will, by their terms, apply to the Offer or the Merger and has not complied with any such laws. Should any person seek to apply any state takeover law, the Purchaser will take such action as then appears desirable, which may include challenging the validity or applicability of any such statute in appropriate court proceedings. In the event it is asserted that one or more state takeover laws is applicable to the Offer or the Merger, and an appropriate court does not determine that it is inapplicable or invalid as applied to the Offer, the Purchaser might be required to file certain information with, or receive approvals from, the relevant state authorities. In addition, if enjoined, the Purchaser might be unable to accept for payment any Shares tendered pursuant to the Offer, or be delayed in continuing or consummating the Offer and the Merger. In such case, the Purchaser may not be obligated to accept for payment any Shares tendered. See "Section 14. Conditions to the Offer."

Antitrust. Under the HSR Act and the rules that have been promulgated thereunder by the Federal Trade Commission (the "FTC"), certain acquisition transactions may not be consummated unless certain information has been furnished to the Antitrust Division of the Department of Justice (the "Antitrust Division") and the FTC and certain waiting period requirements have been satisfied. The acquisition of Shares by the Purchaser pursuant to the Offer is subject to such requirements.

The Company and the Parent expect to file Premerger Notification and Report Forms in connection with the purchase of Shares pursuant to the Offer with the Antitrust Division and the FTC on or about Monday, March 16, 1998. Under the provisions of the HSR Act applicable to the Offer, the purchase of Shares pursuant to the Offer may not be consummated until the expiration of a 15-calendar day waiting period following the filing by the Parent. Accordingly, if the forms are filed on March 16, 1998, the waiting period under the HSR Act applicable to the purchase of Shares pursuant to the Offer will expire at 11:59 P.M., New York City time, on March 31, 1998, unless such waiting period is earlier terminated by the FTC and the Antitrust Division or extended by a request from the FTC or the Antitrust Division for additional information or documentary material prior to the expiration of the waiting period. If the acquisition of Shares is delayed pursuant to a request by the FTC or the Antitrust Division for additional information or documentary material pursuant to the HSR Act, the purchase of and payment for Shares will be deferred until 10 days after the request is substantially complied with, unless the extended period expires on or before the date when the initial

15-day period would otherwise have expired, or unless the waiting period is sooner terminated by the FTC and the Antitrust Division. Only one extension of such waiting period pursuant to a request for additional information is authorized by the HSR Act and the rules promulgated thereunder, except by court order. Any such extension of the waiting period will not give rise to any withdrawal rights not otherwise provided for by applicable law. See "Section 4. Withdrawal Rights." It is a condition to the Offer that the waiting period applicable under the HSR Act to the Offer expire or be terminated. See "Section 14. Conditions to the Offer." So long as the Merger Agreement is in effect and any applicable waiting period under the HSR Act has not expired or been terminated, the Purchaser is obligated to extend the Offer from time to time for a period or successive periods, each not to exceed ten business days after the previously scheduled Expiration Date.

POINT 18: *Here, the arbitrageur learns the specific dates on which the Hart–Scott–Rodino Act's antitrust periods expire.*

The FTC and the Antitrust Division frequently scrutinize the legality under the antitrust laws of transactions such as the proposed acquisition of Shares by the Purchaser pursuant to the Offer. At any time before or after the purchase of Shares pursuant to the Offer by the Purchaser, the FTC or the Antitrust Division could take such action under the antitrust laws as it deems necessary or desirable in the public interest, including seeking to enjoin the purchase of Shares pursuant to the Offer or seeking the divestiture of Shares purchased by the Purchaser or the divestiture of substantial assets of the Parent, the Company or their respective subsidiaries. Private parties and state attorneys general may also bring legal action under federal or state antitrust laws under certain circumstances. Based upon an examination of information available to the Parent relating to the businesses in which the Parent, the Company and their respective subsidiaries are engaged, the Parent and the Purchaser believe that the Offer will not violate the antitrust laws. Nevertheless, there can be no assurance that a challenge to the Offer on antitrust grounds will not be made or, if such a challenge is made, what the result would be. See "Section 14. Conditions to the Offer" for certain conditions to the Offer.

In addition, the antitrust and competition laws of certain foreign jurisdictions require (or, in some instances, provide for on a voluntary basis) notification of the transaction and the observance of pre-consummation waiting periods. The Company and the Parent will make any such required filings (and, if deemed in the Company's and the Parent's interests, any such voluntary filings) with the appropriate antitrust and competition authorities contemporaneously with their filings under the HSR Act or shortly thereafter. Based upon an examination of information available to the Parent relating to the businesses in which the Parent, the Company and their respective subsidiaries are engaged, the Parent and the Purchaser believe that the Offer will not violate any such foreign antitrust and competition laws. Nevertheless, there can be no assurance that a challenge to the Offer will not be made on antitrust or competition grounds or, if such a challenge were made, what the result would be.

POINT 19: *In this section, the arbitrageur can learn about all the legal issues affecting the bid. State takeover laws, regulatory issues, and antitrust aspects of the transaction are frequently discussed in depth here.*

16. Fees and Expenses. Except as set forth below, the Purchaser will not pay any fees or commissions to any broker, dealer or other person for soliciting tenders of Shares pursuant to the Offer.

Credit Suisse First Boston is acting as Dealer Manager in connection with the Offer and as financial advisor to the Parent in connection with the Parent's proposed acquisition of the Company, for which services Credit Suisse First Boston will receive customary compensation. The Parent also has agreed to reimburse Credit Suisse First Boston for its out-of-pocket expenses, including the fees and expenses of legal counsel and other advisors, incurred in connection with its engagement, and to indemnify Credit Suisse First Boston and certain related persons against certain liabilities and expenses in connection with its engagement, including certain liabilities under the federal securities laws. In the ordinary course of business, Credit Suisse First Boston and its affiliates may actively trade the debt and equity securities of the Parent and the Company for their own account and for the accounts of customers and, accordingly, may at any time hold a long or short position in such securities.

The Purchaser and the Parent have retained D.F. King & Co., Inc., as the Information Agent, and First Chicago Trust Company of New York, as the Depositary, in connection with the Offer. The Information Agent may contact holders of Shares by mail, telephone, telex, telecopy, telegraph and personal interview and may request banks, brokers, dealers and other nominee stockholders to forward materials relating to the Offer to beneficial owners.

For acting as Information Agent in connection with the Offer, D.F. King & Co., Inc., will be paid reasonable and customary compensation and will also be reimbursed for certain out-of-pocket expenses and may be indemnified against certain liabilities and expenses in connection with the Offer, including certain liabilities under the federal securities laws. The Purchaser will pay the Depositary reasonable and customary compensation for its services in connection with the Offer, plus reimbursement for out-of-pocket expenses, and will indemnify the Depositary against certain liabilities and expenses in connection therewith, including under federal securities laws. Brokers, dealers, commercial banks and trust companies will be reimbursed by the Purchaser for customary handling and mailing expenses incurred by them in forwarding material to their customers.

17. Miscellaneous. The Purchaser is not aware of any jurisdiction where the making of the Offer is prohibited by any administrative or judicial action pursuant to any valid state statute. If the Purchaser becomes aware of any valid state statute prohibiting the making of the Offer or the acceptance of Shares pursuant thereto, the Purchaser will make a good faith effort to comply with any such state statute. If, after such good faith effort, the Purchaser cannot comply with any such state statute, the Offer will not be made to (nor will tenders be accepted from or on behalf of) the holders of Shares in such state. In any jurisdiction where the securities, blue sky or other laws require the Offer to be made by a licensed broker or dealer, the Offer shall be deemed to be made on behalf of the Purchaser

by the Dealer Manager or by one or more registered brokers or dealers licensed under the laws of such jurisdiction.

NO PERSON HAS BEEN AUTHORIZED TO GIVE ANY INFORMATION OR MAKE ANY REPRESENTATION ON BEHALF OF THE PARENT, THE PURCHASER OR THE COMPANY NOT CONTAINED IN THIS OFFER TO PURCHASE OR IN THE LETTER OF TRANSMITTAL, AND IF GIVEN OR MADE, SUCH INFORMA- TION OR REPRESENTATION MUST NOT BE RELIED UPON AS HAVING BEEN AUTHORIZED.

Pursuant to Rule 14d-3 of the General Rules and Regulations under the Ex- change Act, the Parent and the Purchaser have filed with the Commission the Schedule 14D-1, together with exhibits, furnishing certain additional information with respect to the Offer. The Schedule 14D-1 and any amendments thereto, in- cluding exhibits, may be inspected at, and copies may be obtained from, the same places and in the same manner as set forth in "Section 7. Certain Informa- tion Concerning the Company" (except that they will not be available at the re- gional offices of the Commission).

AMX ACQUISITION CORP.

March 13, 1998

SCHEDULE I

DIRECTORS AND EXECUTIVE OFFICERS OF
THE PARENT AND THE PURCHASER

1. Directors and Executive Officers of the Parent. The following table sets forth the name, and present principal occupation or employment, and material occupations, positions, offices or employments for the past five years of each director and executive officer of the Parent. Unless otherwise indicated, the cur- rent business address of each person is 425 Sixth Avenue, Pittsburgh, Pennsylva- nia 15219. Unless otherwise indicated, each such person is a citizen of the United States of America, and each occupation set forth opposite an individual's name refers to employment with the Parent.

Name	Present Principal Occupation or Employment and Five-Year Employment History
KENNETH W. DAM Director since 1987	Mr. Dam is Max Pam Professor of American and For- eign Law at the University of Chicago Law School. He served as President and Chief Executive Officer of United Way of America in 1992, Vice President for Law and External Relations of IBM Corporation from 1985 to 1992, Deputy Secretary of State from 1982 to 1985 and Provost of the University of Chicago from 1980 to 1982. Other directorships include the Council on Foreign Relations, the Brookings Institution and a number of nonprofit organizations.

Name	Present Principal Occupation or Employment and Five-Year Employment History
JOSEPH T. GORMAN Director since 1991	Mr. Gorman has been Chairman and Chief Executive Officer of TRW Inc. (a global company serving the automotive, space and defense markets) since 1988. From 1985 to 1991 he served as President of TRW and from 1985 to 1988 he was its Chief Operating Officer. In addition to serving as a director of TRW, Mr. Gorman is a director of The Procter & Gamble Company and a member of the BP America Inc. Advisory Board.
JUDITH M. GUERON Director since 1988	Dr. Gueron is President of Manpower Demonstration Research Corporation (MDRC), a nonprofit research organization, a position she has held since 1986. She was MDRC's Executive Vice President for Research and Evaluation from 1978 to 1986. Dr. Gueron was director of special projects and studies and a consultant for the New York City Human Resources Administration before joining MDRC.
SIR RONALD HAMPEL Director since 1995	Sir Ronald has been Chairman of Imperial Chemical Industries PLC (a diversified chemicals manufacturer) since 1995. He was Deputy Chairman and Chief Executive of Imperial Chemical Industries from 1993 to 1995 and Chief Operating Officer from 1991 to 1993. He has been an ICI director since 1985. He is a member of the Listed Companies Advisory Committee of the London Stock Exchange and the Nominating Committee of the New York Stock Exchange and Chairman of the UK Committee on Corporate Governance. Mr. Hampel is a citizen of the United Kingdom.
JOHN P. MULRONEY Director since 1987	Mr. Mulroney has been President and Chief Operating Officer of Rohm and Haas Company (a specialty chemicals manufacturer) since 1986. He has been a director of Rohm and Haas since 1982. In addition to Rohm and Haas, Mr. Mulroney also is a director of Teradyne, Inc.
PAUL H. O'NEILL Director since 1986	Mr. O'Neill has been Chairman of the Board and Chief Executive Officer of the Parent since June 1987. From 1985 to 1987, he was President and a director of International Paper Company. Other directorships include Gerald R. Ford Foundation, Eastman Kodak Company, Lucent Technologies Inc., Manpower Demonstration Research Corporation, National

	Present Principal Occupation or
Name	Employment and Five-Year Employment History

Association of Securities Dealers, Inc. and The RAND Corporation.

SIR ARVI PARBO
Director since 1980

Sir Arvi has been Chairman of WMC Limited (an Australian mining and minerals processing company) since 1974. From 1971 to 1986, he served as Managing Director of WMC Limited and was Chairman of Alcoa of Australia Limited from 1978 to June 1996. Other directorships include Munich Reinsurance Company of Australia Ltd., Sara Lee Corporation and Zurich Australian Insurance Group. Mr. Parbo is an Australian citizen.

HENRY B. SCHACHT
Director since 1994

Mr. Schacht is a director and Senior Advisor of Lucent Technologies Inc., a communication systems and technology company. He was Chairman of Lucent Technologies from February 1996 to February 1998 and its Chief Executive Officer from February 1996 to October 1997. He was also Chairman of Cummins Engine Company, Inc. from 1977 to 1995 and its Chief Executive Officer from 1973 to 1994. Other directorships include Cummins Engine Company, Inc., The Chase Manhattan Bank Corporation, The Chase Manhattan Bank, Johnson & Johnson, and Lucent Technologies.

FORREST N. SHUMWAY
Director since 1988
(also served previously
as a director from 1982
to 1987)

Mr. Shumway retired as Vice Chairman of the Board and Chairman of the Executive Committee of AlliedSignal Inc. in 1987. Prior to 1985, he had served as Chairman and Chief Executive Officer of The Signal Companies, Inc. Mr. Shumway is also a director of Transamerica Corporation.

FRANKLIN A. THOMAS
Director since 1977

Mr. Thomas is a Consultant of TFF Study Group, a non-profit institution focusing on South Africa. Previously, he was President of the Ford Foundation, a position he had held from 1979 until 1996. He was also the President and Chief Executive Officer of Bedford Stuyvesant Restoration Corporation from its founding in 1967 until 1977. Other directorships include Citicorp/Citibank, N.A., Cummins Engine Company, Inc., Lucent Technologies Inc. and PepsiCo, Inc.

**MARINA v. N.
WHITMAN**
Director since 1994

Dr. Whitman is a Professor of Business Administration and Public Policy, School of Business Administration and the School of Public Policy at the University of Michigan. She was Vice President and Group Executive,

Name	Present Principal Occupation or Employment and Five-Year Employment History
	Public Affairs and Marketing Staffs of General Motors Corporation from 1985 to 1992 and Vice President and Chief Economist from 1979 to 1985. She was a member of the President's Council of Economic Advisers from 1972 to 1973. Other directorships include Browning-Ferris Industries, Inc., The Chase Manhattan Corporation, The Procter & Gamble Company and Unocal Corporation.
ALAIN J.P. BELDA	President and Chief Operating Officer. Mr. Belda was elected President and Chief Operating Officer in January 1997. He was President of Alcoa Aluminio S.A. in Brazil from 1979 to 1994. Mr. Belda was elected Vice President of the Parent in 1982 and, in 1989, was given responsibility for all of the Parent's interests in Latin America (other than Suriname). In August 1991, he was named President—Latin America for Alcoa. Mr. Belda was elected Executive Vice President in 1994 and Vice Chairman in 1995. Mr. Belda is a citizen of Brazil.
GEORGE E. BERGERON	Executive Vice President. Mr. Bergeron was named President—Alcoa Closure Systems International in 1982 and was elected Vice President and General Manager—Rigid Packaging Division in July 1990. He was appointed President—Rigid Packaging Division in 1991. Mr. Bergeron was elected Executive Vice President of the Parent in January 1998 and is responsible for corporate growth initiatives.
MICHAEL COLEMAN	Vice President and President—Alcoa Rigid Packaging. Mr. Coleman joined the Parent in January 1998. He had been Vice President—Operations of North Star Steel from 1993 to 1994, Executive Vice President—Operations from 1994 to 1996 and President from 1996 through 1997. Mr. Coleman joined North Star Steel in 1982.
RICHARD L. FISCHER	Executive Vice President—Chairman's Counsel. Mr. Fischer was elected Vice President and General Counsel in 1983 and became Senior Vice President in 1984. He was given the additional responsibility for Corporate Development in 1986 and in 1991 named to his present position. In his current assignment, Mr. Fischer is responsible for Corporate Development and

Name	Present Principal Occupation or Employment and Five-Year Employment History
	the expansion and integration of the Parent's international business activities.
L. PATRICK HASSEY	Vice President and President—Alcoa Europe. Mr. Hassey joined Alcoa in 1967 and was named Davenport Works Manager in 1985. In 1991, he was elected a Vice President of the Parent and appointed President—Aerospace/Commercial Rolled Products Division. Mr. Hassey was appointed President—Alcoa Europe in November 1997.
PATRICIA L. HIGGINS	Vice President and Chief Information Officer. Ms. Higgins joined the Parent in January 1997 and is responsible for the integration and implementation of the Parent's computer initiatives. She began her career at American Telephone & Telegraph Co. in 1977 and was Vice President of International Sales Operations in Network Systems before joining Nynex Corporation in 1991 as Group Vice President, Manhattan Market Area. In 1995, Ms. Higgins moved to Unisys Corporation where she was President, Communications Market Sector Group.
RICHARD B. KELSON	Executive Vice President and Chief Financial Officer. Mr. Kelson was appointed Assistant Secretary and Managing General Attorney in 1984 and Assistant General Counsel in 1989. He was elected Senior Vice President—Environment, Health and Safety in 1991 and Executive Vice President and General Counsel in May 1994. Mr. Kelson was named to his current position in May 1997.
FRANK L. LEDERMAN	Vice President and Chief Technical Officer. Mr. Lederman was Senior Vice President and Chief Technical Officer for Noranda, Inc., a company he joined in 1988. Mr. Lederman joined Alcoa as a Vice President in May 1995 and became Chief Technical Officer in December 1995. In his current position Mr. Lederman directs operations of the Alcoa Technical Center.
G. JOHN PIZZEY	Vice President and President, Alcoa World Alumina. Mr. Pizzey joined Alcoa of Australia Limited in 1970 and was appointed to the board of Alcoa of Australia as Executive Director—Victoria Operations and Managing Director of Portland Smelter Services in 1986.

Name	Present Principal Occupation or Employment and Five-Year Employment History
	He was named President—Bauxite and Alumina Division of Alcoa in 1994 and President—Primary Metals Division of Alcoa in 1995. Mr. Pizzey was elected a Vice President of the Parent in 1996 and was appointed President—Alcoa World Alumina in November 1997. Mr. Pizzey is an Australian citizen.
LAWRENCE R. PURTELL	Executive Vice President—Environment, Health and Safety and General Counsel. Mr. Purtell joined the Parent in November 1997. He had been Corporate Secretary and Associate General Counsel of United Technologies Corporation from 1989 to 1992 and Vice President and General Counsel of Carrier Corporation from 1992 to 1993. Mr. Purtell was Senior Vice President and General Counsel and Corporate Secretary of McDermott International, Inc. from 1993 to 1996. In 1996, he joined Koch Industries, Inc. as Senior Vice President, General Counsel and Corporate Secretary.
ROBERT F. SLAGLE	Executive Vice President, Human Resources and Communications. Mr. Slagle was elected Treasurer in 1982 and Vice President in 1984. In 1986, he was named Vice President—Industrial Chemicals and, in 1987, was named Vice President—Industrial Chemicals and U.S. Alumina Operations. Mr. Slagle was named Vice President—Raw Materials, Alumina and Industrial Chemicals in 1989, and Vice President of the Parent and Managing Director—Alcoa of Australia Limited in 1991. He was named President—Alcoa World Alumina in 1996 and was elected to his current position in November 1997.
G. KEITH TURNBULL	Executive Vice President—Alcoa Business System. Dr. Turnbull was appointed Assistant Director of Alcoa Laboratories in 1980. He was named Director—Technology Planning in 1982, Vice President—Technology Planning in 1986 and Executive Vice President—Strategic Analysis/Planning and Information in 1991. In January 1997 he was named to his current position, with responsibility for company-wide implementation of Alcoa Business System.

2. Directors and Executive Officers of the Purchaser. The following table sets forth the name, and present principal occupation or employment, and material

occupations, positions, offices or employments for the past five years of each director and executive officer of the Purchaser. Unless otherwise indicated, the current business address of each person is 425 Sixth Avenue, Pittsburgh, Pennsylvania 15219. Unless otherwise indicated, each such person is a citizen of the United States of America, and each occupation set forth opposite an individual's name refers to employment with the Purchaser.

Name	Present Principal Occupation or Employment and Five-Year Employment History
GEORGE E. BERGERON	Director and President of the Purchaser since March, 1988. Mr. Bergeron was named President—Alcoa Closure Systems International in 1982 and was elected Vice President and General Manager of the Parent's Rigid Packaging Division in July 1990. He was appointed President of the Parent's Rigid Packaging Division in 1991. Mr. Bergeron was elected Executive Vice President of the Parent in January 1998 and is responsible for corporate growth initiatives at the Parent.
RICHARD B. KELSON	Director, Vice President and Treasurer of the Purchaser since March, 1988. Mr. Kelson was appointed Assistant Secretary and Managing General Attorney in 1984 and Assistant General Counsel of the Parent in 1989. He was elected Senior Vice President—Environment, Health and Safety of the Parent in 1991 and Executive Vice President and General Counsel of the Parent in May 1994. Mr. Kelson was named to his current position at the Parent in May 1997.
LAWRENCE R. PURTELL	Director, Vice President and Secretary of the Purchaser since March, 1988. Mr. Purtell joined the Parent in November 1997. He had been Corporate Secretary and Associate General Counsel of United Technologies Corporation from 1989 to 1992 and Vice President and General Counsel of Carrier Corporation from 1992 to 1993. Mr. Purtell was Senior Vice President and General Counsel and Corporate Secretary of McDermott International, Inc. from 1993 to 1996. In 1996, he joined Koch Industries, Inc. as Senior Vice President, General Counsel and Corporate Secretary.

Facsimiles of the Letter of Transmittal will be accepted. The Letter of Transmittal and certificates evidencing Shares and any other required documents should be sent or delivered by each stockholder or such stockholder's broker, dealer, commercial bank, trust company or other nominee to the Depositary at one of its addresses set forth next.

The Depositary for the Offer is:

By Mail:	By Overnight Courier Delivery:
First Chicago Trust	First Chicago Trust
Company of New York	Company of New York
Attention: Tenders & Exchanges	Attention: Tenders & Exchanges
P.O. Box 2569, Suite 4660	14 Wall Street, 8th Floor
Jersey City, New Jersey 07303	New York, New York 10005

By Hand:	By Facsimile Transmission:
First Chicago Trust	(201) 222-4720
Company of New York	or
Attention: Tenders & Exchanges	(201) 222-4721
c/o The Depository Trust Company	
55 Water Street, DTC TAD	
Vietnam Veterans Memorial Plaza	Confirm by Telephone:
New York, New York 10041	(201) 222-4707

Questions or requests for assistance may be directed to the Information Agent or the Dealer Manager at their respective addresses and telephone numbers listed below. Additional copies of this Offer to Purchase, the Letter of Transmittal and other tender offer materials may also be obtained from the Information Agent or the Dealer Manager.

The Information Agent for the Offer is:

D.F. KING & CO., INC.
77 Water Street, 20th Floor
New York, New York 10005
(212) 269-5550 (Call Collect)
Toll Free (800) 848-3094

The Dealer Manager for the Offer is:

CREDIT SUISSE FIRST BOSTON CORPORATION
Eleven Madison Avenue
New York, NY 10010
Call Toll Free (800) 881-8320

<u>**POINT 20**</u>: *The arbitrageur has a description of the acquiring company's investment banker (adviser), as well as information on the parties to the transaction. During the pendency of the deal, the arbitrageur may want to contact these parties to ask relevant questions.*

Appendix **2**

Wallace Computer Services—
Text of Court Decision

MOORE CORPORATION LIMITED and FRDK, INC., Plaintiffs, v. WALLACE
COMPUTER SERVICES, INC., ROBERT J. CRONIN, THEODORE DIMITRIOU,
FRED F. CANNING, WILLIAM N. LANE, III, NEELE E. STEARNS, JR.,
R. DARRELL EWERS, RICHARD F. DOYLE and WILLIAM E. OLSEN, Defendants.

Civil Action No. 95-472 MMS

UNITED STATES DISTRICT COURT FOR THE DISTRICT OF DELAWARE

907 F. Supp. 1545; 1995 U.S. Dist. LEXIS 18882;
1996-1 Trade Cas. (CCH) P71,287

December 4, 1995, Dated

CORE TERMS: customer, shareholder, vendor, tender offer, pill, antitrust, poison,
win, target, merger, defensive, preliminary injunction, competitive, submarket, acquisition, fiscal, projection, bid, Clayton Act, redeem, tender, enhanced, counterclaim, competitor, business judgment rule, injunction, coercive, proxy, takeover,
out-sourcing

COUNSEL: [**1] Jesse A. Finkelstein, Esq., and Daniel A. Driesbach, Esq., of
Richards, Layton & Finger, Wilmington, Delaware; Of Counsel: Donald I.
Strauber, Esq., Thomas J. McCormack, Esq., William S. D'Amico, Esq., Robert A.
Schwinger, Esq., and Eric Welsh, Esq., of Chadbourne & Parke LLP, New York,
New York; attorneys for plaintiffs.

Michael D. Goldman, Esq., Stephen C. Norman, Esq., and Michael A. Pittenger,
Esq., of Potter Anderson & Corroon, Wilmington, Delaware; Of Counsel: Walter
C. Carlson, Esq., William H. Baumgartner, Jr., Esq., Richard B. Kapnick, Esq., and

Brandon D. Lawniczak, Esq., of Sidley & Austin, Chicago, Illinois; attorneys for defendants.

JUDGES: Murray M. Schwartz, United States District Judge

OPINIONBY: Murray M. Schwartz

OPINION: [*1549] OPINION

Dated: December 4, 1995
Wilmington, Delaware

Schwartz, Senior District Judge

I. INTRODUCTION

Before the Court in this securities and antitrust matter are the parties' cross motions for preliminary injunctive relief and plaintiffs' motion to dismiss defendant's counterclaim. In their motion for a preliminary injunction, plaintiffs Moore Corporation Limited and its wholly-owned subsidiary FRDK, Inc. (collectively, "Moore") [**2] seek to enjoin defendants Wallace Computer Services, Inc. and its Board of Directors (collectively, "Wallace," "Board," or "Wallace Board") from implementing Wallace's antitakeover devices or taking any other actions to impede Moore's tender offer. Moore contends that such antitakeover maneuvers constitute a breach of fiduciary duty to the Wallace shareholders. As principal relief, Moore seeks to compel Wallace to redeem its "poison pill," which according to Moore presents the most serious obstacle to the consummation of the tender offer.

Wallace has counterclaimed that Moore's tender offer, if consummated, would violate Section 7 of the Clayton Act, *15 U.S.C. § 18*. In response, Moore has moved for dismissal of the counterclaim pursuant to Fed. R. Civ. P. 12(b)(6), arguing that Wallace has not alleged sufficient antitrust injury and therefore lacks standing to bring this claim. Wallace has also moved for a preliminary injunction as to this antitrust counterclaim. n1

> n1 Wallace also alleged that both Moore and counterclaim defendant Reto Braun ("Braun"), Moore's Chairman and Chief Executive Officer, have made misleading statements in connection with the tender offer, in violation of Sections 14(d) and (e) of the Securities Exchange Act of 1934 (the "Securities Exchange Act"). Alleging false and misleading statements in violation of Section 14(a) of the Securities Exchange Act, Wallace sought to enjoin Moore's proxy contest concerning the upcoming annual Wallace Board meeting, to be held on Friday, December 8, 1995. The Wallace pre-hearing and post-hearing briefs contained no discussion whatsoever of these allegations. Additionally, Wallace's counsel advised that Wallace was taking no steps to impede the proxy contest. The Court will therefore treat the allegations as withdrawn.

[**3]

Consonant with the high stakes in this case, the parties have erected a voluminous record for the Court's consideration. Prior to, contemporaneous with, and following a preliminary injunction hearing, the Court has been "carpet bombed" n2 with a rash of legal memoranda, over two hundred exhibits, myriad depositions, with separately filed excerpts and highlights from those same depositions, and a salmagundi of other documents. In addition to considering all of the above, the Court also will refer to testimony elicited at a three day preliminary injunction hearing held November 7–9, 1995.

> n2 *Bon-Ton Stores, Inc. v. May Dep't Stores Co., 881 F. Supp. 860, 863 (W.D.N.Y. 1994)* (citing *Consolidated Gold Fields PLC, Inc. v. Anglo Am. Corp., 713 F. Supp. 1457, 1475 (S.D.N.Y.)*, op. amended, *890 F.2d 569* (2d Cir.), cert. dismissed, *492 U.S. 939 (1989))*.

Jurisdiction is based on diversity of citizenship, *28 U.S.C. § 1332,* and federal question jurisdiction, *28 U.S.C. §§ 1331,* 1337(a), *15 U.S.C. §* [**4] *26.* Venue is proper under *28* [*1550] *U.S.C. § 1391(c)* and *15 U.S.C. § 22.* This opinion contains this Court's findings of fact and conclusions of law, pursuant to Fed. R. Civ. P. 52(a); to the extent that findings of fact are placed among conclusions of law, they should be deemed findings of fact.

For the reasons set forth below, the Court will deny Moore's motion for preliminary injunction with respect to the breach of fiduciary duty claim and grant Moore's motion to dismiss Wallace's Clayton Act counterclaim. Wallace's motion for preliminary injunction with respect to the antitrust claims will therefore become moot.

II. THE PARTIES

Plaintiff Moore Corporation Limited is an Ontario, Canada corporation engaged in the business of delivering information handling products ("business forms" or "forms") and services, with its principal place of business in Toronto, Ontario. Docket Item ("D.I.") 1, P 7. Plaintiff FRDK, Inc. is a New York corporation with its principal place of business in Toronto, Ontario. Id. P 8. As a wholly-owned subsidiary of Moore Corporation Limited, FRDK, Inc. was incorporated for the purpose of making a tender offer for all outstanding Wallace stock in connection [**5] with a proxy solicitation and merger. Id. P 8. Counterclaim defendant Braun is the Chairman and Chief Executive Officer of Moore Corporation, Limited.

Defendant Wallace is a Delaware corporation engaged predominantly in the computer services and supply industry, with its principal place of business in Hillside, Illinois. Id. P 9. Defendants Robert J. Cronin ("Cronin"), Theodore Dimitriou ("Dimitriou"), Fred F. Canning ("Canning"), William N. Lane, III ("Lane"), Neele E. Stearns, Jr. ("Stearns"), R. Darrell Ewers ("Ewers"), Richard F. Doyle ("Doyle"), and William E. Olsen ("Olsen") are members of the eight-member Wallace Board of Directors. Of these eight directors, all but Cronin and Dimitriou are independent directors. Cronin presently serves as President and Chief Executive Officer of Wallace. Dimitriou formerly served as Chief Executive Officer, and now serves as Chairman of the Wallace Board.

III. MOORE'S FIDUCIARY DUTY CLAIM

A. Facts

As with all actions alleging breach of fiduciary duty by a target corporation's Board of Directors, a detailed examination of the actions of the Wallace Board is required to provide context to the claim. In February, 1995, [**6] Moore's Chief Executive Officer Braun approached Wallace management proposing a possible business combination between Moore and Wallace. D.I. 176 at 2–3. On March 8, 1995, the Wallace Board instructed its Chief Executive Officer Cronin to advise Braun that Wallace had no interest in a business combination with Moore. Between February and June, 1995, attempts were made by Braun to meet with Cronin over lunch to discuss the matter, but the lunch meeting never occurred. On June 14, 1995, the Wallace Board approved an employment agreement for Cronin that provided Cronin, among other items, a severance package in the amount of $8 million in the event of a change in his job duties. D.I. 107, Deposition of Doyle ("Doyle Depo."), at 52. The substance of this agreement, in all pertinent respects, was identical to a prior agreement between Wallace and Dimitriou, Cronin's predecessor as Chief Executive Officer. Additionally, the Wallace Board adopted a bylaw amendment creating a 60-day notice requirement applicable to shareholders desiring to bring business for consideration at Wallace's annual meeting. Id. at 56.

On July 30, 1995, a Sunday, Moore announced its intention to commence a tender [**7] offer for all outstanding shares of Wallace common stock (together with the associated preferred stock purchase rights that were issued in connection with Wallace's poison pill) at a price of $56 per share, a number which was determined with the advice of Moore's financial consultant Lazard Freres. The value of the proposed transaction was approximately $1.3 billion. D.I. 1, P 20. Moore intends, as soon as practicable after the consummation of the tender offer, to cause Wallace to merge with FRDK, and [*1551] purchase all shares not tendered. Concurrently with the tender offer, Moore has delivered proxy solicitation materials to the Wallace shareholders in order to nominate three individuals to serve as and replace the entire membership of the Wallace Board. Id. PP 21, 22. n3

> n3 On August 2, 1995, FRDK filed a Schedule 14D-1 with the Securities and Exchange Commission ("SEC"), detailing the provisions of the tender offer. D.I. 28 at 19.

The $56 tender offer was an all-cash offer for all shares that would [**8] provide Wallace shareholders a premium of 27% over the market price of Wallace stock value as of the date of the announcement of the offer. Id. PP 24, 25. The offer was conditioned upon, inter alia, (a) the valid tender of a majority of all outstanding shares of Wallace's common stock on a fully-diluted basis on the date of purchase; (b) the redemption, invalidation or inapplicability of the rights allowed under the Preferred Stockholder Rights Plan (the poison pill); n4 (c) Wallace Board approval of the acquisition of shares pursuant to the offer and proposed merger under Section 203 of the Delaware Business Combination Statute ("Section 203"); n5 (d) the proposed merger having been approved pursuant to Article Ninth of Wallace's Restated Certificate of Incorporation ("Article Ninth"), or the inapplicability of such article to the offer and proposed merger; n6 and (e) the availability of sufficient financing to consummate the offer and proposed merger. n7 Id. P 20.

n4 The poison pill was adopted on March 14, 1990, and caused the Wallace Board to declare a dividend of one preferred stock purchase right per share of common stock, payable to each shareholder of record as of March 28, 1990. Each right entitles the holder to purchase from Wallace one two-hundredth of a share of designated stock at a price of $115. Additionally, following the occurrence of certain events, including the acquisition of 20% or more of Wallace's common stock, each holder of a right is entitled to exercise that right by purchasing common stock of Wallace at half-price. D.I. 1, P 29.

[**9]

n5 Section 203 applies to any Delaware corporation that has not opted out of the statute's coverage. It provides that any person acquiring 15% or more of a company's voting stock (thereby becoming an "interested shareholder") may not engage in any business combination, including a merger, for three years after becoming such, unless that person obtains or has obtained certain approvals by the Board of Directors, or the affirmative vote of at least two-thirds of the outstanding voting stock not owned by the interested shareholder. See 8 Del. C. § 203.

n6 Article Ninth, entitled "Certain Business Combinations," is designed to impede coercive and inadequate tender offers. It prohibits certain business combinations by any "interested shareholder" (defined to include any person who directly or indirectly owns 20% or more of the outstanding voting power of Wallace, or an affiliate or assignee thereof), unless the affirmative vote of at least 80% of the combined voting power of the then outstanding shares of Wallace stock is obtained. D.I. 1, PP 34, 35. Like the poison pill, Article Ninth was in place years before the initiation of the Moore tender offer.

n7 Testimony at the November hearing was to the effect that financing had been obtained, with a commitment for the same extending to December 11, 1995.

[**10]

Moore communicated its intent to launch the tender offer to Wallace by leaving a telephone message that Sunday evening at Cronin's home. Upon receiving the information, Cronin contacted the Wallace Board and officers, and a group of advisors met them at their corporate headquarters. On Monday, July 31, Wallace, based on the recommendation of Dimitriou, retained Goldman Sachs ("Goldman") as its financial advisor to review the adequacy of the Moore tender offer. Dimitriou recommended Goldman based on the fact that Goldman had previously done work for Wallace, and that Goldman enjoyed the reputation as being a leading investment firm.

That same day, at 8:30 A.M., Moore filed the complaint in this action seeking the Court to compel the removal of the antitakeover devices and to declare that the proposed merger complied with all applicable laws. See *Moore Corp. v. Wallace Computer Servs., 898 F. Supp. 1089, 1995 WL 590561 (D.Del. 1995).* Wallace moved to dismiss the complaint on the dual grounds that the action was not yet ripe, and that plaintiffs engaged in impermissible forum shopping. The motion was denied. See id. On August 1, 1995, the Wallace Board met for the first time to consider [**11] the offer and to ratify the retention of Goldman as the company's financial advisor. [*1552] Doyle Depo. at 107. n8

> n8 The fee arrangement negotiated between Wallace and Goldman merits a brief description at this point, since Moore argues that the compensation arrangement biased Goldman in favor of finding inadequacy. Under the provisions of the arrangement, if Wallace remained independent, Goldman would receive $500,000 initially, plus additional $1.5 million increments, up to a total of $8 million. If Moore's $56 tender offer succeeded, Goldman would receive 6.2% of the total amount of the offer, up to approximately the same $8 million. However, because the fee is structured on a percentage scale, Goldman would obviously receive more than the $8 million if the eventual offer was for a price over $56 per share.

Cody Smith ("Smith"), a Goldman partner, headed his firm's evaluation of the proposed tender offer. In accordance with requests from Goldman, Wallace management provided a series of documents reflecting [**12] historic information and future projections to Goldman on Monday, July 31, 1995. D.I. 107, Deposition of Michael J. Halloran ("Halloran Depo."), at 72–73. These documents, assembled and presented by Michael J. Halloran ("Halloran"), a Wallace vice president and its Chief Financial Officer, included the following: annual reports for preceding years, Securities and Exchange Commission Form 10K reports, proxy reports, quarterly statements for the first three fiscal quarters of 1995, and any current analysts reports Wallace had on file. Id. Additionally, Halloran provided Goldman with its June, 1995 Strategic Plan (the "Strategic Plan"). Id. at 73–74. All of the figures and data provided to Goldman were prepared exclusively by Wallace.

The Strategic Plan contained projections which were, in large part, dependent upon future acquisitions. However, Smith testified that but for one acquisition, the Strategic Plan acquisition-related projections were not used by Goldman in preparing its report. Transcript of Hearing ("Tr.") 440, 444–45. Goldman made no independent investigation of the figures supplied by Wallace, nor did it make any changes thereto, but did speak with department heads [**13] at Wallace to review their component businesses, the basis of their forecasts, and the evidence supporting their forecasts. Id. at 423.

On August 4th, 1995, Goldman visited the Wallace headquarters in Hillside, Illinois. Wallace provided Goldman with its 1996 budget and additional supporting papers thereto. Wallace also gave Goldman its projections for fiscal year 1996 by quarter, as well as a projection through fiscal year 2000. The numbers set forth in the projections contained adjustments to reflect additional financial information which Wallace had gained in the two month interim since the Strategic Plan was created. Wallace then was asked to provide additional figures to include projections through the year 2002, which Wallace gave Goldman on August 9th. These projections contained more generous assumptions than previously supplied. Wallace explained that these more optimistic figures were given to Goldman because "we realized that we really had not given ourselves credit for some major initiatives we were taking to redo our manufacturing system," which was expected to be completed by the end of the calendar year 1996. Halloran Depo. at 118–119. Both subsequent sets of figures [**14] contained higher projected earnings than the first set.

On August 11, 1995, the Wallace Board met for the purpose of reviewing the adequacy of the Moore offer. Goldman presented its preliminary opinion that $56 was inadequate. The Wallace Board took no action at that time. On August 14, 1995, the Board met again, when Goldman issued its final opinion as to the inadequacy of the Moore offer. n9 The Board unanimously concluded that the offer was inadequate. Their decision was based on the presentation of Goldman and the results from the fourth quarter of fiscal 1995 (May, June and July). Wallace sales had increased 32% to 33% over the prior year and profits had increased 32%. Both the actual figures from the fourth quarter of fiscal 1995 and all of fiscal 1995 were record results and were above those projected by financial analysts. Additionally, the Wallace Board believed that the proposed union between the companies would present [*1553] antitrust concerns. On August 15, 1995, Wallace formally rejected Moore's offer. D.I. 28 at 2.

n9 The report prepared for the August 14th presentation differed from that prepared for the August 11th presentation, because the latter contained two assumptions which were inconsistent with one another, yielding an incorrect result.

[**15]

On October 12, 1995, Moore raised its offer price to $60 per share. Again, the Wallace Board met to consider the offer. Additional material was given to Goldman to provide an updated set of data regarding their financial status. On October 17, 1995, Goldman presented its opinion that the $60 offer was inadequate. Goldman based its opinion in part on the fact that Wallace is presently generating and receiving the benefits of its capital expenditure plan for infrastructure such as the Wallace Information Network ("WIN") system, which has become successful only within the past two years. n10 Tr. 429–30. Further,

Wallace's recent alliance with United Stationers, an office products company, had begun to produce favorable returns. Id. at 430. Goldman also believed that a reorganization or recapitalization plan, which Wallace could adopt, would produce current value which could exceed $60 per share, yet still allow its shareholders to retain their ownership interest in the company, a result the Moore cash-out offer could not achieve. Id. at 431.

> n10 A major asset of Wallace is its recently-developed computer system known as the "Wallace Information Network" ("WIN"). The WIN system is a set of computer programs that links together several other Wallace systems, such as its order entry, order management, manufacturing, inventory management, distribution and billing systems, for the purpose of delivering services and assisting the customer, as well as reducing costs. Tr. 220. The benefits WIN provides largely accrue to large, out-source customers because it enables them to control inventories, manage accounts and identify items for consolidation Moore's internal documents reveal that (1) the WIN system is a superior system; (2) Moore entered into an agreement with Electronic Data Systems in a bid to engage in a technological catch-up which has not been successful, Tr. 60; and (3) Wallace has been beating Moore in head-to-head competition for large, forms-intensive customers with multiple locations.

[**16]

The Board concurred in the Goldman conclusion that the price was inadequate, because recent financial results demonstrated continued improvement and momentum in the marketplace. At neither the August 14th nor the October 17th meeting did Goldman provide Wallace with a range of values that would be adequate or fair. Similarly, Goldman did not inform the Board the margin by which the Moore offers fell short of adequacy, nor did the Board ask. At both meetings, however, Goldman went through its materials with the Wallace Board and answered questions posed by the Board regarding the Goldman analysis. Tr. 421.

A hearing on Moore's motion for a preliminary injunction was held on November 7–9th, 1995. At that time, 73.4% of Wallace shareholders had tendered their shares. Moore alleges that the all cash tender offer, proposed merger, and proxy solicitation cannot be completed unless Wallace agrees to remove or make inapplicable its anti-takeover devices, including its poison pill, Article Ninth, and the protection of Section 203. D.I. 1, P 27. The Board's failure to redeem the poison pill, however, is the gravamen of Moore's prayer for injunctive relief. n11

> n11 The Wallace Board is entitled under its poison pill to redeem the rights or make the poison pill inapplicable to the offer and proposed merger by an amendment to the rights agreement. D.I. 1, P 30. The Board is also empowered under Article Ninth to avoid the shareholder vote requirement by approving the transaction by a majority vote of the Board. Id. P 36. Finally, the Board has the right to opt out of Section 203's protection under Delaware law. Id. P 31. While the court notes that Moore also seeks to compel Wallace

to make inapplicable Article Ninth of its Restated Certificate of Incorporation, and opt out of the protection of 8 Del. C. § 203, Moore's briefs submitted before and after oral argument confine its discussion to the poison pill. Additionally, no portion of oral argument was devoted to these defenses. Accordingly, the Court will so limit its discussion.

[**17]

B. Analysis

1. Standard of Review

Before reaching the substantive issues in this case, the Court must determine the standard of review applicable to the Wallace Board's challenged actions. A shareholder challenge to board actions usually entails one of the following standards of judicial review: the traditional business judgment rule, the Unocal standard of enhanced judicial scrutiny, see *Unocal Corp. v. Mesa Petroleum Co., 493 A.2d 946 (Del. 1985)*, or the [*1554] entire fairness standard, see, e.g., *AC Acquisitions Corp. v. Anderson, Clayton & Co., 519 A.2d 103, 111 (Del. 1986). Unitrin, Inc. v. American Gen. Corp., 651 A.2d 1361, 1371 (Del. 1995)*. Determining the appropriate standard of review is not a task this Court takes lightly. "Because the effect of the proper invocation of the business judgment rule is so powerful . . ., the determination of the appropriate standard of judicial review frequently is determinative of the outcome of [the] litigation." Id. (quoting *Mills Acquisition Co. v. Macmillan, Inc., 559 A.2d 1261, 1279 (Del. 1988)*). While the entire fairness standard has no application to the case presently before the Court, n12 the [**18] business judgment rule and Unocal enhanced scrutiny will apply. Accordingly, the Court will first address the interplay between the two standards of review.

> n12 The "entire fairness" standard of review applies "where a self-interested corporate fiduciary has set the terms of a transaction and caused its effectuation." *AC Acquisitions Corp. v. Anderson, Clayton & Co., 519 A.2d 103, 111 (Del. 1986)*. A reviewing court must review the transaction and determine that the merits satisfy the court of its entire fairness, id., including scrutiny of both "fair dealing" and "fair price." *Mills Acquisition Co. v. Macmillan, Inc., 559 A.2d 1261, 1280 (Del. 1988)*. The "entire fairness" standard applies "only if the presumption of the business judgment rule is defeated," *Grobow v. Perot, 539 A.2d 180, 187 (Del. 1988)* (citing *Aronson v. Lewis, 473 A.2d 805, 812–17 (Del. 1984)*), due to allegations of board self-dealing. See, e.g., *Unitrin Inc. v. American Gen. Corp., 651 A.2d 1361, 1372 (Del. 1995)* ("The Court of Chancery concluded that the Board's implementation of the poison pill and the Repurchase Program, in response to American General's Offer, did not constitute self-dealing that would require the Unitrin Board to demonstrate entire fairness."). Since there are no allegations in the present case of an interested transaction, this standard is inapplicable and will not be discussed.

[**19]

The business judgment rule is a judicially-created doctrine which gives recognition to the fundamental tenet of Delaware General Corporation Law that directors are charged with managing the business and affairs of the corporation. See 8 Del. C. § 141. It is a presumption that in making a business decision, the directors of a corporation act on an informed basis, in good faith and honest belief that the action taken was in the best interests of the corporation. *Aronson v. Lewis, 473 A.2d 805, 812 (Del. 1984).* The bedrock principle embodied in the business judgment rule is the court's reluctance to substitute its judgment for that of a board if the board's decision can be attributed to any rational business purpose. *Sinclair Oil Corp. v. Levien, 280 A.2d 717, 720 (Del. 1971).* The plaintiff bears the initial burden and must establish facts sufficient to persuade the Court that the presumption of the business judgment rule has been rebutted and therefore the Court should substitute its own judgment for that of the Board. See *Unitrin, 651 A.2d at 1374.*

When a board is confronted with a hostile tender offer, it has the obligation to determine whether the offer is [**20] in the best interests of the corporation and its shareholders. The board's duty to the shareholders in this context is no different from its duty in any other situation, and its decision should be entitled to the same deference it would receive in other matters. *Unocal, 493 A.2d at 954.* However, because directors might have some entrenchment motive, described by the Supreme Court of Delaware as the "omnipresent specter that a board may be acting primarily in its own interests, rather than those of the corporation and its shareholders," an "enhanced judicial scrutiny" is applicable to board decisions in the tender offer context. That standard must be satisfied before the board's actions are reviewed under the traditional business judgment rule. Id. This enhanced test places the initial burden upon the board to demonstrate compliance therewith before the presumption of the business judgment rule may be invoked. See *Unitrin, 651 A.2d at 1374.*

Under the enhanced judicial scrutiny test set forth in Unocal, the directors must show they had reasonable grounds for believing that a danger to corporate policy and effectiveness existed, a burden which is satisfied by showing [**21] good faith and reasonable investigation. *Unocal, 493 A.2d at 955* (quoting *Cheff v. Mathes, 41 Del. Ch. 494, 199 A.2d 548, 554–55 (Del. 1964)).* This proof is materially enhanced where the board is comprised of a majority of outside independent directors who have complied with their duties of good [*1555] faith and reasonable investigation. *Unocal, 493 A.2d at 955;* see also *Aronson, 473 A.2d at 812.* However, the board is not empowered with unbridled discretion to defeat any perceived threat by whatever draconian means available. *Unocal, 493 A.2d at 955.* A defensive measure may only survive enhanced judicial scrutiny and fall within the purview of the business judgment rule if it is reasonable in relation to the threat posed. Id.

Once the directors meet their burden under Unocal of showing a threat and response proportional to that threat, their actions will be subjected to review under the traditional business judgment rule. See *Macmillan, 559 A.2d at 1288;*

see also *In re Sea-Land Corp. Shareholders Litigation, 642 A.2d 792, 804 (Del. Ch. 1993)* ("Before a board may receive the normal protection of the business judgment rule, it must demonstrate that its actions [**22] were reasonable in relation to the advantage sought to be achieved or to the threat allegedly posed."). The Supreme Court of Delaware and Chancery Court have repeatedly held that the refusal to entertain an offer may comport with a valid exercise of the board's business judgment. *Paramount Communications, Inc. v. Time, Inc., 571 A.2d 1140, 1152 (Del. 1989) ("Time"); Macmillan, 559 A.2d at 1285 n.35; Smith v. Van Gorkom, 488 A.2d 858, 881 (Del. 1985).*

2. Preliminary Injunction Standard

In addition to bringing its legal position within the strictures of substantive Delaware corporate law, Moore must satisfy the procedural criteria for granting a preliminary injunction. Not surprisingly, at some point, the two burdens become intertwined. In a preliminary injunction proceeding, plaintiff bears the burden of establishing (1) the likelihood of success on the merits; (2) the extent of irreparable injury from the conduct complained of; (3) the extent of irreparable harm to the defendants if the preliminary injunction issues; and (4) effect on the public interest if relief were granted. *Clean Ocean Action v. York, 57 F.3d 328, 331 (3d Cir. 1995);* Opticians Ass'n of [**23] *Am. v. Independent Opticians of Am., 920 F.2d 187, 191–92 (3d Cir. 1990).* In effect, the board must defeat the plaintiff's ability to discharge this burden by demonstrating that even under Unocal's enhanced scrutiny, the board's actions merited the protection of the business judgment rule. See *Unitrin, 651 A.2d at 1375.* Plaintiff's likelihood of success on the merits, therefore, is a function of the board's inability to discharge its Unocal burden. See id.

In accordance with the Unocal analysis utilized by the Supreme Court of Delaware and the standard for a preliminary injunction recognized by the Third Circuit Court of Appeals, the Court will review the facts of the case sub judice under the following analytical framework. As to the likelihood of success on the merits: (1) Were the actions of the Wallace Board defensive? (2) If so, did the Wallace Board satisfy its burden under Unocal? (a) What was the nature of the threat perceived by the Wallace Board by the Moore tender offer? (b) Were the Wallace Board's actions reasonably proportionate to the perceived threat of the Moore tender offer? As to the balance of the equities and the public interest: [**24] (1) Has Moore demonstrated irreparable injury if the relief sought is not granted? (2) Is the extent of Moore's injury if the injunction does not issue greater than the injury to Wallace if the injunction issues? (3) Has Moore shown that the relief sought is not adverse to the public interest?

a) Likelihood of Success on the Merits

i) Were the Actions Taken by the Wallace Board "Defensive"?

A defensive measure taken by the board in response to some perceived threat to the corporation is the sine qua non triggering Unocal's enhanced judicial scrutiny. See *Unitrin, 651 A.2d at 1372.* Whether board action is "defensive" can be determined from a variety of factual circumstances, such as the timing of consideration and implementation of the measure in relation to the initial appearance of the corporate threat. See id. (poison pill, advance notice bylaw provision for shareholder proposals, and stock repurchase program, adopted by board after commencement of tender offer, deemed defensive measures); *Gilbert v. El Paso Co., 575 A.2d 1131, 1136 (Del. 1990)* (golden parachute [*1556] agreements, Employee Savings and Stock Ownership Plans and shareholder supermajority [**25] voting provisions adopted after initiation of tender offer deemed defensive measures). Proper determination of the defensive nature of the board's challenged actions is critical. If a particular measure taken by the board is not found to be defensive, the reviewing court must review the board's action under the business judgment rule. *Id.* at 1143–44 (a business combination plan which predates the outside bid is not a defensive measure and therefore not subject to Unocal's enhanced judicial scrutiny).

In the case sub judice, the allegedly defensive measures taken by the Wallace Board include the following: (1) the failure to redeem the poison pill; (2) the adoption of a "golden parachute" employment contract with Cronin; and (3) the amendment to the Wallace bylaws to require a 60-day advance notice period for shareholder proposals for the Wallace annual meeting. With respect to the failure to redeem the poison pill, the Court finds this to be a defensive measure. Poison pills are, by definition, defensive. Even when they are adopted prior to a takeover bid as a preventative measure, they become defensive when the board fails to redeem them after a hostile tender offer is [**26] commenced. See *Moran v. Household Int'l, Inc., 500 A.2d 1346, 1350 (Del. 1985).*

Evidence adduced at the evidentiary hearing persuaded the Court that the golden parachute component of Cronin's employment agreement was not adopted as a defensive measure. Doyle testified that the Wallace Board fully intended to adopt an employment agreement for Cronin, identical in all pertinent respects to that of Dimitriou, Cronin's predecessor, but for some reason failed to get around to it in a timely fashion. During this period of laxity, Moore had been attempting to lure Wallace management over to its company. Tr. 292. In addition to finding Doyle's testimony to be credible, the facts that such agreements are commonplace among chief executives of major companies and that Cronin's severance package was identical to that of his predecessor, persuade this Court that the adoption of the golden parachute agreement was not a defensive measure. The advance notice amendment to the Wallace bylaws is a mild defensive measure, see *Unitrin, 651 A.2d at 1369.* However, it has played no role in either the tender offer or the proxy contest, which explains why it was not briefed or argued by either party. [**27] Accordingly, enhanced judicial scrutiny will be limited to the Wallace Board's failure to redeem the poison pill.

ii) Unocal's Enhanced Judicial Scrutiny

(A) Did the Moore Offer Pose a Threat to Wallace?

Unocal's first inquiry focuses upon the existence and nature of the threat to the target company. *Unocal, 493 A.2d at 955.* Under this inquiry, the target board must demonstrate that after reasonable investigation, the board determined, in

good faith, that the tender offer posed a threat to the corporation or its shareholders which warranted the adoption of a defensive measure. See *Unitrin, 651
A.2d at 1375.* An affirmative and precise determination of a threat must be
demonstrated before moving to the second inquiry under Unocal, as this first inquiry informs the second. See *Unitrin, 651 A.2d at 1384* ("the nature of the threat
associated with a particular hostile offer sets the parameters for the range of permissible defensive tactics."); see also *Time, 571 A.2d at 1154* ("The obvious requisite to determining the reasonableness of a defensive action is a clear
identification of the nature of the threat."). The Unocal Court also held that
[**28] the presence of a majority of outside directors will materially enhance the
board's proof on this issue. *Unocal, 493 A.2d at 955.*

Wallace argues that the Moore tender offer posed a serious threat to Wallace
in that (1) the $56 and $60 offers are inadequate, (2) the offer is squarely contrary
to Wallace's successful business strategy, and (3) the tender offer is illegal under
the antitrust laws. Moore argues that the tender offer poses no threat to Wallace
because, at least as to inadequacy, the Wallace Board never undertook to dis-
cover what an adequate or "fair" price for Wallace stock would be. Thus, Moore
argues, Wallace has no basis upon which to determine that the allegedly inadequate [*1557] price constitutes a threat. Second, Moore argues that the alleged
threat to Wallace's business plan is not legally cognizable, and dismisses as un-
warranted Wallace's analogy to *Time, 571 A.2d 1140.* Third, Moore argues that
the alleged antitrust concerns do not constitute a threat to Wallace, because, as
Wallace itself admits, the antitrust litigation was commenced solely for the purposes of deterring the consummation of Moore's offer.

Since Unocal, Delaware courts have struggled to [**29] determine what
threats cited by target management as justification for defensive measures are
legally cognizable. Early decisions presented easy cases for an affirmative determination of a threat. For example, in Unocal itself, the threat posed by the offer
was due to the coercive nature of the offer. n13 See *Unocal, 493 A.2d at 956*
(two-tier, "front-loaded" cash tender offer for approximately 37% of company's
outstanding stock is inadequate and coercive, and posed a threat to shareholders);
see also *El Paso, 575 A.2d at 1145* (coercive, two-tier, partial tender offer is "serious" threat to shareholders). In those cases, the threat is obvious: shareholders
will feel compelled to tender their shares to avoid being treated less favorably in
the second stage of the transaction. See *Time, 571 A.2d at 1152.*

> n13 A "coercive" offer is a term of art used to describe an offer which has
> the effect of compelling shareholders to tender their shares out of fear of
> being treated less favorably in the second stage. A classic example of a co-
> ercive offer is a partial, front-loaded tender offer. In that case, a shareholder
> might elect to tender immediately, since he cannot be guaranteed the same
> terms should he elect not to tender and the tender offeror succeeds. At that
> point, as a minority shareholder, he might be treated adversely. A "nonco-
> ercive" offer, on the other hand, is one which does not create that compul-
> sion. An example of a noncoercive tender offer would be an all shares, all
> cash, fully negotiable tender offer, where all shareholders are treated
> equally, no matter when they tender. For a detailed explanation of these

terms, see *City Capital Assoc. v. Interco Inc., 551 A.2d 787, 798 (Del. Ch. 1988).*

[**30]

An inadequate, non-coercive tender offer may also pose a legally cognizable threat in two ways. First, the target corporation may be inclined to provide the shareholders with a more attractive alternative, but may need some additional time to formulate and present that option. During the interim, the threat is that shareholders might choose the inadequate tender offer only because the superior option has not yet been presented. See, e.g., *City Capital Assoc. v. Interco Inc., 551 A.2d 787, 798 (Del. Ch. 1988)* (retention of poison pill is appropriate response to give target time to develop an alternative plan to maximize shareholder value). Second, in addition to the threat of inadequacy, the board might also find that the danger that shareholders, tempted by the suitor's premium, might tender their shares in ignorance or mistaken belief as to management's representations of intrinsic value and future expectations. See, e.g., *Time, 571 A.2d at 1153* (threat posed by the fact that "shareholders might elect to tender into Paramount's cash offer in ignorance or in a mistaken belief of the strategic benefit which a business combination with Warner might produce."); see also [**31] *Unitrin, 1994 Del. Ch. LEXIS 187, 1994 WL 698483* at *6 (Del. Ch. Oct. 13, 1994)* ("Board action may be necessary to protect stockholders from a 'low ball' negotiating strategy, or to allow the board to make an important decision over the management of the corporation. There are no limited categories of threats posed by an unsolicited offer, but the board's perception of a threat must be reasonable.") (citations omitted), rev'd on other grounds, *651 A.2d 1361.* n14

> n14 In an effort to delineate different types of threats for the purposes of Unocal, the Time Court quoted the collected views of commentators as set forth in Ronald J. Gilson & Renier Kraakman, Delaware's Intermediate Standard for Defensive Tactics: Is There Substance to Proportionality Review?, 44 Bus. Law. 247, 267 (1989). Types of threats include the following:
>
> (i) opportunity loss . . . [where] a hostile offer might deprive target shareholders of the opportunity to select a superior alternative offered by target management [or, we would add, offered by another bidder];
> (ii) structural coercion, . . . the risk that disparate treatment of non-tendering shareholders might distort shareholders' tender decisions; and
> (iii) substantive coercion, . . . the risk that shareholders will mistakenly accept an underpriced offer because they disbelieve management's representations of intrinsic value.
>
> *Time, 571 A.2d at 1153 n.17.*

[**32]

[*1558] In determining whether the Wallace Board made a good faith determination after reasonable investigation that the Moore offer posed a threat, the

Court is guided by a recent and closely analogous decision of the Supreme Court of Delaware in *Unitrin, 651 A.2d 1361*. There, the court determined that the Unitrin board reasonably perceived a threat to the corporation from the suitor's offer in that shareholders might mistakenly tender without knowledge as to the projected future value of the shares. The board cited several reasons for its determination of a threat: the board's belief that (1) Unitrin stock was worth more than the 50–⅜ offer price; (2) the tender offer price did not reflect Unitrin's long term business prospects as an independent company; (3) the "true value" of Unitrin was not reflected in the current market price of its common stock; (4) because of its strong financial position, Unitrin was well positioned to "pursue strategic and financial opportunities"; and (5) the merger with American General would have anticompetitive effects and thus raise antitrust concerns. *Id. at 1370*. The court deferred to the board's reasonable perception of the threat. Id.; cf. [**33] *Shamrock Holdings, Inc. v. Polaroid Corp., 559 A.2d 278, 289–90 (Del. Ch. 1989)* (noncoercive, all cash, all shares, inadequate tender offer constitutes a cognizable threat since target was on verge of winning a judgment in excess of $5 billion, an asset with a present value shareholders would be unable to value).

With these principles in mind, the Court turns to the evidence proffered by Wallace to determine whether it demonstrates the Board's good faith belief, made after reasonable investigation, that the Moore offer posed a legally cognizable threat. First, the procedure followed by the Wallace Board in assessing each offer by Moore demonstrates reasonable investigation for purposes of Unocal. When Moore's first offer of $56 was made, the Wallace Board met three times within two weeks to review the terms of the offer and assess its merits. Wallace retained Goldman as its investment banker to review the financial aspects of the proposed transaction. Goldman prepared its analysis by using projections which were reasonably related to past growth and historical data which was provided by Wallace management. Collectively, the Board considered Wallace's current business plans [**34] and strategies, its financial projections, its current financial results and future projections, and the opinion of Goldman in arriving at its decision that the $56 offer was inadequate. Further, several individual members of the Board took the position that, based on their knowledge and experience, the offer seemed to be a "low ball" offer. n15 The same investigative procedure was followed when Moore raised its offer price to $60. Updated financial information was given to Goldman which represented the actual, rather than projected, 1995 figures. After Goldman analyzed the information, Goldman again arrived at the conclusion that the $60 offer was also inadequate. The Board considered the presentation of Goldman and arrived at its conclusion that the second offer was also inadequate.

n15 Characteristic of the opinions of Wallace Board members as to the future success of the company is the following excerpt from the testimony of Mr. Doyle:

I think that Wallace, personally, is the epitome of what a successful American company ought to be. If we go back to the middle sixties, Wallace decided that it would change basically—would start to change from being basically a

manufacturing and production company to a sales/marketing-oriented company that was very customer-oriented. It has—today, it is, in my judgment, the best company in its field with respect to technology. It has an exceptionally dedicated and high-morale work force. It has a good experienced management. It has an excellent balance sheet with very little debt and a large cash position. It's in a—in a market where many of its competitors are in trouble and, therefore, Wallace has great opportunity for success over the next five, ten years.
Tr. 459-60.

[**35]

The Wallace Board's decision reflected consideration of a variety of factors which were also reflected in the Goldman report, including the belief that the fourth quarter of fiscal 1995 (May, June and July, 1995), promised to be a good one. That belief became a reality: sales had increased 32% to 33% over the prior year, and profits had increased 32%. The fact that Wallace is generating [*1559] and receiving the benefits of its capital expenditure plan, specifically the WIN system, as well as Wallace's recent alliance with United Stationers which had begun to produce favorable returns, were also considered. These data suggested to the Board that Wallace could achieve returns greater than Moore's offer, while allowing the shareholders to retain their ownership interest. Accordingly, the Court cannot conclude that the Wallace Board lacked good faith or acted unreasonably in its investigation of the Moore offer.

Moore argues that the Wallace Board has not demonstrated good faith and reasonable investigation, on the ground that the preparation performed by Goldman was unreliable because of the optimistic figures provided by Wallace management. Specifically, Moore argues that Goldman based its [**36] future earnings projections on management's assumption that 30% of future profits and 38% of future sales were expected to be derived from acquisitions. However, the associated costs, share dilution, and amortization of goodwill in connection therewith were not similarly figured into its projections, and thus the results, reflecting the benefits but not the costs, were "useless." Smith, however, specifically denied using the acquisition-related figures, with the exception of one projected acquisition, testimony which was unrebutted by Moore. The testimony of Halloran corroborated Smith's statement. Tr. 375, Defense Exhibit ("DX") 33B.

Additionally, the Court finds that the financial projections assumed by Wallace were not unrealistic. In its Strategic Plan, which was provided to Goldman, Wallace had assumed certain growth percentages which proved to be conservative with respect to actual numbers. Halloran Depo. at 172–73. When Wallace was asked to provide updated figures to Goldman, Halloran determined the percentage of actual growth of the company by using actual numbers representing the growth for fiscal 1994 and fiscal 1995. That percentage was then used to project future growth [**37] through the year 2002. To the extent that any prediction of future values has any indicia of trustworthiness, this was a reasonable means to project future values. This finding is bolstered by the fact that its previous projections, based on projected growth in the 1995 strategic plan, had been lower than actual results. Furthermore, Wallace's projections for growth into fiscal years 1996 and 1997 were lower in most instances than the actual growth Wallace experienced in fiscal 1995. n16 While these statistics might be misleading since the Court cannot ascertain the viability of future markets in those areas, at the very least, they indicate a principled assessment of future growth, which hardly rises to the level of bad faith. n17

> n16 For example, in the Business Forms Division, fiscal 1995 actual growth rate was 21%, as compared to its projected growth rate for fiscal 1996, at 14% and for fiscal 1997, at 10%. The same conservative approach was taken with other segments of Wallace's business. In its Continental Division, the 1995 actual growth rate was 24%. Its projected growth rates for fiscal years 1996 and 1997, respectively, were 17% and 15%. Similarly, in its TOPS Division, the actual growth rate for fiscal 1995 was 45%, while its projections for fiscal 1996 and 1997 were, respectively, 14% and 5%.

[**38]

> n17 For example, Mr. Cronin testified that some of the markets in which Wallace is engaged are declining. The business forms industry is predicted to decline between 3% and 5% per year, according to industry analysts. Tr. 317. Thus, a declining market would probably require Wallace to predict declining sales and profits growth in that area.

Furthermore, the Wallace Board could reasonably conclude, based on the upward trend in earnings per share, that the company was well-positioned to reap economic benefits in the future, which would support their initial reaction that the Moore offer seemed "low ball." A review of the earnings per share growth data from recent quarters demonstrates this trend. n18 For the first quarter of fiscal 1995, Wallace reported $0.52 earnings per share growth. This number increased to $0.60 for the second quarter of fiscal 1995, to $0.64 for the third quarter, and finally reached $0.70 for the fourth quarter. Figures for the first quarter of fiscal 1996, recently released, confirmed this upward trend: earnings per share growth reached [*1560] $0.85. n19 Additionally, [**39] the results from the first quarter of fiscal 1996, as compared to the same quarter of fiscal 1995, surpassed management's projections. Management projected a 34% increase in sales and a 50% increase in earnings for the first quarter of fiscal 1996 over the same quarter for 1995. Tr. 409–10. The actual figures for the first quarter of fiscal 1996 were 35.4% and 63.5%, respectively. n20 See D.I. 181 at Exh. A. n21

> n18 The following series of numbers excludes takeover-related costs.

> n19 Moore argues that these increasing numbers demonstrate a phenomenon other than Wallace's continued success in the business. In particular, Moore argues that the recent strike at Ampad, a Wallace competitor, caused Wallace to receive a percent of the industry's business it would otherwise not have enjoyed. Second, Moore argues that Wallace's unexpected

ability to pass on the increase of paper costs to customers yielded unexpected profits. The Court is unpersuaded, in light of the fact that Wallace is so well-positioned in the industry with its technologically advanced computer services system, that these external events were the primary cause of Wallace's upward growth trend.

[**40]

n20 On November 20, 1995, Wallace reported results from the first quarter of fiscal 1996 as follows:

Wallace Computer Services, Inc. . . . . reported that sales for its first quarter ended October 31, 1995 increased 35.4 percent to $214.4 million compared to $158.4 million for the first quarter last year. Before takeover expenses, net income rose 65.6 percent to $19.3 million compared to $11.6 million last year, and earnings per share rose 63.5 percent to 85 cents compared to 52 cents per share achieved in fiscal 1995. These results exceeded the company's most recent forecast and all analyst projections. D.I. 181, at Exh. A.

n21 The Court also recognizes that these increases in growth have been somewhat retarded by the pendency of the Moore bid. As Wallace's November 20, 1995 press releases states, "the hostile takeover bid was delaying the signing of some new contracts, and in its absence, results could be even higher." D.I. 181 at Exh. A.

Finally, as the Unocal court noted, the target board's proof under Unocal is materially enhanced where board's approval [**41] was comprised of a majority of outside independent directors who exercised good faith and reasonable investigation. n22 *Unocal, 493 A.2d at 955.* Their "independent" status, coupled with the substance of and procedures utilized in their review of the Moore offers, satisfies this Court that Wallace has met its initial burden under Unocal to demonstrate, by proof of good faith and reasonable investigation, that the Moore offer posed a threat to Wallace and its shareholders.

n22 The eight-person Wallace Board is comprised of two insiders, Cronin and Dimitriou (the former Chief Executive Officer treated as an insider), and six independent directors. The independent directors are successful businessmen with proven track records. Mr. Doyle has held positions as Senior Vice President, Chief Financial Officer, Chief Administrative Officer and a member of the board at various major domestic corporations. Mr. Olsen is the former President of IGA, a wholesale and retail grocery company. Mr. Canning is the former President of the Walgreen Company, a drug retailer. Mr. Lane is Chairman of both General Binding and Lane Industries. Mr. Ewers is the former Executive Vice President of Wrigley, a chewing gum manufacturer. Mr. Sterns is the former President of a major company. Suffice it to note that all the members of the Wallace Board have substantial experience in serving as high level executives and board members. There was no evidence that Wallace management had either the ability or desire to influence the thinking of the independent directors with respect to the adequacy of the offer.

[**42]

This case presents a factual scenario different from that which normally occurs. In most cases, the target seeks to persuade the Court that the hostile tender offer posed a threat to the company's future plans and the company's shareholders which justified the defensive measures until the expected benefits of the plan come into fruition. Here, however, the directors seek to prove that the hostile tender offer poses a threat of a different nature. The favorable results from the board's past actions are now beginning to be translated into financial results which even surpass management and financial analyst projections, and the financial data which manifests these results are facts only known to them. Therefore, Moore's tender offer poses a threat that shareholders might tender their shares without appreciating the fact that after substantial capital investment, Wallace is actually witnessing the beginning of the pay-off of its business strategy. The Court therefore finds that Moore's tender offer poses a threat to Wallace that shareholders, because they are uninformed, will cash out before realizing the fruits of the substantial technological innovations [*1561] achieved by Wallace. Accordingly, [**43] the Court turns its attention to the second Unocal inquiry, which evaluates the proportionality of the target board's response.

(B) Did the Actions of the Wallace Board Constitute a Reasonable Response?

The second prong of the Unocal enhanced scrutiny requires that once the threat has been identified, the board must prove that its defensive measure[s] constituted a response which was reasonably proportionate to the magnitude of the threat. *Unocal, 493 A.2d at 955.* A claim for breach of fiduciary duty arising out of a board's failure to redeem a poison pill are reviewed under the enhanced scrutiny provided by Unocal. *Moran, 500 A.2d at 1356; Stahl v. Apple Bancorp, Inc., 1990 Del. Ch. LEXIS 121, 1990 WL 114222* at *6 (Del. Ch. Aug. 9, 1990). Reasonableness turns on an assessment by the directors of the nature of the tender offer and the effect such offer would have on the corporate enterprise. *Unocal, 493 A.2d at 955.* Factors relevant to this assessment include (1) inadequacy of the price offered; (2) nature and timing of the offer; (3) questions of illegality; (4) the impact on "constituencies" other than the shareholders (i.e., creditors, customers, employees, and perhaps [**44] even the community generally); (5) the risk of nonconsummation; and (6) the qualities of the securities being offered in the exchange. Id.

Wallace argues that since the Moore tender offer has commenced, it has only taken three actions: (1) rejected the Moore offers for $56 and $60 per share, (2) authorized the commencement of antitrust litigation, and (3) declined to redeem the poison pill. Wallace argues that these actions are clearly reasonable and proper, given the gravity of the threat posed by Moore's offer. Wallace asserts that the decision not to redeem the poison pill is not draconian, because it in no way presents any obstacle to Moore's proxy contest. Moore argues that a fortiori, no threat exists, but that in any event, Wallace's actions were not reasonably proportionate. Since the Wallace Board never informed itself as to what a "fair" or "adequate" price would be, Moore reasons, it was poorly positioned to determine whether a threat due to inadequacy exists as an initial matter, thus obfuscating any meaningful determination of proportionate response, and concomitantly negating any justification for keeping the poison pill in place.

As an initial matter, the [**45] Court notes that poison pills serve legitimate functions which create no fiduciary duty issue. For example, if a hostile tender offer is commenced at a share value which the board, in good faith and after reasonable investigation, determines to be "inadequate," the board may justifiably leave the pill in place for a period of time so as to enable it to take steps necessary to protect and advance shareholder interests. See, e.g., *City Capital, 551 A.2d at 798.* Such permissible actions include negotiation on behalf of the shareholders with the offeror, recapitalization or restructuring as an alternative to the offer, Revlon-style auctioning, should Revlon duties be triggered, or the arrangement for an otherwise better and value-maximizing alternative than that posed by the tender offer. Id.; see also *Stahl, 1990 Del. Ch. LEXIS 121, 1990 WL 114222* at *8 (failure to redeem pill was reasonable in relation to threat since it preserved the board's ability to explore alternatives to enhance shareholder value). After the period in which such alternatives may be considered has ended, and the board has determined that such alternatives are not feasible or, at any rate, not better for the shareholders, [**46] the legitimate role of the poison pill has expired. *City Capital, 551 A.2d at 798.* At that point, the only function the pill serves is to prevent the shareholders from exercising their right to tender, as the poison pill, once activated, effectively forecloses the consummation of the tender offer.

However, failing to redeem a poison pill can be justified by considerations other than maximizing current share value. In Time, the Supreme Court of Delaware noted, "Absent a limited set of circumstances as defined under Revlon, a board of directors, while always required to act in an informed manner, is not under any per se duty to maximize shareholder value in the short term, even in the context of a takeover." *Time, 571 A.2d at 1150.* The Time court further observed that "directors are not [*1562] obliged to abandon a deliberately conceived corporate plan for a short-term shareholder profit unless there is clearly no basis to sustain the corporate strategy." *Id. at 1154;* see also *Mai Basic Four, Inc. v. Prime Computer, 1988 Del. Ch. LEXIS 161, 1988 WL 140221* at *4 (Del. Ch. Dec. 20, 1988) ("Prime has recently obtained new management and is only now on the verge of reaping the economic benefits [**47] of its recent acquisition of Computervision. As a result, the projections by Prime's management for the future are optimistic."); compare, *Sutton Holding Corp. v. DeSoto, Inc., 1990 Del. Ch. LEXIS 15, *23, 1990 WL 13476* at *8 (Del. Ch. Feb. 5, 1990) (management's failure to attempt to maximize shareholder value, and reliance on a modest restructuring plan which had been prepared in the ordinary course of business, falls short of the business plan of Time, and thus ordering of the immediate redemption of the poison pill would ordinarily be required).

Delaware courts have recognized that at some point, the failure to redeem a poison pill can constitute a fiduciary breach. "Our cases, however, also indicate that in the setting of a noncoercive offer, absent unusual facts, there may come a time when a board's fiduciary duty will require it to redeem the rights and to permit the shareholders to choose." *City Capital, 551 A.2d at 798–99* (failure to redeem the poison pill, to enable board to implement restructuring plan projected to produce modest increase in share value, constituted an unreasonable response to the threat posed by noncoercive tender offeror); see also *Grand Metro. Public Ltd. v. Pillsbury [**48] Co., 558 A.2d 1049, 1057–58 (Del. Ch. 1988)* (failure to redeem poison pill in order to implement board's restructuring plan projected to offer greater share value was unreasonable in relation to threat posed by noncoercive tender offer, since projected benefits of plan may never come into fruition).

While Unocal gave no direct guidance to courts applying the proportionality test, the Court did expressly define the outer parameter of board action by condemning any action which is "draconian" as not reasonably proportionate to the perceived threat. *Unocal, 493 A.2d at 955.* Draconian measures have been described as measures which are coercive or preclusive with respect to the outside bid. See *Unitrin, 651 A.2d at 1387–88.* Board actions that are coercive in nature or force upon shareholders a management-sponsored alternative to a hostile offer, even if the threat is valid, may be struck down as unreasonable and nonproportionate responses. See *Time, 571 A.2d at 1154–55* ("Time's responsive action to Paramount's tender offer was not aimed at 'cramming down' on its shareholders a management-sponsored alternative, but rather had as its goal the carrying forward of a preexisting [**49] transaction in an altered form. Thus, the response was reasonably related to the threat."). If a defensive measure is not preclusive or coercive, Unocal requires the action to fall within a "range of reasonableness." *Unitrin, 651 A.2d at 1387–88; Paramount Communications Inc. v. QVC Network Inc., 637 A.2d 34, 45 (Del. 1993)* ("QVC"). As the Unitrin court noted, "proper and proportionate defensive responses are intended and permitted to thwart perceived threats," and the board need not wait for the actual takeover to be commenced, when it reasonably perceives the takeover threat to be imminent:

When a corporation is not for sale, the board of directors is the defender of the metaphorical medieval corporate bastion and the protector of the corporation's shareholders. The fact that a defensive action must not be coercive or preclusive does not prevent a board from responding defensively before a bidder is at the corporate bastion's gate.

Unitrin, 651 A.2d at 1388. The rationale for this "range of reasonableness" standard, as explained by the Unitrin court, is that directors need a degree of latitude in discharging their fiduciary duties when defending [**50] against threats to the company. That latitude, combined with an appropriate amount of judicial restraint, results in a reviewing court's upholding the board's defensive actions, provided the actions are not coercive or preclusive. See *id. at 1388.*

In Unitrin, the board's response to the hostile tender offer was found not to be preclusive or coercive. The challenged actions taken were the adoption of poison pill, advance notice provision in bylaws for shareholder [*1563] proposals, and a repurchase program. The Unitrin board determined that the inadequate price of the offer and potential antitrust complications caused the American General offer to be a threat. Discarding the antitrust concerns as frivolous, see *Unitrin, 1994 Del. Ch. LEXIS 187, 1994 WL 698483,* at *8, the Chancery Court determined that the inadequate price threat was "mild" because the offer was negotiable both in price and structure. Id. at *7. However, even in the face of a mild threat, the Chancery Court upheld the board's adoption of the poison pill because the board reasonably believed the price was inadequate and feared that the shareholders would not realize that the long term value of Unitrin was not reflected in the market [**51] price of the stock. Id. at *8. This finding was not contested on appeal to the Supreme Court of Delaware. *Compare, QVC, 637 A.2d at 49–50* (defensive measures designed to protect desired merger with Viacom deemed draconian in light of "threat" posed by QVC all cash tender offer for majority of Paramount shares, offering aggregate premium of over $1 billion).

In the present case, retention of the poison pill is not draconian. The Board's decision not to redeem the pill is not coercive or preclusive. First, retention of the pill will have no discriminatory effect on shareholders, as is generally the result in any situation involving a coercive offer. See *Unitrin, 651 A.2d at 1388* ("A selective repurchase of shares in a public corporation on the market, such as Unitrin's Repurchase Program, generally does not discriminate because all shareholders can voluntarily realize the same benefit by selling."). Second, and more important, retention of the pill will have no effect on the success of the proxy contest. See *Moran, 500 A.2d at 1357* ("We reject appellants' contentions . . . that the Rights Plan fundamentally restricts proxy contests."); see also *Unitrin, 651 A.2d at 1383* [**52] (concluding that a proxy contest is not precluded by the existence of a poison pill, supermajority voting requirement and fully implemented stock repurchase plan); *Time, 571 A.2d at 1155* (Time board's response to the Paramount bid was not preclusive because Paramount was still able to make an offer for the combined Time-Warner entity or amend the conditions of its offer to eliminate the requirement that the Time-Warner agreement be nullified). Here, the poison pill is only triggered upon the acquisition of 20% of the shares of Wallace stock. Therefore, so long as Moore maintains a stock ownership percentage below that amount, it may safely wage its proxy contest free from the dramatic effect of the poison pill.

Since the Court finds that the retention of the poison pill was not a coercive or preclusive response, it must merely be satisfied that it fell within a "range of reasonableness" to survive Unocal scrutiny. *QVC, 637 A.2d at 45–46.* The evidence demonstrates that the Wallace Board reasonably believed that the shareholders were entitled to protection from what they considered to be a "low ball" offer. See, e.g., *Unitrin, 1994 Del. Ch. LEXIS 187, 1994 WL 698483* at *8 ("It is the prerogative [**53] of the directors of a Delaware corporation to determine that the market undervalues the price of its stock and to protect its stockholders from offers that do not reflect the long term value of the corporation under its present management plan."). After substantial capital investment spanning several years, Wallace had finally begun to reap the financial benefits from its WIN system. Cf. *Mai Basic Four, 1988 Del. Ch. LEXIS 161, 1988 WL 140221* at *4 ("Prime has recently obtained new management and is only now on the verge of reaping the economic benefits of its recent acquisition"). These benefits, however, were reflected in data which remained peculiarly within the province of the Wallace Board. Shareholders, at the time of the Moore offer, were unable to appreciate the upward trend in Wallace's earnings which have been set forth in detail above. Given this situation, the Wallace Board's response can hardly be deemed unreasonable. In light of the foregoing, the Court concludes the Wallace Board has demonstrated that its retention of the poison pill falls within the range of reasonableness required under Unocal. See *Unitrin, 651 A.2d at 1388.* n23

n23 The Wallace Board also had concerns as to whether the acquisition of Wallace by Moore would violate federal antitrust law. Although this Court has, for preliminary injunction purposes, concluded that it would not, as appears infra, one cannot say there was not legitimate substance to this concern. If there were antitrust standing, it is unknown what result would obtain after a full-blown trial.

[**54]

[*1564] Having concluded that retention of the poison pill was proportionate to the threat the Wallace Board believes Moore's tender offer poses, the poison pill is entitled to review under the business judgment rule. The burden now shifts "'back to the plaintiffs who have the ultimate burden of persuasion [in a preliminary injunction proceeding] to show a breach of the directors' fiduciary duties.' In order to rebut the protection of the business judgment rule, the burden on the plaintiffs will be to demonstrate, 'by a preponderance of the evidence that the directors' decision were primarily based on [(1)] perpetuating themselves in office or [(2)] some other breach of fiduciary duty such as fraud, overreaching, lack of good faith, or [(3)] being uninformed.' *Unocal, 493 A.2d at 958* (emphasis added)." *Unitrin, Inc., 651 A.2d at 1390* (internal citation omitted).

Moore has not carried its burden. It is held the decision of the Wallace Board not to redeem the poison pill was a valid exercise of its business judgment.

b) Hardship to Moore, Wallace, and the Public Interest

While Moore has not succeeded in showing a likelihood of success on the merits, the Court will briefly [**55] discuss the other requirements for a preliminary injunction. In ruling on a preliminary injunction, the Court must weigh the extent of hardship to the plaintiff if the requested relief is not granted against the hardship to the defendant if the relief is granted. See *Clean Ocean Action, 57 F.3d at 331.* Moore argues that if the Court does not issue a preliminary injunction, Moore will continue to suffer the consequences of the Wallace Board's breach of fiduciary duty by not having its tender offer put to the shareholders. Furthermore, Moore argues, the availability of the proxy contest does not negate Moore's right to an equitable remedy, especially since Wallace plans to rely on its defensive supermajority voting requirements to block the offer and thwart the overwhelming desires of the shareholders. Wallace argues that Moore has failed to put forward any evidence of injury since the option of a proxy contest is still available to Moore. Furthermore, Wallace argues it will suffer irreparable injury in that the company will cease to exist if the tender offer were to succeed, and there could therefore never be a trial on the merits. Finally, since this would be a cash-out merger, [**56] the Wallace shareholders will be deprived of their right to participate in the emerging glowing financial results of Wallace. A preliminary injunction would also grant Moore access to Wallace's WIN system, a move which could not later be "unscrambled." It is Wallace's technology which is enabling it to beat Moore in head-to-head competition. If a preliminary injunction were granted, there is a real possibility that Moore would gain access to that technology prior to trial. If that were to happen, Wallace will have lost its technological advantage and with it, its competitive edge.

The Court finds Wallace's arguments persuasive. First, Moore has not demonstrated irreparable injury if the preliminary injunction does not issue. Moore may still wage its proxy contest. Second, and perhaps most importantly, to the extent that Moore would suffer injury if relief were denied, Wallace's injury if the injunctive relief is granted would be far greater. At the preliminary injunction stage of a hostile tender offer case, the Court must be extremely cautious when determining whether to grant the relief, given the dramatic consequences of the action. Cf. *United States v. Spectro Foods Corp.*, [**57] *544 F.2d 1175, 1181 (3d Cir. 1976)* ("The power to issue a preliminary injunction, especially a mandatory one, should be sparingly exercised."). Finally, the public interest favors neither side.

IV. WALLACE'S ANTITRUST COUNTERCLAIM

A. Antitrust Standing

1. Background

Moore concedes that "on a motion to dismiss for failure to state a claim, all allegations [*1565] in the pleadings must be accepted as true." *Schrob v. Catterson, 948 F.2d 1402, 1405 (3d Cir. 1991)*; see also *In re Solar Mfg. Corp., 200 F.2d 327, 333 (3d Cir. 1952)* (applying same standard to counterclaims), cert. denied, *345 U.S. 940 (1953)*. The Court will assume the veracity of the facts as averred by Wallace in the context of Moore's motion to dismiss.

According to Wallace's allegations, Moore and Wallace compete in the manufacture and sale of business forms. Wallace Counterclaim, Count One, P 13, D.I. 40. Wallace asserts in its antitrust counterclaim that "if Moore were to acquire Wallace, the effect of such acquisition may be substantially to lessen competition in the relevant product and geographic market, thus violating Section 7 of the Clayton Act, *15 U.S.C. § 18.*" D.I. 40, Counterclaim [**58] at P19. Wallace also avers that unless the Court enjoins Moore's takeover attempt, Wallace will suffer irreparable harm flowing from the antitrust infirmity, including but not limited to, "loss of independent decision making authority, loss of trade secrets, loss of employees, and loss of customers." Id. at P 20.

2. Analysis

Under Section 16 of the Clayton Act, "any person, firm, corporation, or association shall be entitled to sue for and have injunctive relief . . . against threatened loss or damage by a violation of the antitrust laws . . . ." *15 U.S.C. § 26.* As an antitrust plaintiff, Wallace must, however, allege and ultimately prove that it would suffer threatened loss or damage constituting an "antitrust injury." *Cargill,*

Inc. v. Monfort of Colorado, Inc., 479 U.S. 104, 113, 93 L. Ed. 2d 427, 107 S. Ct. 484 (1986); The Treasurer, Inc. v. Philadelphia Nat'l Bank, 682 F. Supp. 269, 273 (D.N.J.), aff'd mem. op., *853 F.2d 921 (3d Cir. 1988).* Antitrust injury involves injury "of the type the antitrust laws were intended to prevent and that flows from that which makes defendants' acts unlawful." *Cargill, 479 U.S. at 109* (citing *Brunswick Corp. v. Pueblo [**59] Bowl-O-Mat, Inc., 429 U.S. 477, 489, 50 L. Ed. 2d 701, 97 S. Ct. 690 (1977)).*

Prior to the Cargill decision, Supreme Court precedent under the Clayton Act required a Clayton Act plaintiff to demonstrate the threat of "antitrust injury" when suing for damages. *Brunswick Corp., 429 U.S. at 489.* However, there raged a debate in the lower courts as to whether a Clayton Act injunctive plaintiff needed to establish antitrust injury when seeking injunctive relief. See, e.g., *CIA Petrolera Caribe, Inc. v. ARCO Caribbean, Inc., 754 F.2d 404, 407–08 (1st Cir. 1985)* (plaintiff need only show threat of injury emanating from the antitrust violation); *Board of Regents v. National Collegiate Athletic Assoc., 707 F.2d 1147, 1151 (10th Cir.), aff'd, 468 U.S. 85, 82 L. Ed. 2d 70, 104 S. Ct. 2948 (1983)* (Brunswick standing limitation not fully applicable to suit for injunctive relief); but see, e.g., *Local Beauty Supply, Inc. v. Lamaur Inc., 787 F.2d 1197 (7th Cir. 1986)* (plaintiff need show "antitrust injury" to fulfill standing requirement); *Schoenkopf v. Brown & Williamson Tobacco Corp., 637 F.2d 205 (3d Cir. 1980)* (same). This debate extended to merger cases involving [**60] standing of target companies to assert Clayton Act violations as well. See, e.g., *Laidlaw Acquisition Corp. v. Mayflower Group, Inc., 636 F. Supp. 1513, 1516–17 (S.D. Ind. 1986)* (target plaintiff has standing to sue in antitrust case); *Gearhart Indus., Inc. v. Smith Int'l, Inc., 592 F. Supp. 203, 211 n.1 (N.D. Tex.)* (same), aff'd in part, modified and vacated in part, *741 F.2d 707 (5th Cir. 1984);* but see, e.g., *Central Nat'l Bank v. Rainbolt, 720 F.2d 1183, 1186–87 (10th Cir. 1983)* (target corporation lacked standing in antitrust case to sue for injunctive relief); *A.D.M. Corp. v. SIGMA Instruments, Inc., 628 F.2d 753 (1st Cir. 1980)* (same); *Carter Hawley Hale Stores, Inc. v. Limited, Inc., 587 F. Supp. 246, 250 (C.D. Cal. 1984).*

In Cargill, the Supreme Court finally repaired the rent in the Circuits over this issue. The Court held that a plaintiff seeking an injunction under Section 16 of the Clayton Act must show a threat of "antitrust injury" in order to fulfill the standing requirement. In that case, the nation's fifth-largest beef packer, Monfort of Colorado ("Monfort"), sought an injunction in a challenge to a merger between the nation's second and [**61] [*1566] third-largest beef packers. *Cargill, 479 U.S. at 106.* The Court first acknowledged that under the Clayton Act's statutory scheme, its standing analysis for injunctive relief would "not always be identical" to standing analysis for damages. *Id. at 111 n.6.* Notwithstanding this caveat, the Court went on to declare it to be "anomalous . . . to read the Clayton Act to authorize a private plaintiff to secure an injunction against a threatened injury for which he would not be entitled to compensation if the injury actually occurred." *Id. at 112.* Following this reasoning, the Court held that a plaintiff seeking injunctive relief under Section 16 of the Clayton Act must allege antitrust injury. *Id. at 113.*

A survey of both case law and scholarly commentary subsequent to the Cargill decision spurs this Court to conclude that the target of a hostile takeover has no standing to bring a Section 7 Clayton Act claim. See e.g., *Anago, Inc. v.*

Tecnol Medical Prod., Inc., 976 F.2d 248 (5th Cir. 1992) (target has no standing to bring Clayton antitrust claim), cert. dismissed, *114 S. Ct. 491 (1993); Burnup & Sims, Inc. v. Posner, 688 F. Supp. 1532 (S.D. Fla. 1988)* (same); [**62] *Burlington Indus., Inc. v. Edelman, 666 F. Supp. 799 (M.D.N.C. 1987)* (same), aff'd, *1987 WL 91498* (4th Cir. June 22, 1987); II Phillip Areeda & Herbert Hovenkamp, Antitrust Law, P 381b, at 332 (Rev. Ed. 1995) (same); Andrew Zuckerman, Standing of Targets of Hostile Takeovers to Enjoin Their Acquisition on Antitrust Grounds, 1992/1993 Ann. Sur. Am. Law 447 (same); but see contra Joseph F. Brodley, Antitrust Standing in Private Merger Cases: Reconciling Private Incentives and Public Enforcement Goals, *94 Mich. L. Rev. 1 (1995).* This line of cases and commentary has cited various grounds pursuant to Cargill to justify a lack of target standing in Clayton Act cases.

For example, courts have regarded any alleged injury suffered by a target in a merger as being inherent to the merger process rather than flowing from any anticompetitive effect of the merger. See *Burnup, 688 F. Supp. at 1534; Burlington, 666 F. Supp. at 805.* Another rationale for finding a lack of target standing is the view that rather than suffering injury, the target and its shareholders ultimately benefit from any increased prices or decreased competition stemming from the merger. *Anago, [**63] 976 F.2d at 251; Burlington, 666 F. Supp. at 805.* Finally, courts have even found that disingenuous antitrust suits may be brought by targets to thwart the loss of control to be suffered by management, as opposed to any motives relating to antitrust. In that vein, courts have not shied from the type of cynicism first articulated by Judge Friendly:

Drawing Excalibur from a scabbard where it would doubtless remain sheathed in the face of a friendly offer, the target company typically hopes to obtain a temporary injunction which may frustrate the acquisition since the offering company may well decline the expensive gambit of a trial . . . .

Missouri Portland Cement Co. v. Cargill, Inc., 498 F.2d 851, 854 (2d Cir.), cert. denied, *419 U.S. 883, 42 L. Ed. 2d 123, 95 S. Ct. 150 (1974).* See also *Burnup, 688 F. Supp. at 1534* ("The suit must be understood in its true sense, an attempt by the incumbent management to defend their own positions, not as an attempt to vindicate any public interest.").

Demonstrating a resistance to change even in light of Cargill, precedent from the Second Circuit Court of Appeals takes the opposite view. See Consolidated Gold [**64] *Fields PLC v. Minorco, S.A., 871 F.2d 252 (2d Cir. 1989)* (target corporation found to have standing to sue for Clayton Act violation), cert. dismissed, *492 U.S. 939, 110 S. Ct. 29, 106 L. Ed. 2d 639 (1989).* In Consolidated Gold Fields, the court held that the plaintiff target would suffer antitrust injury because its "loss of independence [was] causally linked to the injury occurring in the marketplace." *Consolidated Gold Fields, 871 F.2d at 258.* However, the loss of independent decision making, intrinsic to any takeover case, runs counter to Cargill's mandate that "plaintiffs must show more than simply an 'injury causally linked' to a particular merger." *Cargill, 479 U.S. at 109* (citing *Brunswick, 429 U.S. at 489*).

[*1567] This principle is further illuminated in the Consolidated Gold Fields dissenting opinion, where Judge Altimari posed the following hypothetical:

Each of the injuries [such as loss of decision making power] alleged by Gold Fields would occur if the combining corporations controlled a total market share of only 2% [implying no anticompetitive result], or if the entity attempting the takeover was not a competitor of the target.

Consolidated Gold Fields, [**65] *871 F.2d at 264* (Altimari, J., dissenting). The dissent also pointed to a further flaw in the Consolidated Gold Fields reasoning, where the majority expressly relied on a decision which did not have the benefit of the Supreme Court's reasoning in Cargill and whose continued vitality was therefore limited. Id. (citing *Grumman Corp. v. LTV Corp., 665 F.2d 10 (2d Cir. 1981)*).

The Third Circuit Court of Appeals has recognized that articulation of a precise formulation for antitrust standing is a continuing struggle, as standing is a somewhat "malleable concept." *Alberta Gas Chemicals, Ltd. v. E.I. du Pont de Nemours and Co., 826 F.2d 1235, 1239 (3d Cir. 1987),* cert. denied, *486 U.S. 1059, 100 L. Ed. 2d 930, 108 S. Ct. 2830 (1988).* In Alberta Gas, the Third Circuit analyzed antitrust standing under Section 7 of the Clayton Act. Plaintiff Alberta Gas was a methanol producer who challenged the merger of a competitor, DuPont, with another company that produced methanol, Conoco. *Id. at 1236–37.* Alberta Gas claimed injury resulting in that it allegedly lost sales when the merger induced Conoco to no longer participate in the push to stimulate market demand for [**66] methanol. *Id. at 1237.* Applying Cargill, the court declined to find this type of loss as connected with or resulting from DuPont's market power in the methanol-producing industry. *826 F.2d at 1241.* Refusing to take a lenient stance on what constitutes antitrust injury, and instructive to the case sub judice, the court also noted that the same type of harm, i.e., non-antitrust harm, would have occurred if any acquiror decided to curtail the target's production and marketing plans. Id.

The Third Circuit appellate court has not faced squarely the issue of target antitrust standing. However, with the above weaknesses in the Consolidated Gold Fields majority's reasoning, as well as the strict approach countenanced by the Alberta Gas court, I conclude that the Third Circuit Court of Appeals would join the Anago line of cases rather than follow Consolidated Gold Fields. The purpose of the requirement of antitrust injury is to ensure that the harm alleged by a plaintiff corresponds to the rationale for finding a violation of the antitrust laws in the first place. *Ansell, Inc. v. Schmid Laboratories, Inc., 757 F. Supp. 467, 484* (D.N.J.), aff'd, *941 F.2d 1200* [**67] *(3d Cir. 1991).* In the event of a Moore takeover, Wallace alleges it will be harmed by a loss in independent decision making authority, loss of customers, loss of employees, and loss of trade secrets. These alleged injuries do not occur because of the potential lessening of competition; rather, they occur due to a change in corporate control. See *Burlington Indus., 666 F. Supp. at 805.* In other words, these sequelae can occur with the consummation of any merger, even those that are not violative of the Clayton Act, and are divorced from any considerations that less competition may exist in the open market. Id.

In sum, because Wallace has not alleged injury "of the type the antitrust law were intended to prevent," the Court will grant Moore's motion to dismiss Count I of Wallace's counterclaim.

Ordinarily, this opinion would stop here and the Wallace motion to preliminarily enjoin the merger on antitrust grounds would not be treated. However, the plain fact is the circuits have divided on the issue of antitrust standing. The Fifth Circuit, Anago, and the Fourth Circuit, Burlington Indus. (summary affirmance), have concluded a takeover target does not have antitrust [**68] standing while the Second Circuit in Consolidated Gold Fields has concluded the opposite. Antitrust standing is a prudential, not constitutional limitation on federal court jurisdiction. As such, it is not surprising that the Circuits have reached opposite conclusions. Similarly, while I believe there should be this prudential limitation on antitrust jurisdiction, [*1568] those possessed of a higher commission might feel otherwise. In an abundance of caution, in order to facilitate appellate review should that contingency occur, the merits of the Wallace motion for preliminary injunction based on an alleged antitrust violation will be addressed.

B. Preliminary Injunction - Wallace's Antitrust Counterclaim

Wallace has moved to preliminarily enjoin a proposed merger with Moore. As stated above, Wallace asserts in its Section 7 counterclaim that "if Moore were to acquire Wallace, the effect of such acquisition may be substantially to lessen competition in the relevant product and geographic market. . . . " D.I. 40, Counterclaim at P 19. Wallace alleges that for most customers in the relevant product and geographic markets, the only acceptable vendors are Wallace, Moore and the [**69] Standard Register Company; thus, the acquisition of Wallace by Moore would transform a three-firm market into a two-firm market. Id. at PP 16–17. Wallace identifies the relevant product market to be the sale of forms and forms services to large, forms-intensive multi-location customers. Tr. 564.

I. Facts

a) Wallace's Evidence

As an obligatory preamble for setting the stage for its definition of the relevant product market as the forms and form services market encompassing large, forms-intensive customers with multiple locations, Wallace offered a historical backdrop to contextualize the current market conditions. Over the past two decades, the business forms market has been pressured to redefine itself in response to evolving customer needs, technology, and availability of raw resources. According to Douglas Fitzgerald, Wallace's Vice President of Marketing, a business customer in the mid-1970s would typically manage most or all of its forms needs in-house. Tr. 98–100. The customer would invariably initiate a given form's inception, design, and utilization; ultimately the customer would print the form on-site or solicit bids to have a vendor (such as Wallace) print [**70] a supply of forms. Once the forms were mass produced and/or shipped to the customer, the customer would warehouse the forms and monitor the form's inventory level and restock at the appropriate time.

In this so-called traditional method of forms management, vendors competed on the basis of price and quality, as well as service, which was evaluated primarily by the turn-around time measured between time of placement of order and delivery. Tr. 100. Over time, the business forms market has mushroomed beyond the mere printing and delivery of forms. Fitzgerald described two trends at the heart of this market transition: first, the proliferation of computers has created a corresponding need for forms and other related supplies. Second, a trend towards "out-sourcing" has evolved: having the vendor assume the forms-management responsibilities formerly achieved internally. For some customers, out-sourcing their forms management functions is efficient and results in significant cost savings. For example, a Wallace customer, Pacific Bell, credits an annual savings of $2 million to its out-sourcing of forms management services. Tr. 105.

Currently, the trend towards customer out-sourcing is [**71] a force to be reckoned with, and business forms vendors fiercely compete by offering an ever-expanding breadth of services. To do so effectively, forms providers such as Wallace offer a smorgasbord of options tailored specifically to the customer's particular needs. For example, in response to the changing demands of the forms marketplace, Wallace provides on-site forms management, i.e., a Wallace employee(s) is stationed at the customer's workplace to perform such diverse tasks as forms design, forms utilization review (e.g., elimination of duplicative forms), forms inventory management, distribution, and purchasing.

Fitzgerald identified a subset of customers who demand out-sourcing services as "large, forms-intensive n24 customers with multiple locations" ("[*1569] LFICwMLs"). Tr. 106. According to Fitzgerald, these customers typically solicit contract bids for forms and forms-related services from various competing vendors. The LFICwML will submit to each vendor-candidate a request for information or a proposal outlining the required forms and accompanying services it seeks. Many of the needs presented by the customer require the vendor to showcase its best attributes, i.e., [**72] provide concrete reasons why one vendor should be considered superior over another. In Wallace's experience, a LFICwML may solicit requests for proposals or bids from as little as two to as many as "multiple dozens" of vendors. Tr. 261. Sometimes, if Wallace is a finalist in the bidding contest, it may lower its proposed price in order to be more competitive, especially if the other finalists are Moore or Standard Register. Tr. 262. However, Wallace does not generally lower its bid price if it is a finalist against vendors other than these; Wallace perceives Moore and Standard Register to be its main competitors, while it views the others as lacking the breadth of service and sophisticated out-sourcing capabilities to be considered competitive when courting LFICwMLs. Wallace did acknowledge, at least in one instance, however, the existence of a LFICwML, Kaiser Permanente, that elected to solicit bids for its forms and forms management functions from regional vendors and not Moore, Wallace, or Standard Register. Tr. 209.

> n24 Forms-intensive has been described by one Wallace witness as referring to either the significance of the form within the customer's organization, or to the volume of forms within the organization, or both. Testimony of Michael Leatherman, Tr. 255.

[**73]

Notwithstanding its view as to its major competitors. Wallace admitted that there are other suppliers who serve LFICwMLs, such as Duplex, Ennis, Reynolds & Reynolds. Vanier, GIS, Better Business Forms, Bowater, Williamette, Jerome

Business, Rittenhouse, Avery Dennison, and Ross Martin. Tr. 135–45, 155, 159, 161–62, 165–68. These suppliers may merely provide forms without forms management services, or forms management services without forms, or a mixture of forms and forms management services. Further, when Wallace wins a contract bid, the bid may be "split" or shared with one or more of these or other competitors. Tr. 129–30. For example, Wallace prints Domestic Air Bill forms for the Federal Express corporation, where Standard Register prints its International Air Bills. Tr. 155.

To compete effectively for customers, Wallace has developed state-of-the-art computer technology allowing customer orders to be automatically routed to the optimum warehouse location, where storage and shipping are bar-code driven. Tr. 117. Inventory and quality control programs track and assure accuracy of order filling; customers are provided with summary invoicing that organizes order data in a concise [**74] format.

Additionally, Wallace has developed the WIN computer system. Fitzgerald described this program as allowing "customers access to a variety of sophisticated forms management services." Tr. 171. Generally, a customized WIN program is offered to Wallace customers who purchase a combination of products that exceeds $1 million. A similar program with lesser customization called Select Services, is offered to Wallace customers with accounts of over $400,000 but less than $1 million. Tr. 213. Customers who utilize either of these programs are charged via pricing methodology that accounts for both product and service. Charges for the services provided are not broken down separately, rather, they are incorporated into a single price incurred for both product and correlative service. Tr. 174.

The WIN program is Wallace's flagship computer program. As described above, it links together order entry, order management, manufacturing, inventory, distribution, and billing systems. Tr. 220. With all of these functions coordinated and available in a single software format, WIN allows Wallace to provide LFICwMLs, many of whom are out-source customers, with tools to streamline their forms [**75] management. If a Wallace customer qualifies for the WIN program, that customer can promptly access the gamut of WIN services on the customer's own personal computer. Tr. 251. Michael Leatherman, a Wallace Senior Vice President and its Chief Information Officer, testified that Wallace invested $34 million over a nine-year period to cultivate the WIN software, basically [*1570] from scratch, as its software needs were sui generis. Tr. 240. Leatherman was unaware of any commercially available software that could readily supplant the WIN software.

Wallace counts its WIN system as a trump card in the competition against its competitors. Since the WIN system has become available, Wallace has won LFICwML accounts from other vendors, including Moore. Tr. 268–70. One of Moore's consultants has admitted that the WIN system "could put Wallace four years ahead of [Moore] in terms of order management." DX 60 at 834454. Moore has been struggling intensively to improve its own computer system, retaining Electronic Data Systems as an adscititous partner in systems development. Tr. 60. Moore's costs in its quest for computer system enhancement have been staggering: in 1995, Moore budgeted $44 million, [**76] and for 1996, it has budgeted

$35 million. McKay Depo. at 111, D.I. 149. Despite these efforts, Moore has suffered delays in implementing enhanced computer systems, with consequential disappointing earnings figures in its U.S. Forms Division. Tr. 60.

i) Wallace's Customers

As anecdotal testimonial support, Wallace also offered evidence from two of its satisfied customers. John W. Rountree, an administrator at Public Service Electric and Gas Company of New Jersey ("PSE&G"), testified that his company uses about 1200 forms in its day-to-day operations. Rountree stated that PSE&G is a satisfied WIN system user, and that it has out-sourced both the printing and managing of its forms. When asked hypothetically if Moore acquired Wallace, and Moore raised prices by five percent for the same services PSE&G currently received, Rountree answered that if no other vendor could provide those services, PSE&G would pay the increased price. Tr. 338.

Similarly, Frank Cuomo, Purchasing Manager with the Pershing Division of Donaldson, Lufkin and Jenrette Securities Corporation, testified that his company uses several hundred forms. Like his PSE&G counterpart, Cuomo is a satisfied WIN customer, [**77] and takes advantage of Wallace's forms management services for its national needs. Unlike his PSE&G counterpart, however, Cuomo also uses local vendors for forms purchases where no forms management is needed, so as to not be totally dependent on a single supplier. Tr. 356. In the hypothetical event of a Moore takeover and price hike, Cuomo would likewise absorb a price increase of five percent for the same services he currently receives from Wallace. Tr. 353.

ii) Wallace's Antitrust Expert

Dr. Jerry Hausman, a Professor of Economics at Massachusetts Institute of Technology, testified as Wallace's expert on the antitrust claim. Hausman's expert opinion was based on econometric analyses n25 he performed on raw data provided to him by Wallace. Hausman had Wallace collect all of their bidding data for their LFICwMLs, specifically those with annual contracts worth $500,000 or more. These data were culled for the time period commencing January 1, 1994 up through the present.

n25 An econometric study is the "use of statistical techniques to analyze economic data." Testimony of Jerry Hausman, Tr. 541.

[**78]

Initially, Hausman explained that for the statistical population of large (greater than $500,000) contracts on which Wallace chose to bid during the above time period, the four largest incumbent contract holders were Moore at 44%, Wallace at 18%, Standard Register at 15%, and Uarco at 12%. Tr. 547, DX 56. After the bidding process closed, these incumbent contracts were awarded anew, with a resultant reshuffling into new proportions: Wallace subsequently won over 50% of the contracts, Moore won about 15%, Standard Register won 12%. Uarco was not able to hold onto any contracts at all. Tr. 547–48, DX 57.

From these data, Hausman concluded that the three companies, Moore, Standard Register, and Wallace, are "very important competitive companies," Tr. 548, and are "primarily responsible for servicing large, multi-location customers that wish to out-source the forms function," Tr. 545. He added that the increase in contract wins for Wallace in [*1571] light of the concurrent decrease for Moore shows that these two entities significantly compete head-to-head. He pointed out that the statistics also showed that Wallace competed against Moore about 75% of the time. Tr. 552.

Hausman additionally [**79] looked to information generated by Moore itself. On a document entitled "Target Competitor Forms Management Accounts," Moore compiled a list of target customers in the eastern United States whose forms management programs were not administered by Moore as of late summer 1995. DX 51, Deposition of Kathleen W. Sakal at 65. Of these target accounts coveted by Moore, 34 accounts were deemed as having a potential value of $1 million or more. Hausman looked at these accounts and concluded that Wallace and Standard Register each held 38% of those million dollar contracts; together they constituted the majority of Moore competitors.

Hausman conceded, however, that there are other LFICwMLs that are serviced primarily by vendors other than Moore, Wallace, and Standard Register. His review of DX 7 demonstrated that many LFICwMLs had contract with other vendors: (company—vendor) Woodward & Lothrop - Duplex; Alex & Alex - Duplex; Alex Brown & Co. - Duplex; Beneficial Management - shared between Wallace and Federal; Schering-Plough - NCR; Wyeth Labs - Federal; Certainteed - shared between Amberst local jobber n26 and Moore; Smith Kline - Duplex; Show Boat - Janice Group; Sun. Co - Ross Martin; [**80] Caesars - Ross Martin; Fleet Bank/Shawmut - Duplex; Bankers' Trust - Howard Press; Canada Life - Reynolds & Reynolds; Cole Haan Shoes - Creative Business Forms; Blue Cross/Blue Shield of Maine - uses its own in house program; Bloomingdale's - Uarco; United Technologies - Uarco; NEC - Uarco; Northeast Utilities - Duplex; United Utilities - Duplex; CenterBank - Duplex; United Illuminating - Duplex; Service America - Uarco; Fag Bearings - Uarco; Mercedes Benz Credit - Jobber; Perrier Group of America - Duplex; Cincinnati Bell Info. Systems - Better Business Forms; Tech Data - Reynolds & Reynolds; People Gas - Better Business Forms; Tampa Electric Co. - Better Business Forms; Glaxo/Burroughs - Wellcome - shared between Uarco and Standard Register; Guilford Mills - Jordan Graphics; Overnite Transportation - NCR; Philip Morris USA - Reynolds & Reynolds; Owens & Manor - Reynolds & Reynolds; Crawford Co. - Duplex; Turner Broadcasting - Reynolds & Reynolds. DX 7; Tr. 588–91.

n26 Jobbers have been described as forms distributors that do not manufacture the forms they distribute. Tr. 179.

[**81]

Finally, Hausman deduced further conclusions from the data supplied him by Wallace. His econometric analysis showed that Wallace's gross margin (defined as price minus cost) was lower when Moore was bidding than when Moore was not bidding. DX 12 at P 11; Tr. 566. When Wallace went head-to-head against Moore in the bidding process, Hausman found the Wallace gross margin was lower by about seven to eight percent. Tr. 566. From this, Hausman concluded that "if Moore were not going out head-to-head against Wallace, . . . on average, prices to customer will go up by between seven and eight percent." Tr. 567. Hausman based his conclusion on the premise that if Moore takes over Wallace, Wallace and Moore will be bidding together rather than as competitors; competition between these two companies will therefore be eliminated. Further, he opined that this elimination of competition will not just affect pricing; the technological rivalry between these two competitors will also be abolished, with a resultant inertia in the improvement of overall services.

Despite his econometric prowess. Hausman could not offer a definition of Wallace's market share as to LFICwMLs. Neither could he "sort out" [**82] what percentage of the total forms sales market is represented by LFICwMLs. Tr. 573. He could not testify as to how many LFICwMLs there are in the U.S. market; other Wallace testimony elucidated that there are approximately 170 Wallace WIN and Select Service customers who fall into this alleged submarket. Tr. 252–254.

[*1572] b) Moore's Evidence

i) Expert Testimony

Not surprisingly, Moore presented economist Dr. Sumanth Addanki from the National Economic Research Associates whose testimony was at stark variance with that of Dr. Hausman. Addanki concluded that the relevant market within which to analyze Moore's acquisition of Wallace is no smaller than the U.S. market for the sale of business forms and related services. Tr. 641. He characterized this market as "unconcentrated, vigorously competitive," with customers having a variety of alternative ways to meet their business forms and services needs. Tr. 641. He found that some of these alternatives include local suppliers, regional suppliers, and national suppliers.

Addanki also reasoned that there is no logical basis for discerning a discrete product submarket of LFICwMLs, and that no one in the industry tracks market share [**83] in such a theoretical arena. Tr. 653. Rather than the size of the customer, number of customer locations, or dollar amount spent on forms and forms management services, he concluded that the primary distinguishing factor is the type of industry within which the customer works and how the customer organizes its forms procurement processes. He found large customers and small customers expressing similar demands regardless of their size, albeit with idiosyncracies varying from customer to customer.

Addanki's review of bidding data for both Moore and Wallace revealed that vendors are often called upon by large customers to bid on supply requirements without any forms-related management services. American Express, Frank Parsons Paper, and Melville Corp. requested quotes from Moore excluding forms management services. See Sakal Depo. at 41, 47, 53. Further, many large customers are supplied on a "noncontract" or ad hoc basis, as in Wallace's relationship with United Parcel Service, DiscoverCard Services, and State Farm Insurance. See PX 229. Other customers request contracts ranging in duration from one to five years, with the capability of being terminated upon notice by either [**84] party. Some customers rely on multiple suppliers for their forms need, such as Avis, Homedco, Federal Express, Bank One, Nationwide Insurance and Boeing. See Fitzgerald Depo. at 200, 204, 214–15, 269–71, 315–17, 325. From this, Addanki concluded the following:

There is no single set of requirements that distinguishes 'large forms-intensive customers with multiple locations.' Rather, these customers can, and do, satisfy their forms need in a variety of alternative ways, out-sourcing as little or as much of the management and distribution functions as they choose, arranging their forms procurement process accordingly, buying forms locally, regionally or centrally as needed.

Addanki Expert Report, PX 119 at 7–8.

Like Wallace's Vice President Fitzgerald, Addanki also described the forms industry as one in transition. Demand for traditional core products in the forms industry, such as single and multi-ply forms, and continuous feed forms, is declining because of technological progress and its impact on customer demands. Shipments of these core products declined by five percent in 1992 and by approximately 4 percent in 1993. PX 119 at 9. As one alternative to paper forms, [**85] customers have the option to perform many of their business functions via electronic mail (e-mail) and transmission over local and wide area computer networks. PX 119 at 5.

Additionally, LFICwMLs have increasingly restructured and consolidated their forms use and forms suppliers, thus intensifying the competitive pressures between vendors in the forms industry. Corporations such as Andersen Consulting, CSC Index, and Price Waterhouse offer management consulting to re-engineer a given business entity, including the revamping of information systems and the forms generated by those systems. Id. at 12. In sum, Addanki opined that the market for business forms today is vigorously competitive because vendors must continue to grow their sales despite the declining demand for core products. Id.

Finally, as a corollary to forms customers consolidation of their purchases, Addanki identified a growing trend in which many informed and sophisticated forms customers [*1573] assert their bargaining power by demanding and obtaining favorable pricing by playing one vendor against its competitors. Tr. 683. These factors also exert pressure on the forms vendors to create new methods of servicing customers' [**86] forms needs more completely.

Along with his qualitative evaluation of competition in the business forms industry, Addanki quantified his economic data. Following U.S. Department of Justice Merger Guidelines, Addanki used the Herfindahl-Hirschman Index ("HHI") to measure concentration in the relevant product market he identified as the business forms industry in the United States. He postulated that there are over 600 vendor participants in this market, with the top 20 vendors accounting for 67% of total sales. PX 119 at 16. As HHI calculations require, each vendor's market share was mathematically squared and then all the squared shares were added. Addanki calculated the HHI of the current market as 432.5. If Moore acquires Wallace, the HHI would increase to 527, an increase of 95 points. Tr. 651. According to

Addanki, this figure, well below the Merger Guideline's safe harbor level of 1000, represents an unconcentrated market where a competitively healthy amount of alternative suppliers are available to customers. In terms of real dollars and cents, the entire business forms market in the United States is approximately $7.5 billion dollars; Moore's and Wallace's combined sales total [**87] approximate $1.3 billion or less than 18% of the total business forms market.

Based on his evaluation of data supplied by Moore, Addanki concluded that the acquisition of Wallace by Moore would not cause competitive harm in the forms industry in the United States.

ii) Other Moore Evidence

Gregory Lynch, Vice President of Moore's Financial Services Group, testified that in the course of its marketing and sales development plans, Moore identified a list of what could be considered LFICwMLs (as defined by Wallace) as potential clients. Out of a possible 2000 LFICwMLs, Moore targeted a limited number (125) of "rational accounts," which were defined in Moore's National Account Pocket Dossier as accounts valued at a potential for $1 million or more. DX 3 at C6130516. In this National Account Pocket Dossier, Moore estimated its market share for these types of accounts as 25%; the remaining 75% were served by other suppliers. Id. at C6130555. Recently, Moore has shifted its focus to customers who potentially spend over $250,000 in forms and forms-related services. Tr. 626. Moore also classifies its customers into three "vertical segments" by industry type rather than merely [**88] by account value: Financial Services, Health Services, and Government Services.

Lynch testified as to the competitive nature of the forms and forms services marketplace. In his experience, each individual customer is different and pursues a strategy related to its own needs and goals. Tr. 618. He agreed that there are many alternatives to supplying customers' needs available to Moore's customers, and the range of alternatives itself is ever increasing. He also agreed that the industry has witnessed a trend where customers out-source functions not related to their core business. Although there are businesses that still produce and manage forms internally, using in-house print shops and in-house employees, other businesses may decide to out-source the production of forms, but retain forms management in-house. Other customers out-source both forms management and production.

Lynch also testified that, in his experience, his customers are very well informed. Customers insist on "30 day out clauses" which allow them to change suppliers after 30 days. Tr. 624. Competitive conditions in the industry itself are responding to the multiplicity of customer demands. Of increasing importance is [**89] the emergence of forms jobbers and distributors, middleman organizations which sell but do not manufacture forms. The industry has witnessed these vendors teaming up with warehousing and distribution firms that provide inventory, distribution, and billing systems. Tr. 178–79; 621–22. Paper mills themselves have also recently entered the competitive fray with various offerings.

Effects of the potpourri of alternatives available to Moore customers has not escaped [*1574] Moore's notice. When Moore informs a customer of a price hike, Moore increasingly runs the risk that the customer will defect to another vendor or vendors. Lynch cited several instances where Moore lost large accounts to smaller vendors when Moore attempted to raise prices: a large contract with a uniform company in Cincinnati was lost to Miami Business Forms; a $4 million American Express contract was lost to a five person organization called General Credit; contracts with CIGNA and Bank of New York were lost to Williamette. Tr. 623.

2. Likelihood of Success on the Merits

Before this Court can preliminarily enjoin Moore's proposed merger based on this issue, Wallace, as movant and counterclaimant, must first establish [**90] that it has demonstrated a likelihood of success on the merits of its Section 7 claim. See *Clean Ocean Action v. York, supra, 57 F.3d 328, 331 (3d Cir. 1995); Allis-Chalmers Mfg. Co. v. White Consol. Indus., Inc., 414 F.2d 506, 510 (3d Cir. 1969),* cert. denied, *396 U.S. 1009, 24 L. Ed. 2d 501, 90 S. Ct. 567 (1970).* Section 7 of the Clayton Act proscribes mergers or acquisitions "where in any line of commerce or in any activity affecting commerce in any Section of the country, the effect of such acquisition may be substantially to lessen competition, or tend to create a monopoly." *15 U.S.C. § 18.* Accordingly, to demonstrate a likelihood of success on the merits, Wallace must fulfill two criteria: first, it must show that it is more probable than not that acquisition of Wallace by Moore will affect a "line of commerce" in "any Section of the country." These respective determinations are informed by the elucidation of a relevant product market and a relevant geographic market. *Brown Shoe Co. v. United States, 370 U.S. 294, 324, 8 L. Ed. 2d 510, 82 S. Ct. 1502 (1962).* Wallace argues that the relevant product market is the forms and forms services market encompassing large, [**91] forms-intensive customers with multiple locations; it posits the geographic market as the entire United States.

Second, Wallace must show that it is more probable than not that the Moore takeover may substantially lessen competition in the relevant product and geographic markets; the mere possibility of substantial impairment to competition will not suffice. *Fruehauf Corp. v. FTC, 603 F.2d 345, 351 (2d Cir. 1979);* see also *United States v. Marine Bancorporation, Inc., 418 U.S. 602, 622–23, 41 L. Ed. 2d 978, 94 S. Ct. 2856 (1974)* (Clayton Act Section 7 "deals in probabilities" rather than "ephemeral possibilities"). Of equal note, however, is that Wallace need not prove the fruition of actual anticompetitive effects of the acquisition, *FTC v. Procter & Gamble Co., 386 U.S. 568, 577, 18 L. Ed. 2d 303, 87 S. Ct. 1224 (1967),* as Section 7's underlying purpose is to "arrest apprehended consequences of intercorporate relationships before those relationships could work their evil," *Brunswick Corp. v. Pueblo Bowl-O-Mat, 429 U.S. 477, 485, 50 L. Ed. 2d 701, 97 S. Ct. 690 (1977).*

a) The Relevant Product and Geographic Markets

A necessary predicate to a finding of a violation [**92] of Section 7 of the Clayton Act is the definition of the relevant product market and relevant geographical market. *United States v. E.I. du Pont de Nemours & Co., 353 U.S. 586, 593, 1 L. Ed. 2d 1057, 77 S. Ct. 872 (1957).* These market determinations confer the requisite context within which the Court can analyze whether there has been a substantial lessening of competition. Id.

i) Relevant Geographic Market

The United States Supreme Court has defined relevant geographic market as the region "where, within the area of competitive overlap, the effect of the merger on competition will be direct and immediate." *United States v. Philadelphia Nat'l Bank, 374 U.S. 321, 357, 10 L. Ed. 2d 915, 83 S. Ct. 1715 (1963).* Both parties agree that the relevant geographic market in this case encompasses the entire United States, Tr. 564, 641, and the Court so finds.

ii) Relevant Product Market

Determination of the relevant product market quite often is the major battleground in Section 7 litigation, and this case is no exception. See 3 Julian O. von Kalinowski, [*1575] Antitrust Laws and Trade Regulation, § 18.01[2] (1995). Another commentator concurs:

However [**93] wide or narrow the range of inquiry for appraising a merger, market definition is frequently critical. For example, viewed in a wider product. . . market than the minimum necessary to include the merging firms, a merger will appear to have a less significant effect. In contrast, when the products . . . of the merging firms differ, a definition wide enough to bring the merging firms into the same market makes the merger. . . more likely to be seen as troublesome.

Phillip Areeda & Louis Kaplow, Antitrust Analysis, P 506, at 814–15 (4th ed. 1988).

The criteria relating to product market definition have been set forth by the Supreme Court in the seminal decision *Brown Shoe Co. v. United States, 370 U.S. 294, 8 L. Ed. 2d 510, 82 S. Ct. 1502 (1962).* The Court held that "the outer boundaries of a product market are determined by the reasonable interchangeability of use [by consumers] or the cross-elasticity of demand between the product itself and substitutes for it." *Id. at 325.* Interchangeability of use implies that one product or service is approximately equivalent to another; discounting any degree of preference for the one over the other, either product would work [**94] just as well. *Allen-Myland, Inc. v. International Business Machines Corp., 33 F.3d 194, 206 (3d Cir. 1994),* cert. denied, *130 L. Ed. 2d 615, 115 S. Ct. 684 (1994).* Cross-elasticity of demand refers to whether the demand for the second good or service would respond to change in the price of the first. Id. In short, "defining a relevant product market is a process of describing those groups of producers which, because of the similarity of their products [or services], have the ability—actual or potential—to take significant amounts of business away from each other." *SmithKline Corp. v. Eli Lilly & Co., 575 F.2d 1056, 1063 (3d Cir.),* cert. denied, *439 U.S. 838, 58 L. Ed. 2d 134, 99 S. Ct. 123 (1978).*

The Supreme Court has also recognized that under appropriate circumstances, a broad product market may be parsed into well-defined submarkets, each comprising a discrete line of commerce unto itself for Section 7 purposes. *Brown Shoe, 370 U.S. at 325.* If such a submarket(s) does exist, the Court must scrutinize not only the broad, overall market, but must also "examine the effects of a merger in each such economically significant submarket to determine if there is a reasonable probability [**95] that the merger will substantially lessen competition." Id. The Brown Shoe Court set forth seven "practical indicia" for lower courts to consider when determining whether a submarket exists: "industry or public recognition of the submarket as a separate economic entity, the product's peculiar characteristics and uses, unique production facilities, distinct customers, distinct prices, sensitivity to price changes, and specialized vendors." Id. All of these indicia need not be present for a well-defined submarket to exist. *General Foods Corp. v. FTC, 386 F.2d 936, 941 (3d Cir. 1967), cert. denied, 391 U.S. 919, 20 L. Ed. 2d 657, 88 S. Ct. 1805 (1968).*

iii) Application of the Brown Shoe Criteria: Wallace's Proposed Submarket

The record evidence shows that the parties are sharply divided on their characterizations of the relevant product market. Moore, the aggressor corporation and antitrust defendant, argues for an expansive definition of the relevant product market, as being "comprised of the sales of all business forms and forms management services." Expert Report of Sumanth Addanki, PX119 at 8. In its Securities and Exchange Commission filing Form 10-K [**96] for 1994, Moore views itself as serving the "information needs of businesses, government and other enterprises." PX 122 at 5. Similarly, in its Form 10-K, Wallace describes itself as a corporation engaged "predominantly in the computer services and supply industry." PX 26 at 3. Both companies overlap in the supply of products and services, such as business forms, labels, commercial printing, direct mail, and office supplies.

Even if Moore's broad characterization of the relevant product market were accurate, definition of a relevant product submarket [*1576] would not be foreclosed under Brown Shoe. Wallace contends that there exists a well-defined submarket in this case: "the sale of forms and forms services" to "large, multi-location customers.," Tr. 564. Wallace argues that application of the Brown Shoe factors conclusively demonstrate that the relevant product market is a submarket within the broad market definition proposed by Moore, and that this submarket is a "line of commerce" unto itself for purposes of the Clayton Act. *Ansell Inc. v. Schmid Laboratories, Inc., 757 F. Supp. 467, 471–74 (D.N.J.)* (applying the Brown Shoe criteria to determine relevant product market), [**97] aff'd mem. op., *941 F.2d 1200 (3d Cir. 1991).*

(A) Industry or Public Recognition of the Submarket as a Separate Economic Entity

Recognized sources of evidence of industry or public recognition include (1) statements of the merging parties and their own market surveys, annual reports, marketing materials, and preacquisition reports; (2) Industry or trade association publications; (3) the existence of a discrete trade association for the product or services involved; (4) perceptions and statements of major customers; and (5) Industry classification codes of the United States Census Bureau. Von Kalinowski, 3 Antitrust Laws and Trade Regulation § 18.02[2] (1995)(collecting cases).

In support of its proposed submarket definition of LFICwMLs, Wallace relies heavily on the first type of evidence: statements and marketing materials of the parties in this case. The record, however, shows that neither company has historically considered LFICwML as a category unto itself. The best evidence Wallace offers is differential treatment of customers according to account size based on dollar value; even then, there seem to be no well defined or accepted parameters. Wallace demonstrated [**98] that only accounts valued at $1 million or above qualify for participation on the WIN system; another Wallace customer category includes those accounts valued at over $400,000. For reasons known only to Wallace, its economics expert used yet another dollar value for his analyses, i.e., $500,000.

Moore documentation was equally all over the scale. In one document, the National Accounts Pocket Dossier, Moore targeted accounts worth $1 million or more for intensive sales promotion and marketing, DX 3 at C6130564, although these efforts have been apparently redefined to include accounts with a floor value of $250,000. In another document compiled for similar purposes, Moore lumped together accounts both small and large, valued from thousands of dollars up through millions of dollars. DX 7. Significantly, in only one instance did either company define a market share for a sub-category of the entire forms industry; Moore chose a cutoff figure of $250,000. DX 61.

The evidence also showed in specialized circumstances, that rather than segregating LFICwMLs as a submarket, Moore analyzes its customer base in terms of vertical segments by industry type, such as Financial Services, Health [**99] Care, and Governmental. Common sense dictates there will be similarity in forms needs within a given industry sector, such as the banking industry, as contrasted to other, diverse types of businesses, such as hospitals. Finally, and perhaps most significantly, both parties agreed that it is not unusual for a customer to split its forms and forms servicing loyalties among different vendors. As a result, a "large" customer in terms of corporate demographics does not necessarily translate into large business forms customer whose account dollar value corresponds to the breadth of its business form needs. In other words, even assuming there exists a subset of customers defined as LFICwMLs, a given LFICwML may not surrender all of its business form and form service requirements to a single or even primary vendor. Instead of falling into well-defined submarkets based on corporate size, locations, or dollar value of account, business forms and form service customers are aligned along a continuum of diverse needs. Accordingly, the Court finds that there is no industry or public recognition of submarket composed of LFICwMLs.

(B) The Product's Peculiar Characteristics and Uses

Both parties [**100] presented convincing evidence of the overwhelming importance of [*1577] serving a forms and forms service customer's distinct needs. Because customers needs are as diverse as the customers themselves, there is no one forms product or forms service (or set of products and/or services) that can be readily distinguished as its own category. Even if the Court were to accept the premise that LFICwMLs compose a circumscribed subset of forms and forms service customer, the record shows that there is no single product and/or service that is marketed to these target customers alone. A relatively small business forms customer with only one location may desire the same forms and forms management services as a LFICwML, albeit on a different scale.

Although out-sourcing may be considered a particular type of service frequently utilized by LFICwMLs, the gamut of out-sourcing options available apply to customers large and small alike.

Typically, under this Brown Shoe factor, courts have distinguished products with specialized end uses or characteristics from similar products. See, e.g., *Ansell, Inc. v. Schmid, 757 F. Supp. at 473* (different packaging and distribution of latex condoms enough to distinguish [**101] between product lines); *United States v. American Tech. Indus. Inc., 1974 Trade Cas. P74,873 (M.D. Pa. 1974)* (artificial Christmas trees considered a separate market from natural Christmas trees). In the case sub judice, there is no basis in the record for discerning any distinct products or services sold to LFICwMLs as compared with those sold to other types of business forms and forms management customers.

(C) Unique Production Facilities

This Brown Shoe factor requires the Court to evaluate whether business forms and forms management services for LFICwMLs require unique facilities or technology different than that which underlies forms and forms-related services demanded by non-LFICwMLs. See *General Foods Corp. v. FTC, 386 F.2d 936, 943 (3d Cir. 1967)* (production facility for steel wool markedly different from facilities for other cleaning devices), cert. denied, *391 U.S. 919, 20 L. Ed. 2d 657, 88 S. Ct. 1805 (1968)*. Wallace argues that the services demanded by LFICwMLs are "mainly produced by using integrated and sophisticated computer systems" such as WIN. Tr. 543. The record demonstrates that many LFICwMLs, especially those that out-source their [**102] forms management functions, derive great benefit from a vendor's sophisticated computer technology.

However, the record also shows many LFICwMLs as contracting with companies other than Moore, Wallace, or Standard Register. DX 7. Although Wallace characterizes these other forms vendors as "second-tier" because of a perceived lack of technological out-sourcing capability, the objective evidence demonstrates that even with "inferior" technology (as compared to WIN), these vendors still compete effectively for LFICwML contracts. The Court finds that the evidence does not support a finding that these types of customers are served by unique production facilities as typified by the Wallace facility.

(D) Distinct Customers

An oft-cited case, *Reynolds Metals Co. v. FTC, 114 U.S. App. D.C. 2, 309 F.2d 223 (D.C. Cir. 1962)*, sets forth a clear paradigm of a distinct customer class. In that case, the parties disputed whether a class of customers who purchased decorative aluminum foil used in the floral industry could be considered unique. The court found that:

the sole purchasers of florist foil are the nation's 700 wholesale florist outlets and, through these, the 25,000 [**103] retail florists throughout the country. Despite a clearly lower price for florist foil, . . . other end users of decorative foil have not joined the identifiable mass of florist foil purchasers in noticeable numbers.

309 F.2d at 228.

Like the aluminum foil manufacturer in Reynolds, Wallace also attempted to portray LFICwMLs as somehow coalescing into a distinct class of customers. The record evidence, however, shows the opposite to be true: the needs of the customers differ greatly by industry type and idiosyncratic customer preference. For customers that could be described as LFICwML, Moore adduced evidence showing that its forms and forms service demands defy simple classification. For example, American Express requested a bid from Moore for forms and no [*1578] forms services. Avis, Homedco, and Federal Express were cited as companies that prefer to rely on multiple forms and forms service suppliers. Furthermore, Wallace's Chief of Information Systems testified that a particular LFICwML's needs can vary greatly depending on the customer, one may handle its own forms management in-house, and another may out-source those same functions. Tr. 254–56.

Diversity of forms, forms service [**104] needs, and out-sourcing are not limited to the LFICwML type of customer. In a document generated by Moore well before the initiation of litigation, Moore identified forms and forms management needs for its smaller customers ranging by account size of $5,000 to $250,000. PX 131 at M4631332. The catalog of products and services primarily used and available to these smaller customers paralleled those described by Wallace as peculiar attributes of LFICwMLs: e.g., custom and stock forms, mailing systems, forms handling equipment, forms management services, warehousing and distribution, and electronic data interchange. Because there appears to be no easy demarcation of forms and forms management attributes as between LFICwML and other smaller customers, as well as within the population of LFICwMLs itself, the Court finds that there is no distinct class of LFICwML customers under Brown Shoe.

(E) Distinct Prices

During the hearing, and in its briefs, Wallace emphasized its pricing strategy for LFICwMLs who purchase a bundle of forms management services as an accompaniment to its forms purchases. Such LFICwMLs incur a unified charge that incorporates both product and service; [**105] a separate breakdown of price per form and price per service is not available. However, Wallace also presented evidence that other LFICwMLs choose to manage their own forms; it follows that these LFICwMLs are charged no differently for their forms purchases than any other customer who purchases only forms. While a subgroup of LHCwMLs may encounter a distinct pricing scheme, the Court finds that the industry does not price its forms and forms management services based merely on a customer's being pigeonholed as a LFICwML.

(F) Sensitivity to Price Changes

Wallace offered testimony of two selected WIN customers who expressed a loyal degree of satisfaction in their corporate relationship with Wallace. Both PSE&G and Pershing witnesses admitted without hesitation that if Wallace raised its prices by five percent, they would incur the additional cost and remain Wallace customers.

On the other hand, in equally anecdotal fashion, Moore offered concrete evidence where it had informed some of its LFICwMLs of a price increase, the customers fled to another vendor. In light of these competing offerings, the Court cannot conclusively find that LFICwMLs react uniformly with respect to price [**106] changes in the forms and forms services industry.

(G) Specialized Vendors

This final Brown Shoe criterion looks to whether a product or service is sold or marketed by a unique class of vendor. For example, in *United States v. Healthco, Inc., 387 F. Supp. 258 (S.D.N.Y.), aff'd mem. op., 535 F.2d 1243 (2d Cir. 1975)*, the court distinguished between submarkets for dental equipment and dental sundries. This distinction was based in part on the two industries' different methods for distributing and marketing those products. Dental equipment was marketed via specialized dental dealers and salespeople and was personally detailed to dental customers; dental sundries were frequently marketed and sold via mail-order. *Id. at 261, 265.* Thus, the court justified the different submarkets in part on the existence of the two different types of vendors.

Wallace has similarly argued that only three specialized vendors, Moore, Wallace, and Standard Register, offer a complete menu of options capable of serving the forms and forms management needs of LFICwMLs. Pointing to the worst case scenario of a LFICwML that completely out-sources its forms and forms management services, Wallace [**107] convincingly showed that extremely sophisticated vendor technology is required to be competitive, and that Moore, Wallace, and Standard Register offer the [*1579] most competitive, state of the art technology available. The PSE&G customer's testimony highlighted this assertion: as a completely out-sourced customer, dependent on a single vendor, the witness regarded only the larger forms companies Moore, Standard Register, Wallace, and Uarco as viable vendors for PSE&G's out-sourcing needs. Tr. 333.

If the evidence showed all LFICwMLs as desiring to out-source the majority of their forms and concomitant services, the Court would agree that only a limited number of "specialized" vendors exist to serve those customers. However, as discussed supra, the evidence showed that LFICwMLs operate along a continuum of out-sourcing needs. Some require little or no out-sourcing; others prefer to liberally out-source. The evidence also showed that a significant number of LHCwMLs contract with vendors not designated by Wallace as specialized, such as Duplex, Vanier, Williamette, Federal, Reynolds & Reynolds, Ross Martin, and Better Business Forms. See, e.g., DX 7. Consequently, the Court cannot agree [**108] that only specialized vendors support the forms and forms management needs of LFICwML.

(H) Barriers to Entry

In *Ansell, Inc. v. Schmid Laboratories, Inc., 757 F. Supp. 467, 474–75, (D.N.J.), aff'd mem. op. 941 F.2d 1200 (3d Cir. 1991)*, the Third Circuit Court of Appeals affirmed the district court's augmentation of the Brown Shoe criteria with consideration of another factor, barriers to entry. See also *Cargill, Inc. v. Monfort of Colorado, Inc., 479 U.S. 104, 120 n.15, 93 L. Ed. 2d 427, 107 S. Ct. 484 (1986)* ("It is also important to examine the barriers to entry into the market, because 'without barriers to entry it would presumably be impossible to maintain supracompetitive prices for an extended time.'") (citation omitted). Low barriers to entry into the market invite entry by new competitors and also expose firms well established in the market to the threat of potential entry. This in turn can induce those firms to hold prices, services, quality, and developments at competitive levels. See 3 Von Kalinowski, supra, at § 26.02[4]. The converse is also true: high entry barriers reduce the potential for increased competition by dissuading smaller [**109] firms from aggressively competing. *FTC v. Proctor & Gamble, 386 U.S. at 578.*

Wallace presented extensive videotape, testimonial, and documentary evidence featuring the superiority of its WIN computer system. Focusing on Moore's struggle to create comparatively competitive technology, Wallace argues that a new entrant into the purported LFICwML submarket would face several years of computer research and development to become competitive. Once again, however, Wallace overlooks the heterogeneity of forms and forms-management needs among the LFICwML user population. For customers like PSE&G who totally outsource forms management, the WIN system is unparalleled. The costs of building a comparable information system would be monumental and no doubt form a high barrier to entry for those customers.

However, further down the consumer spectrum is Pershing, who uses both WIN and local/regional forms vendors; these smaller vendors compete effectively without WIN-type technology for a subset of Pershing's forms business. Depending on how much or little forms services a LFICwML decides to out-source, the evidence shows vendors with lesser technological capabilities successfully vying for [**110] those customers. See e.g., DX 7. Wallace has demonstrated that its WIN and Select Service LFICwMLs number around 170. Moore has placed the total number of LFICwMLs at 2000; Wallace's share of these customers is less than ten percent. Even if one assumes that Moore and Standard Register each serve twice as many LFICwML customers as Wallace (a generous assumption), 50% of the LFICwML market remains served by vendors beside Moore, Wallace, and Standard Register. Therefore, even without computer technology approaching that of the WIN system, other vendors compete effectively for a large share of LFICwMLs. A vendor need not surmount as ambitious a hurdle as Wallace erects to enter the forms and forms services market for LFICwMLs.

In sum, the evidence has failed to support Wallace's contention that the relevant product [*1580] market in this case constitutes the sale of business forms and forms-related services to large, multi-location customers. Mindful that the Brown Shoe factors are "practical indicia," and not intended to be mechanically applied, the Court has considered the factors and finds that they fall short of identifying LFICwMLs as a discrete segment of the forms and forms-related [**111] services market that can fairly be considered a well-defined submarket. See *Bon-Ton Stores, Inc. v. May Dep't Stores Co., 881 F. Supp. at 875.* At best, Wallace, leading the pack in technological innovation responsive to the needs of large, form-intensive customers with multiple locations, is beginning to successfully carve out a niche in an industry in transition. That transition has not yet matured to the point where there is an identifiable submarket. Instead, at this time, because customer needs for forms and forms-related services fall along a continuum without regard to corporate size or location, the realities of the forms and forms-related services industry, Wallace has not established that there is a submarket beyond the broader relevant product market in this case, i.e., the entire U.S. market for business forms. n27

n27 The parties have not argued for the Court's consideration of the relevant product market under the U.S. Department of Justice Merger Guidelines ("Merger Guidelines"), which call for analysis of factors similar to some noted in Brown Shoe. Courts have frequently looked to these Merger Guidelines (most recently promulgated in 1992) as an advisory aid in determining the relevant product market, see *57 Fed.Reg. 41552 (1992)*; see e.g., *Allis-Chalmers Mfg. Co., 414 F.2d at 524*; *Ansell Inc. v. Schmid, 757 F. Supp. at 475*. Because neither party has advanced evidence or data supporting a relevant product market using Merger Guideline analysis, the Court will refrain from considering whether the Merger Guidelines would have yielded that same conclusion as reached under decisional law. However, as discussed infra, Moore has offered evidence under the Merger Guidelines as to the effects of a Moore-Wallace merger on competition within the relevant market.

[**112]

b) Substantial Lessening of Competition

Once the relevant product and geographic markets circumscribing the area of effective competition have been defined, the Court must analyze whether the effect of the merger "may be substantially to lessen competition." *Brown Shoe, 370 U.S. at 328* (quoting *15 U.S.C. § 18*). Inquiry into the likely effect of a Moore-Wallace merger on competition starts with an evaluation of the level of economic concentration in the U.S. market for business forms. While statistics reflecting market share controlled by industry leaders are the focal point of the Court's analysis, the Court is also mindful that statistics must be viewed in light of the particular market's structure, history, and probable future. *Brown Shoe, 370 U.S. at 322 n.38.*

The Department of Justice Merger Guidelines reference the Herfindahl-Hirschman Index ("HHI"), a statistical formula used to calculate and compare market concentration pre- and post-merger. As indicated by Moore's expert Addanki, a market's HHI is calculated by adding the squares of the market shares of those vendors participating in the market. See Merger Guidelines § 1.5. The Merger Guidelines contemplate [**113] a product market to fall into one of three categories: unconcentrated (HHI below 1000), moderately concentrated (Hill between 1000 and 1800), and highly concentrated (HHI above 1800). Id. at § 1.51.

Finding the relevant product and geographic market to be the forms industry in the entire U.S., Addanki looked at market shares of the top 20 forms vendors (who account for approximately 67% of the forms market dollars). He found the pre-merger HHI value at 432, indicating an unconcentrated market. Following an acquisition of Wallace by Moore, the post-merger HHI value would be 527, indicating that the forms industry market would remain unconcentrated. According to the Merger Guidelines, an unconcentrated product or service market post-merger is indicative of a market "unlikely to have adverse competitive effects." Merger Guidelines § 1.51. Based on his statistical analysis and qualitative market considerations discussed above, Addanki concluded that a Wallace-Moore merger is unlikely to cause competitive harm. He reported that post-acquisition, forms and forms-related service customers will still enjoy realistic alternatives to which they can readily turn for their needs. DX 119 [**114] at 17. Addanki [*1581] further opined that in such a competitive environment, a Wallace-Moore combination could neither successfully exercise unilateral market power, nor facilitate coordination and collusion among remaining vendors. See Merger Guidelines § 2.2 (cautioning against the danger that, post-acquisition, a merged firm may be able to unilaterally elevate the price and suppress the output of a product and still capture any sales lost due to that price rise, if buyers will substitute another product that is now sold by the merged firm); *Hospital Corp. of Am. v. FTC, 807 F.2d 1381, 1386 (7th Cir. 1986)* (courts must consider whether acquisition will make it "easier for the firms in the market to collude, expressly or tacitly, and thereby force price above or farther above the competitive level"), cert. denied, *481 U.S. 1038, 95 L. Ed. 2d 815, 107 S. Ct. 1975 (1987)*.

In direct contrast, Wallace's expert, Hausman, offered no such market share or market concentration statistics in his data, all of which incorrectly assumed a relevant product submarket of sales of large, forms-intensive customers with multiple locations. In fact, Hausman explicitly disclaimed any knowledge [**115] of Wallace's market share of LFICwMLs and what percentage of the total forms sales market is represented by LFICwMls. Notwithstanding his incomplete information base, Hausman concluded that were Moore to acquire Wallace, Moore would be able to raise prices of forms and forms-related services to LFICwML by seven or eight percent, a figure Hausman termed as statistically significant.

First, Hausman drew his conclusion based on 51 bidding situations in 1994 and 1995 where Wallace bid on LFICwML contracts valued at $500,000 or greater. Tr. 584. Where Wallace successfully competed directly against Moore for such contract bids, the data showed that Wallace had enjoyed a lesser gross profit margin by seven or eight percent. These figures are corroborated by the testimony of Wallace's Chief Executive Officer Cronin. Cronin confirmed that when competing directly against Moore as finalists for a customer contract, Wallace's corporate strategy involved lowering its bid price to be more competitive. With respect to other competitors, however, Wallace did not lower its prices as much or even at all. Hausman's data also showed that for this same time period, Wallace was able to win over 46% of [**116] Moore's LFICwMLs with its bidding tactics.

From the data, Hausman then assumed the converse to be true: post-acquisition, with Wallace eliminated from the marketplace, Moore would be able to raise its contract prices by this same seven or eight percent. Hausman postulated this effect to be the sine qua non of substantially lessened competition. The Court will assume Wallace has preliminarily established that when Moore competes against Wallace for LFICwMLs, those customers will receive a lower price than if the two entities did not compete. However, the Court cannot credit Hausman's other empirical assertions, unsupported by market share data, that no matter how broadly or narrowly one defines the market, there would be a substantial lessening of competition post-acquisition. Hausman cannot draw his conclusion in a vacuum; market definition provides the necessary context within which the lessening vel non of competition must be evaluated. *United States v. E.I. du Pont de Nemours & Co., 353 U.S. 586, 593, 1 L. Ed. 2d 1057, 77 S. Ct. 872 (1957).*

The Court is unaware of any precedent where a substantial lessening of competition was found without regard to definition of a relevant [**117] product market, submarket, market share, or market concentration. To the contrary, an antitrust plaintiff cannot prevail by simply alleging a lessening of competition within a limited subset of customers; plaintiff must also evaluate the significance of this impact in the "universe" of the relevant product market. *United States v. Gillette Co., 828 F. Supp. 78, 83 (D.D.C. 1993).* Here, as stated above, Wallace has not shown any probability of establishing its proposed submarket of LFICwML within the entire U.S. business forms industry; the only realistic market definition supported by the evidence, at least at this stage of the litigation, it the broad U.S. forms industry. The Court is willing to assume arguendo that there is a subset of LFICwMLs that would only look to Moore, Standard Register, or Wallace for [*1582] their forms and forms-management services, and that these will pay higher prices if there is a Moore takeover of Wallace. Even so, Wallace's failure to show that the lessening of competition for these customers would have the effect of substantially lessening competition in the overall relevant product market is fatal.

Similarly, the Court is willing to assume as true [**118] that if Moore were to merge with Wallace, Moore's arch-rival in the technology and service arena would be removed from the competitive mix. However, the evidence showed that other competitors are "attempting to create similar services" to the WIN system, Tr. 256–57, some of which "compete[] favorably with WIN," PX 128 at 2. Moore has demonstrated that it views competitors other than Wallace as posing real and significant competitive threat; it therefore is unlikely that Moore will be content with the status quo in terms of staying competitive on the technological and service fronts.

In short, the uncontroverted evidence shows that the relevant product market in this case is currently unconcentrated and will remain so even if Moore acquires Wallace. HHI calculations confirm that the merger falls within the safe harbor as defined by the Department of Justice Merger Guidelines. In addition, most likely stymied by both lack of time and the transitional nature and state of flux of the forms industry, Wallace did not present a requisite showing under decisional law that competition in the relevant product market will be substantially lessened in the event of a Moore takeover. Accordingly, [**119] the Court finds that Wallace has failed to show a likelihood of success on the merits of its Section 7 Clayton Act counterclaim.

3. Irreparable Injury and Harm to Public Interest

Wallace has presented uncontroverted testimony that customers have deferred their award of contracts to Wallace because of the uncertainty of the pending takeover offer. If these customers eventually choose other vendors, Wallace will certainly suffer the damage in the form of lost profits. Moreover, Wallace correctly asserts if Wallace is merged into Moore, Moore will gain access to its proprietary computer technology, thereby negating its technological advantage and consequent competitive superiority. The Wallace technological and correlative competitive superiority could never be reclaimed if an eventual trial should result in a finding that Moore violated Section 7 of the Clayton Act. In contrast, the injury Moore would suffer if the merger were preliminarily enjoined on antitrust grounds is loss of incremental profit anticipated by reason of the merger. The Count concludes that if the merger goes through and there is no injunction, Wallace will suffer far more irreparable injury than Moore.

Those [**120] form intensive customers with multiple locations who require the full panapoly of forms and form services, which can only be met by Moore, Wallace and Standard Register, will incur higher costs if in fact there is a merger of Moore and Wallace. In that sense, since those customers are part of the public, the public interest would be served by grant of an injunction.

4. Balancing of All Four Preliminary Injunction Factors

The Court has found Wallace has failed to satisfy the first criteria for grant of injunctive relief in that it has not demonstrated a likelihood it will prevail on the merits at a final hearing. However, the Court has found Wallace did carry its burden in demonstrating that the irreparable harm it will suffer far exceeds the irreparable injury to Moore if the injunction does not issue. Similarly, the fact that there will a decrease in competition for even a limited subset of business forms customers weighs in favor of finding that Wallace has carried its burden in demonstrating the public interest will be served if an injunction were granted on antitrust grounds.

AT&T Co. v. Winback and Conserve Program Inc., 42 F.3d 1421, 1429 (3d Cir. 1974), instructs [**121] that "the injunction should issue only if the plaintiff (movant for the injunction) produces evidence sufficient to [*1583] convince the district court that all four n28 factors favor preliminary relief." In a footnote in the same opinion, the above-quoted language was blunted with the instruction that the "district court should award preliminary injunctive relief only upon weighing all four factors." *Id. at 1427, n.8.* Weighing all four factors and recognizing that three of the criteria counsel for issuance of the injunction, the fact remains that without both a probability of success on the merits and irreparable injury to the movant, a preliminary injunction should not issue. Accordingly, if the entire section IV(B) were not dicta, an order would be entered denying the Wallace motion for preliminary injunction.

n28 Relativity of harm to the plaintiff and defendant has been combined into one factor in the text.

V. CONCLUSION

The Court has found Wallace carried its burden under the Unocal enhanced [**122] judicial scrutiny test and Moore has not rebutted the presumption that the Wallace Board acted properly under the Business Judgment Rule in refusing to redeem its poison pill. As a consequence, an order will be entered denying Moore's motion for preliminary injunction.

The Court has also held a target in a hostile tender offer cannot challenge a proposed merger with the acquiror on the ground the merger would violate federal antitrust laws because it lacks antitrust standing. In order to facilitate appellate review in the event the Third Circuit Court of Appeals were to hold a target does have antitrust standing, this Court concluded that the requested Wallace injunction should not issue.

An order will be entered denying Moore's motion for preliminary injunction and granting Moore's motion to dismiss the Wallace antitrust counterclaim.

ORDER

At Wilmington this 4th day of December, 1995, for the reasons set forth in the accompanying Opinion issued this date,

IT IS ORDERED:

1.   Plaintiff's motion for preliminary injunction is denied.

2.   Plaintiff's motion to dismiss the defendant Wallace's antitrust counterclaim is granted.

3.   Defendants' motion for preliminary injunction [**123] is denied as moot.

Murray M. Schwartz

United States District Judge

Index

LaVergne, TN USA
05 February 2010
172209LV00005B/11/A